# The New Early Years Foundation Stage

# The New Early Years Foundation Stage

## CHANGES, CHALLENGES AND REFLECTIONS

*Edited by Pat Beckley*

McGraw Hill Education

Open University Press

Open University Press
McGraw-Hill Education
McGraw-Hill House
Shoppenhangers Road
Maidenhead
Berkshire
England
SL6 2QL

email: enquiries@openup.co.uk
world wide web: www.openup.co.uk

and Two Penn Plaza, New York, NY 10121-2289, USA

First published 2013

A catalogue record of this book is available from the British Library

ISBN-13: 978-0-33-524698-4 (pb)          .
ISBN-10: 0-33-524698-2 (pb)
eISBN: 978-0-33-524699-1

*Library of Congress Cataloging-in-Publication Data*
CIP data applied for

Typesetting and e-book compilations
by RefineCatch Limited, Bungay, Suffolk

# Praise for this book

'This contemporary and relevant text explores, from multiple perspectives, the key challenges facing early years practitioners at a time of unprecedented change in education. It systematically explores and offers insights into the many agencies including education, health and social care that work together to enable high quality early years practice to be developed. By drawing on a range of professionals in the field, it challenges the reader to critically analyse the characteristics of effective early learning and to consider the key underpinning pedagogy that informs it. It is accessible to a wide audience including students, researchers, teacher trainers and practitioners. I would strongly recommend it as a set text on our "outstanding" Primary and Early Years PGCE course.'

Derval Carey-Jenkins, Principal Lecturer: PGCE Primary and Early Years Course Leader, University of Worcester, UK

'This contemporary book focusing on the new Early Years Foundation Stage will be an essential read for those studying and delivering early years curriculum and pedagogy. The book draws on theory, research, policy and practice and ensures that the chapters have significance to all early years practitioners. It challenges the reader to think reflectively about the EYFS and what is appropriate provision to support and develop young children's learning. The book is effectively organised into four relevant parts and is a very accessible read, often exemplifying high quality provision through interesting research observations, case studies and scenarios.'

Dr Avril Brock, Principal Lecturer in Early Childhood Education, Leeds Metropolitan University, UK

# Contents

## PART 3

### The specific areas of learning and development

## PART 4

### Advanced early years pedagogy

# Notes on the contributors

**Dr Pat Beckley (editor)** taught in primary schools, leading age phases in the 3–11 range, before going into higher education at Bishop Grosseteste University, Lincoln. Her current role is the Academic Coordinator for the 3–7 cohorts on the PGCE Primary course. This draws on her experience running a large inner city early years unit and supporting colleagues in her work as an Advanced Skills Teacher. Doctoral research interests concerned *Challenges and Resolutions to Early Years Literacy Approaches in two selected sites in Norway and England.* Her current research, with colleagues from six other European countries, is focused on young children's wellbeing. She is an executive member of TACTYC (Association for the Professional Development of Early Years Educators).

**Nigel Appleton** is Dean of the School of Teacher Development at Bishop Grosseteste University, Lincoln where he is responsible for initial and continuing teacher education. He began his career as a mathematics teacher before moving into higher education at what is now the University of Cumbria, where he worked in initial teacher training.

**Jan Ashbridge** is Senior Lecturer teaching early childhood education and English at the University of Cumbria. She is an experienced early years teacher and was also a senior advisory teacher for the Foundation Stage for Cumbria LEA. Jan has been involved in planning and delivering training to students and early years educators across the North West of England in all aspects of young children's learning and is committed to helping practitioners develop the knowledge and skills they need to promote successful learners.

**Emma Butcher** has been a teacher at Redcliffe Children's Centre and Maintained Nursery School, Bristol since 2008. She has been grappling issues on a Masters module in special needs education and is currently studying on a Masters module for Bristol early years maths specialist.

**Elizabeth Carruthers** is headteacher of Redcliffe Children's Centre, Nursery School and Research and Professional Development Base in Bristol. She has worked in all phases of education which includes being a local authority Foundation Stage advisor and a numeracy consultant with the National Strategy (NS). Her research interests and publications are in the area of early years education and play, wild forest experiences for children and the pedagogy of children's mathematical graphics. She is presently studying for a PhD at Bristol University.

**Liz Creed** is currently working as a psychological well-being practitioner within a primary care setting for the National Health Service, providing brief guided self-help interventions using cognitive behaviour therapy (CBT) techniques. Expertise needed for this involved psychological therapies training at the University of York. Prior to this Liz gained clinical experience working for child and adolescent mental health services. Liz began her training with an Msc Foundations of Clinical Psychology by the University of Wales and is developing her career through further CBT training at Newcastle University to become a psychotherapist.

**Julie Kitchen** taught children in Nursery, Reception and Key Stage 1 classes for fifteen years, after gaining a BEd (Hons) in 1990. She was awarded an MA (Ed) after conducting practitioner research into children's early independent writing and gained Early Years Professional Status (EYPS) in 2007. Julie became a training manager for EYPS at EM Direct in Grantham and then a visiting tutor and full-time Lecturer in education studies and early childhood studies at Bishop Grosseteste University. Julie is currently Head of an initial teacher training programme, delivering employment-based routes to qualified teacher status (QTS).

**Rachel Sparks Linfield** has worked in education for over 25 years, teaching through-out the Foundation Stage, Key Stages 1 and 2 and in higher education at both the University of Cambridge and Leeds Metropolitan University. She has written a wide range of books and articles for early years and primary practitioners, and non-fiction texts for children.

**Estelle Martin** has extensive experience as a professional in early years education and care across the disciplines including local authority policy development, nursery education, further and higher education, teacher education, social services day care, psychology services (child and adolescent mental health) and post-graduate counselling training and education. Formerly at Canterbury Christ Church University as Programme Director for the BA Early Childhood Studies, she is currently a Lecturer in Early Childhood and Education Studies at Anglia Ruskin University. Estelle is an assessor and tutor for the EYPS, also lecturing on the BA Early Childhood Studies degree at University Campus Suffolk. Her research interests focus on emotional and social development in childhood. Estelle's doctoral research has included children's participation and the role of emotions and learning in early childhood.

**Jane Murray** was an early childhood teacher for twenty years in three English local authorities before moving to her present role as Senior Lecturer in Early Years Education at the University of Northampton. Jane currently teaches across a range of early childhood and initial teacher education undergraduate courses as well as leading on the University of Northampton's MA in Education (Early Years) modules and pathway. Jane's research interests are in early childhood and education; she has several publications which focus predominantly on research, enquiry and epistemological issues in education and early childhood.

**Jackie Musgrave** is a senior lecturer in the Centre for Early Childhood at the University of Worcester. She is also a visiting lecturer at Warwick University where she teaches child health to early childhood studies students. Jackie started her working life as a registered general nurse and then trained as a registered sick children's nurse at Birmingham Children's Hospital. She moved into the community and worked as a practice nurse and developed an interest in the care of children with asthma. In 1998, Jackie moved into education and taught on a range of child care qualifications. After eight years of teaching and managing the Early Years Foundation Degree in a college of further education, she moved to her current role in April 2012. Jackie's research interests include the care and education of children aged birth to 3 and the effect of health on children's education and holistic development. Her current research is for her doctorate studies and she is exploring how practitioners create inclusive environments in day care settings for children with chronic medical conditions such as anaphylaxis, asthma, diabetes and eczema.

**Dr Kathy Ring** has extensive experience in the field of early years education. Following full-time positions as teacher, deputy headteacher and lecturer, she now combines her part-time role as a senior lecturer in early years education at York St John University with independent consultancy. She is an associate of early education. Kathy continues to research and write about how young children learn and how this can best be supported in educational settings. Her current focus is on how practitioners create opportunities for skill development across the multi-modality of children's engagement with their worlds.

**Anita Soni** has published two books on the Early Years Foundation Stage (EYFS). She works part time at the University of Birmingham in the educational psychology department and also works as an educational psychologist with a range of primary schools and children's centres in the West Midlands. Anita is interested in working with children and their families in their early years of life, between 0 and 5 years. She is enthusiastic about developing the skills of the children's workforce, especially those working in children's centres, and early years provision in the maintained, voluntary and independent sectors. This includes teachers, managers, teaching assistants, family support workers, early years practitioners and childminders. She has used a range of approaches to enable this including training, group supervision and consultation. Anita's particular interests are early years, children's centres, the Key Person approach, personal, social and emotional development and supervision.

**Corinne Syrnyk** is an assistant professor of psychology at St Mary's University College in Alberta, Canada. Having studied in both Canada and the UK, she has made contributions to the fields of psychology, early childhood studies and education. With international teaching experience, her preferred subjects include introductory and advanced child psychology and contemporary issues in the early years. Her research interests centre around children with social, emotional and behavioural disorders (SEBD), specifically the programmes and methods of intervention that are in place to support these children, along with the individuals who provide this support. She also conducts research and publishes in the areas of early language comprehension and early word learning.

# Foreword

The new Early Years Foundation Stage offers a revised framework for practitioners working in settings with young children and with it come certain challenges and issues on its implementation. This book provides students, academics and those concerned with early years, with reflections from professionals covering a range of backgrounds including higher education, children's centres and agencies linked to provision for young children, using their expertise in education, health, social care and psychology. The chapters form insights into elements of practice, with foundations in relevant pedagogy, and are brought together by Dr Pat Beckley from Bishop Grosseteste University.

Jan Ashbridge and Julie Kitchen provide an overview of principles underpinning provision. Anita Soni and Liz Creed give a perspective with a psychology basis, to explore children's experiences as individuals. Areas of learning are discussed by professionals who are leading researchers in their field, for example Kathy Ring on literacy and Elizabeth Carruthers and Emma Butcher on mathematics. Rachel Sparks Linfield discusses understanding the world and Estelle Martin considers expressive arts and design. Health and social aspects are scrutinized by Corinne Syrnyk, Jane Murray and Jackie Musgrave.

The book provides a wealth of experience and expertise and provides an essential reference for those who are privileged to be involved with the welfare, learning and education of young children.

*Nigel Appleton*
*Dean of the School of Teacher Development*
*Bishop Grosseteste University,*
*Lincoln*

# Acknowledgements

This book has evolved from a desire to share experiences, findings, reflections and research concerning children's early years at a time when the revised EYFS is being discussed and implemented. I am most grateful to my well-respected colleagues who have contributed so kindly by writing chapters to provide further insights into their particular fields of interest. This has been achieved despite other commitments in work and in their personal lives and is appreciated. The insights discussed support others working in early years and help further early years pedagogy and practice. Thanks also go to colleagues working at Bishop Grosseteste University and staff at Molescroft Primary School for sharing their outstanding practice.

# Introduction

This book provides a timely exploration of challenges and changes of issues for the early years. It incorporates discussions of the *Statutory Framework for the Early Years Foundation Stage*, hereafter referred to as the 2012 EYFS framework (DfE, 2012) and reflections from experienced professionals who share their knowledge and understandings of aspects of their practice and their reflections of it. Those involved in early years practice, whether at home, in private facilities, nurseries, schools, local authorities, higher education, health or other provision and agencies, have taken on board the new guidelines and implemented them, building on and adapting existing values and beliefs. The views of the professionals writing the chapters should provide welcome insights into pedagogy and practice and may enable readers to reflect upon their own principles regarding early years.

## Characteristics of effective learning

The 2012 EYFS framework identifies characteristics of effective learning. Three aspects are given which cover playing and exploring, active learning and creating and thinking critically. These three key aspects are further broken down into sub-headings that are: playing and exploring, focusing on children's engagement – finding out and exploring, playing with what they know, being willing to have a go; active learning based on children's motivation – being involved and concentrating, keeping trying, enjoying achieving what they set out to do; and creating and thinking critically focused on thinking – having their own ideas, making links, choosing ways to do things. These characteristics of effective learning are explored further in the framework and examples are provided within the EYFS principles underpinning practice concerning a unique child, positive relationships and enabling environments. The characteristics are discussed throughout this book in further detail. Part 1 concerns the underpinning philosophy and pedagogy for early years. Characteristics of effective learning are apparent in Chapter 1 where Liz Creed discusses a variety of theories concerning child development and the importance of promoting an appropriate atmosphere where children can flourish and the crucial nature of this facet. In Chapter 2 Jan Ashbridge describes how the organization and management of the enabling environment can facilitate the characteristics. In Chapter 3 Julie Kitchen discusses the role of the adult in providing appropriate interactions with children and differing approaches and views about how this can be addressed. Part 2, Chapters 4 to 6 written by Anita Soni and Pat Beckley, concern the prime areas of learning and development. Here strategies are interwoven within discussions to foster reflections of how the characteristics can be incorporated into practice within the three areas of personal, social and emotional development, physical development and communication and language. In Chapter 4 Anita considers carefully how the successful implementation of the personal, social and emotional development aspect is vital in ensuring children thrive. She notes her concerns and offers reflections on practice. Pat continues these discussions with reflections on pedagogy and practice for the elements of physical development and communication and language in Chapters 5 and 6. The aims of the characteristics are further included in Part 3, where considerations of issues focus on the four specific areas of learning and development in Chapters 7–10, written by Kathy Ring, Elizabeth Carruthers, Emma Butcher, Rachel Sparks Linfield and Estelle Martin.

Finally, in Part 4 pertinent issues are discussed further. Corinne Syrnyk, in Chapter 11, considers ways children who have difficulties accessing the characteristics can be supported in the early years. In Chapter 12 Jane Murray focuses on the thinking characteristic while providing a convincing rationale for the importance of this aspect and including examples from practice. Jackie Musgrave successfully combines aspects of engagement, motivation and thinking in Chapter 13 based on health and development. She argues the importance of these aspects for children's wellbeing. The two year review for young children is also considered carefully, with implications for those involved. To complete this section Pat considers wider implications of pedagogy and practice, incorporating differing views on appropriate approaches and possible future challenges.

## Early years principles

The principles underpinning the early years are discussed in detail in Part 1. Liz's considerations of various theories of child development and her personal experiences of the effect early childhood has on development and later life are included. These are closely linked to a unique child, where an understanding of children as individuals through knowledge of relevant theories and research supports preparations for helping and interacting with the child as an individual. Enabling environments are explored in Jan's chapter. Her wealth of experience in running, supporting and leading courses based on early years settings is used to provide reflections on possible considerations when planning an appropriate learning environment. Julie completes this section with reflections concerning the adult around the child. Her work builds on partnerships with parents where strategies such as working together to gain knowledge of children's prior learning and development, a welcoming environment, supporting fathers, liaising as an ongoing process and sharing assessments are used as a basis for consideration of how practitioners can develop interactions with children to be of most benefit.

## Areas of learning and development

The areas of learning and development in the 2012 EYFS framework differ from the previous framework in 2008 in that there are now 'Prime' and 'Specific' areas. The prior aspects, that is personal, social and emotional development, communication, language and literacy, problem-solving, reasoning and numeracy, knowledge and understanding of the world, creative development and physical development have been changed in the 2012 document to prime areas of personal, social and emotional development, physical development, communication and language and specific areas of literacy, mathematics, understanding the world and expressive arts and design. It is apparent that communication and language and the area concerning literacy have been split into separate areas. Physical development has been placed as a prime area and problem-solving, reasoning and numeracy have become mathematics. The new areas of learning and development are discussed in individual chapters in Parts 2 and 3. It is felt that the changes were the result of a belief, based on recent research, that the prime areas were crucial at an early age whereas the specific aspects could be addressed at a later age if necessary.

## Challenges, changes and reflections

Change can be viewed in a variety of ways, for example it might be welcomed, met with indifference or feared. Changes to existing practice might be easily implemented or may require much deliberation and collaboration to incorporate new initiatives or strategies. Practitioners may embrace different ideas or the incorporation of new views may require a complete re-think or reflection of values and beliefs held. Challenges may arise when there is an uncertainty about the changes or lack of confidence in implementing new practices. This book aims to support those involved in early years by sharing views and addressing some of the areas of concern felt. This aim is continued in Part 4 where key challenges highlighted are discussed and reflected upon.

## Reference

DFE (Department of Education) (2012) *Statutory Framework for the Early Years Foundation Stage: Setting the Standards for Learning, Development and Care of Children from Birth to Five*. www.education.gov.uk/publications/standard/AllPublications/Page1/DFE-00023-2012 (accessed 27 March 2013).

# Part 1

## The foundations of early years

Part 1 covers the key principles underpinning early years provision, featuring key theories of child development and prominent innovators of practice, appropriate enabling environments and main considerations when providing such environments. The section closes with reflections of practice for adults around the child, building on relationships and partnerships with parents and carers and the collaboration this fosters. It includes discussions of different ways in which adults working in settings with young children can promote interactions and scaffold and promote learning with them. Chapter 1, written by Liz Creed, concerns differing approaches used to facilitate learning and differing beliefs and theories concerning young children's development. Consideration is given to theories which have influenced perceptions of child development and how best to organize and manage provision. Prominent examples of provision, such as Montessori, are also discussed. Theories and ways of formulating an appropriate environment for children to flourish concern those interested in the welfare and care of young children. There is also discussion of how promoting a child's positive self-image is crucial to encouraging their development. Working with young children is ever-changing because of the need to respond to new initiatives, relevant innovations – including technological advances – and the results of collaborations with colleagues locally and on a global scale, bringing fresh ideas about ways to help children.

Chapter 2, 'The environment for learning' written by Jan Ashbridge, poses arguments concerning changes that have taken place in an early years setting since the mid-1970s and considers the rationale for such changes. Issues arising from the new EYFS framework are discussed, with relevant questions to ponder from personal experiences. Notions of quality of settings and what this entails reflect society's views of what is important for young children. Some examples of differing notions of what constitutes quality provision and how this can be represented in practice are considered in Jan's chapter. The importance of play-based learning is highlighted with links made to provision for courses for those involved in working with early years children, for example through initial teacher training. The enabling environment, emphasized in recent governmental documentation for early years, is explored through physical and emotional aspects, linking to guidelines from the 2012 EYFS framework. Jan highlights the need to promote an environment where the importance of the value of partnerships with parents and carers is evident through the organization and management of the facility. Aspects of the early years learning environment are discussed, such as outdoor learning. The chapter closes by raising challenges for the professional who is organizing the provision and possible explanations for the complexity of the role with numerous issues to be considered.

Chapter 3, 'The adults around the child' written by Julie Kitchen, delves into relationships by exploring adult/child and child/child interactions. It builds on relationships with parents and carers to acknowledge prior learning and development, working together to support the child as an individual in the most appropriate ways. Julie considers different interpretations of the support given to children by the professional involved. She draws on her research to provide pertinent examples of pedagogy in practice concerning the role of the adult.

The section opens with a discussion of the child as unique and the factors involved in this area, written by Liz Creed.

# 1

# Early years pedagogy into practice
Liz Creed

## Introduction

The chapter considers contemporary historical, socio-economic and political perspectives on early years provision, incorporating discussions of key figures who have influenced early years provision. This is explored in reference to the outcomes for children, their wellbeing, learning and progression. The chapter covers the factors involved in devising an appropriate environment for children to flourish, including play-based learning, from the pedagogical basis discussed. It suggests ways in which this stimulating environment can be accommodated and enhanced. The importance of reflective practice to continually review and enhance provision for young children is highlighted, with the inclusion of relevant research findings and governmental initiatives.

## Background to early years pedagogy

Early years pedagogy is an evolving phenomenon, responding to influences from numerous areas. *The Penguin English Dictionary* (Garmonsway and Simpson, 1971) states pedagogy is the 'art and practice of teaching'. This definition of the term could be open to change as it develops into an awareness of wider perspectives and is impacted by the underpinning beliefs and values of those involved. The document *Researching Effective Pedagogy in the Early Years* by Siraj-Blatchford et al. (2002: 27) considers 'Pedagogy is often referred to as the *practice* (or the *art*, the *science* or the *craft*) of teaching but in the early years an adequate conception of educative practice must be wide enough to include provision of learning environments for play and exploration', original emphasis). In this way, what is deemed appropriate practice in the early years is also open to reflection and change. The General Teaching Council (GTC, 2010: 2) suggested pedagogy is

> both the means of enhancing student learning and the source of teachers' professional identity. As professionals, teachers use expert judgement to recognise and resolve the dilemmas in teaching and learning . . . At their best, teachers are also able to reflect on and evaluate their practices, and to make rationally and ethically defensible judgements that go beyond compliance, pragmatic constraints or ideological preferences.

The teaching role is one of many professional roles concerned with children's progress in an early years setting. The EYFS framework can be used as a basis for provision with professionals using their judgements as to how best to implement this into their practice and provision.

Globalization is a factor in changing views of appropriate provision for early years children. The greater ease of collaboration, networks and sharing ideas supports the development of a broadening outlook of different strategies and approaches, with fresh perspectives facilitating a review of existing ways of working. This will be explored further in Chapter 14 'Challenges and convergence'.

The new 2012 EYFS (DfE, 2012), introduced following the Tickell Review, provides a framework and guidance for professionals when working with young children. The framework was produced after gaining the views of those involved in early years learning. Historically, in 1870 members of the Houses of Parliament debated the age for starting school. The importance of earning a living was considered with beginning and leaving statutory schooling early as a solution. Statutory schooling at 5 years old was established. The Hadow Report (Consultative Committee on Education, 1931) encouraged children's active engagement in activities and experiences, rather than that they should be perceived as empty vessels to be filled with facts. The Plowden Report (CACE, 1967) observed that young children would be best served by an educational system which provided nursery education for all whose parents wished for it. Concerns about standards were followed by the Bullock Report (DES, 1975) which advocated a number of measures to achieve high standards plus monitoring of standards to ensure they were achieved. In PM James Callaghan's Ruskin speech (Callaghan, 1976) he stated a monitoring of resources should occur to maintain a proper standard of performance. Research focusing on children's transition from a pre-school unit to a Reception class by Cleave, Jowett and Bate (1982) revealed differences between the two settings in the organization and types of activity provided for the children. In the National Curriculum (1988) the core curriculum covered English, mathematics and science. In 1995 the National Commission for Education developed the notion that investment of taxpayers' money in increased support for children aged 3–8 years would ensure that all children would achieve a good standard of basic skills at an early age, which would provide a foundation for later learning. Concerns were raised by some professionals over the 'top-down' emphasis evident in their settings, where pressure was exerted for children to be encouraged to use skills too early and there was a focus on outcomes to be attained.

Government guidelines such as the reports *Starting with Quality* (DES, 1990) and *Desirable Outcomes for Children's Learning on Entering Compulsory Education* (DfE, 1998) heralded welcome support for professionals working in early years provision that emphasized the importance of these crucial early years. It helped to promote the esteem of the roles of those working with younger children and began to raise awareness of this important phase in children's lives. It fostered further discussions of the quality of provision during this time, what this might entail and how it could be resourced and delivered. In 2000 the *Curriculum Guidance for the Foundation Stage* (QCA/DfEE, 2000) established the Foundation Stage as a valued aspect of the provision for children and gave credence for the stage as a crucial part of children's development, identifying it as highly important in its own right. Younger children were catered for in a separate document, *Birth to Three Matters* (Sure Start, 2002) which gave the foundations of four aspects: the strong child, the skilful communicator, the competent learner and the healthy child. The EYFS (DCSF, 2008) provided a framework for early years provision and covered the underpinning rationale and purpose of the findings with strategies for six areas of learning. It combined the rationale for the youngest age phase with those of 3–5 years to provide a seamless framework for provision. It was underpinned by four areas: a unique child, positive relationships, enabling environments and learning and development. The learning and development aspect incorporated a structure for children's development in learning from birth to 5 years and included: personal, social and emotional development, communication, language and literacy, problem-solving, reasoning and numeracy, knowledge and understanding of the world, creative development and physical development. This was complemented by an assessment strategy, the EYFS profile (QCA, 2008). This sought to bring together a common framework for the delivery of provision and an assessment of children's progress. It supported enabling children to have smooth transitions when required through this common set of documentation. Following findings from the Tickell Review adjustments were made to respond to views of those working with the framework and those involved with early years provision and possible changing needs. Reflections of appropriate practice have responded to theories of child development and research findings.

The policy and legislation outlined above are derived from theories of child development, and have detailed the optimum conditions for effective child development in various areas, such as social, emotional and cognitive development, and provided detail regarding factors which influence this development both by enhancing or hindering this process. There has been a range of theories put forward to outline the main factors in child development, many of which differ in assigning relative importance to factors influencing development. In light of this, key theorists and their respective recommendations and findings relating to fostering child development are explored throughout this chapter.

The following section notes key theorists who have influenced provision and its pedagogy and practice.

## Key theorists

### Locke (1632–1704)

Locke considered nurture or external forces as routes for development. He believed interactions with people and the environment affected children's development, and that parents were the first educators.

Locke theorized that people are born with a 'blank slate', meaning infants and children learn from experiences rather than being innately provided with skills and knowledge of themselves and the world. He therefore placed great importance on early life experiences, stating should infants and children have negative or unhelpful experiences they would suffer the consequences of this throughout their adult life. In discussing his concept of 'associations of ideas', Locke suggested it was crucial for children to be taught positive associations in order to develop effectively. He suggested early experiences are more important than those later in life, as it is these early experiences that form the first key lessons in learning about the self. In this way he proposed education as key in development, suggesting a good character and intelligence in adulthood is primarily derived from receiving a good education as a child. However he also proposed infants and children are born with some innate talents and capabilities, and following this argument suggested it was necessary for parents to observe their children's natural abilities and interests, and tailor learning to these rather than imposing their own views on children's activities and engaging them in activities they dislike.

In his ([1693] 1996) treatise *Some Thoughts Concerning Education and of the Conduct of the Understanding*, Locke discussed three distinct methods to educate children effectively, namely ensuring the development of a healthy body through maintaining a healthy diet and sleep pattern, the formation of a virtuous character specifically related to a child's ability to think rationally, and the choice of an appropriate educational curriculum further focused around encouraging critical thinking and an interest in learning and obtaining knowledge.

## Rousseau (1712–1778)

Rousseau believed that education should not be concerned with particular techniques of imparting information but rather with developing a child's character and moral sense, to enable them to make their own judgements about what is right or wrong. He proposed educators should enable children to learn moral behaviour through experiencing the consequences of their actions, and ensure children are able to do this in a safe way.

Rousseau proposed the importance of developmentally appropriate education, suggesting child development occurs in stages, namely three different stages of childhood. He suggested that during the first stage of childhood up to 12 years children are governed by their emotions and impulses, followed by the second stage between 12 and 16 years in which reason develops, and the third stage from 16 onwards when the child develops into an adult. He believed that at early stages of development children learn through their interaction with the world, particularly through the senses. He therefore proposed that educators should encourage development through enabling children to explore their environment, and that educators should optimize learning by helping children to explore things through their senses encouraging them to draw inferences based on these. Rousseau placed importance on developing children's ability to think and reason in younger childhood; however, he also placed importance on teaching children to understand complex human emotions, particularly sympathy, in later developmental stages.

## Freud (1856–1939)

Freud proposed children develop through a series of stages, highlighting in particular stages of personality and moral development, or the 'psychosexual stages of development'. In these stages, Freud proposed, children are influenced by differing constructs of the psyche which are both unconscious and conscious to varying degrees, namely the Id, Ego and Super-Ego. Freud suggested infants are initially governed by the unconscious Id, which seeks to gain immediate gratification and have its needs met, leading infants to seek out experiences based on the 'pleasure principle'. In this stage, Freud proposed infants have not yet developed ideas of socially appropriate behaviour, and behave in accordance with their wishes and demands.

Freud proposed that as children develop, so does the Ego in order to moderate the demands of the Id in accordance with the child's outer world or environment. In this way, the Ego aims to find a balance between the Id's drive for immediate gratification and what is realistic and reasonable; therefore it is a part of the Id modified by the external influence of the outside world.

Freud also proposed the Super-Ego develops later, which works in conflict with the Id, seeking to motivate a child to behave in a socially acceptable manner. Freud suggested this construct controls a child's sense of right and wrong, leading to feelings of guilt as a punishment in instances of misbehaviour. He suggested the Super-Ego acts as a parental figure, and takes on the influence of individuals in such a role, such as teachers and educators, for example. With the Id and Super-Ego striving for opposing goals, Freud proposed the Ego manages conflicts and discrepancies between the two.

During a child's stages of development, from infancy into puberty and adulthood, Freud argued the Id, Ego and Super-Ego influence a child to varying degrees, eventually leading to effective management of drives by the Ego and an emotionally well-adjusted adult. However, should conflicts between the constructs occur which are not resolved during each of the stages of development, Freud suggested it may be possible for a child to become stuck, or fixated, at one of the stages. This would lead to maladjustments in personality development, leading to the development of 'neuroses' or problems with emotional wellbeing. He therefore suggested it is necessary for caregivers to attend to children's needs effectively in order to help them move through these developmental stages appropriately.

## Dewey (1859–1952)

Dewey argued that social interaction is needed for children to learn. He believed that pupils thrive in an environment where they actively interact with the curriculum and their surroundings. In addition to his views on child development, he also stated his views regarding effective education of children. He stated that effective education would present new information in a way that allows children to relate this to past experiences in order to optimize its meaning, and effective teaching would provide opportunities for hands-on learning and experiential education.

## Watson (1878–1958) and Skinner (1904–1990)

Watson and Skinner's views fall under the heading of Behaviourism, a movement in psychology which highlighted the importance of scientific investigation to further understanding of human behaviour and development through drawing conclusions based on observable behaviours. This was a reaction to previous theories in psychology where the focus was often centered on constructs of the mind, which behaviourists argued could not be helpfully understood as they did not lend themselves to direct observation.

In discussing child development, behaviourist theories proposed children learn through imitation and 'conditioning'. Bandura's (1969) Social Learning Theory proposed children's behaviour can be modified through observation and imitation or modelling of various role models. Research (Bandura et al., 1961) highlighted children observing role models' aggression are more likely to then act aggressively themselves than when they have observed role models reacting compassionately or indifferently. Skinner also discussed the role of imitation in the development of language, stating children learn language as a result of imitation of language to which they are exposed.

Skinner also discussed the role of 'conditioning' in childhood learning, proposing children learn through reward and punishment of certain behaviours. Therefore if behaviour is punished, either through delivering punishment or withdrawal of a pleasurable item, this behaviour reduces. Whereas when behaviour is rewarded or reinforced, either through directly being given a reward, or a negative stimulus being removed, this behaviour is likely to increase in frequency. Therefore, children learn to behave in certain ways through the consequences of their behaviour. In addition to this, behaviour is also influenced through 'extinction', which occurs when a previously reinforced behaviour is no longer reinforced, causing the behaviour to become exhibited less frequently.

When considered in the context of child development this has implications for children and their caregivers, in suggesting that to increase the likelihood of a child displaying wanted behaviours, these must be reinforced so that the likelihood a child will engage in these behaviours is increased initially. Their use must also continue to be reinforced otherwise the behaviours may begin to diminish.

## Piaget (1896–1980)

Piaget (1929) proposed that children develop through a series of stages. He named them the Sensori-motor (birth–2 years), Pre-operational (2–4 years), Intuitive (4–7 years), Concrete operational (7–11 years) and Formal operational (11–16 years) stages of development. Piaget suggested children learn initially through interaction with objects around them, stating this mode of learning is much more effective for child development than passively listening to information. As a child moves through the proposed stages of development, they become increasingly able to solve problems mentally without the need to deal with objects directly. This allows the child to move away from purely dealing with the actual, to being able to consider the possible.

Piaget also emphasized the importance of social interaction in fostering effective child cognitive development, stating that through this children develop language which enables them to communicate their own ideas and communicate with others, enabling them to learn others' ideas and perspectives and therefore further their own knowledge.

## Kohlberg (1927–1987)

Kohlberg devised a theory of moral development where morality could be viewed in stages from 1–6 in sequence towards higher order reasoning, and proposed that by progressing through these stages of development children become able to deal with moral dilemmas more effectively. Kohlberg expanded on Piaget's work, proposing the process of moral development was primarily concerned with justice, and continued throughout an individual's lifetime.

Kohlberg's stages begin with the pre-conventional stages found in childhood. Stage 1, which he suggested is driven by ideas of obedience and punishment, leads children to be concerned with how to avoid punishment, which is followed by stage 2 in which children become concerned with self-interest or 'what's in it for me?' leading them to consider morality and what is right in terms of what is in their own best interest. Kohlberg suggested the conventional stages occur in adolescence and adulthood, and stages 3 and 4 are concerned with filling certain social roles and adhering to social conventions such as laws. Finally, in the post-conventional level occurring in adulthood, Kohlberg proposed stages 5 and 6 are characterized by individuals developing abstract moral reasoning, being able to view rules and laws as changing and flexible, and being able to develop a moral code outside of that proposed by societal conventions. In these stages, individuals are seen as able to recognize that views about morality vary according to each person and community.

## Vygotsky (1896–1934)

Vygotsky stressed the importance of social interactions to promote children's development. He proposed children learn primarily through social interaction with others in a number of different contexts, and that this active involvement in activities encourages achievement at a higher level. Vygotsky stated children learn and develop through considered interaction with an 'expert' individual who is able to guide learning effectively. He suggested children learn most effectively when new information is presented to a level just above their current level of understanding. Should new information be too advanced, the child would struggle to assimilate this with previously understood information. However, should the information not be challenging enough, the child would fail to continue to develop their knowledge further. The difference between what was possible unaided and what was achievable with support is called the zone of proximal development (ZPD). The adult (expert) has an engineered conversation with the child (novice) in which the adult constructs questions that the child is able to respond to. The questions may develop in complexity in stages, and through the process of reflection and providing answers the child is able to make appropriate learning connections around meanings of the experiences encountered. Vygotsky claimed there was a gap between a child's actual development and their potential development. This would be followed by internalization where a child could reflect upon what was discovered. Therefore, by providing new information just ahead of a child's current level of knowledge and enabling a child to take time to reflect on this new information, an 'expert' or educator is able to allow a child to reach their potential for development.

## Bruner (1915–)

Bruner's observations of childhood learning lead him to propose children learn new information and master new skills through a process he referred to as 'scaffolding'.

In this he suggested children, and also adults, are able to learn any skill as long as information is structured appropriately through the learning process, and suggested effective teaching should return to material previously presented at certain intervals, providing more advanced knowledge at every stage. He proposed three stages of learning, or 'modes of representation', known as enactive, iconic and symbolic representation. Upon being presented with new information, learners progress through these stages to the deepest level of understanding at symbolic representation.

Bruner also held views regarding children's cognitive and social development, and similarly to Vygotsky, proposed that social interaction plays a key role in this development and language acquisition. In his view children acquire language in order to communicate with others, and do so primarily through effective and meaningful parent–child interactions. From his social constructivist viewpoint, he suggested the importance of social interaction and communication in child development.

## Bowlby (1907–1990)

In his 'Attachment Theory' (Bowlby, 1969), Bowlby highlighted the importance for development of an effective mother–child relationship in a child's early life. Bowlby stated that it is necessary for a mother and infant to form a bond with each other within a short period of time after birth, and proposed that an effective, caring bond ensures the child's emotional wellbeing. However should the mother not be available during this time, or should the bond developed be less than adaptive and optimal, the child would suffer developmentally later in life and experience difficulties with emotional wellbeing.

Bowlby suggested infants become attached to individuals who are sensitive and responsive in their interactions with them, and who remain as consistent caregivers during a period from around six months to two years after birth. With adaptive attachments, in which caregivers continue to respond to children's needs sensitively and effectively during this time, children are able to begin to explore their world moving away from their caregivers to develop knowledge and understanding of the world around them, while returning to caregivers as a secure base. In this way, children have the safety and security necessary from which to confidently explore their world.

In cases where children have less than optimal attachments, problems in emotional wellbeing can develop as children do not have a safe and secure base to explore from, and do not have caregivers who are responsive to their needs.

Bowlby described how caregivers' responses to children and infants can lead to the development of patterns of attachment, therefore influencing an individual in later life as attachment patterns formed early in life can often be replicated with close individuals in adulthood.

## Maslow (1908–1970)

Maslow also proposed certain stages of development; however, he argued that these were organized in a 'hierarchy of needs' in which humans develop through being motivated to fulfil increasing levels of need.

This hierarchy begins with physiological needs such as food, water, shelter and sleep, moving on to the need for safety including personal and financial security, and health and wellbeing. The next level of need is for love and belonging, for example through intimate relationships, friendships and family relationships. Humans then move on to the need for esteem, including self-esteem and confidence, respect for themselves and others. Maslow termed the final stage 'self-actualization', with humans striving to realize their full potential. This can be specific to each individual; however Maslow stated that in order to achieve this, an individual must not just achieve but master the previous needs.

Maslow stated that each stage must be achieved before an individual is able to strive for the next stage, and in cases where any one of the four lower stages (physiological, safety, love/belonging, esteem) are not met this results in anxieties and tension.

**Reflections**

Which theories do you feel influence your philosophy of early years learning?

How are they demonstrated in practice?

Are there a combination of theories underpinning your philosophy and practice?

## Factors affecting child development: research

In addition to these theories of child development, research can also inform us of factors influencing children and their cognitive, social and emotional development. Bowlby ([1953] 1969) developed his 'maternal deprivation hypothesis' in which he proposed that children suffer cognitively, socially and emotionally without an effective, warm and caring bond with their mother. Research (Ainsworth et al., 1978; Goldfarb, 1947; Spitz, 1946) has indicated support for this, identifying how infants who did not have a secure maternal attachment, or were raised in foster care/institutions with poor attachments to caregivers showed poor development in all areas. Research (van Ijzendoorn et al., 1992) indicates that secure attachments to multiple caregivers, including fathers, siblings and wider family members, encourages effective child development. Peer relationships are also considered important for children's development, as is indicated through research (Cowen et al., 1973; Gilmartin, 1987; Kochenderfer and Ladd, 1996) which has demonstrated that rejection and bullying by peers leads to poor social and emotional development, and problems in later life with confidence and self-esteem.

## Early experiences and influence on later life

In considering factors contributing to effective child development, in which the benefits can be seen through effective social, emotional and cognitive development of a child, it is also important to consider the impact of this early experience on the individual throughout their lifespan. We have seen how theorists have identified important conditions enabling children to achieve their full potential during childhood, and factors which can hinder this. This is important in itself; however, what is also greatly important is an understanding of how such early experiences influence an individual in adulthood, as a key aim of education is to ensure a child is given the opportunity to develop into a successfully functioning adult.

With this in mind, let us consider theory identifying the relationship between early experiences and functioning in later life; in particular, a theory proposed by Beck (1976) regarding early experiences and the development of emotional disorders. In his Cognitive Model of Emotional Disorders (1976), Beck proposed that early experiences lead an individual to develop beliefs about themselves, others and the world around them. He proposed that these beliefs are absolute, such as 'I am worthy', 'Others are critical', or 'The world is an unsafe place'. He suggested that individuals develop a number of beliefs, and that these can be either helpful or unhelpful. When beliefs develop which are unhelpful, or negative, they lead an individual to experience emotional distress; therefore to alleviate or protect against this an individual develops rules or assumptions, which guide their behaviour to ensure these beliefs do not impact negatively upon them. For example, if an individual receives messages as a child from caregivers that it is selfish to ask for things they want, they may develop beliefs such as 'I am bad' or 'I am selfish'. Rules in this instance would prompt the individual to put others first, or deny themselves of things they want or need, and appear as statements such as 'I should always put others' needs before my own' or 'I ought not to express my own needs'. In this way, these rules are often rigid and inflexible standards a person feels they must adhere to. Such a rule could be seen to influence behaviour in that a person who believes they should not assert their own needs may seek to please others and deny themselves the things they need. When considering the impact of this it is possible to see that through developing unhelpful beliefs, an individual may become vulnerable to difficulties with emotional wellbeing in later life. For example, this individual may feel happy while meeting others' needs, but may be prone to depression and feelings of guilt when it is necessary to take care of themselves. Also the long-term consequences of this behaviour may lead the individual to develop problems in relationships, for example due to difficulty expressing their own needs they may not have their own needs met by others, which may lead to resentment and tension in relationships.

In accordance with this model, psychological vulnerability is linked to situations which may occur in an individual's life leading to a person's rules being threatened or broken, for example when this individual asks for their needs to be met or does something to please themselves. In the event of this event or trigger occurring, an individual would then experience emotional distress, for example anxiety or depression.

This theory falls under the Cognitive Movement in psychology, and later contributed to the formation of Cognitive Behaviour Therapy through convergence with Behaviourism as a treatment for emotional disorder, and targets an individual's faulty thinking patterns or cognitive distortions, and maladaptive coping patterns or behaviours to alleviate distress.

**Reflections**

Do you follow a positive cognitive behaviour pattern?

How can this positive pattern of thinking be promoted in a setting with young children?

## Conclusion

In light of the above discussion, it is very important not to underestimate the impact of childhood experiences and development on an individual throughout their life, both in terms of their social and emotional wellbeing, but also for their cognitive development, and academic and professional achievement. It is therefore essential for caregivers and educators to find out about relevant theory and research highlighting ways of fostering effective child development in all areas, and to ensure their own practice is informed by this wealth of information.

Some individuals have developed their own approaches to working with young children, using their pedagogical perspective to implement their perceptions of appropriate practice. The new EYFS provides a framework in which to work with young children. It is the professional who uses that information and incorporates this into the context of service provision, the partnerships fostered, the community involved around the setting, resources and, of course, the experiences and needs of the children in their care.

## References

Ainsworth, M.D.S., Blehar, M.C., Waters, E. and Wall, S. (1978) *Patterns of Attachment*. Hillsdale, NJ: Erlbaum.

Bandura, A. (1969) Social learning theory of identificatory processes. In D.A. Goslin (ed.) *Handbook of Socialization Theory and Research*. Chicago: Rand McNally.

Bandura, A., Ross, D. and Ross, S.A. (1961) Transmission of aggression through imitation of aggressive models. *Journal of Abnormal and Social Psychology*, 63: 575–82.

Beck, A.T. (1976) *Cognitive Therapy and the Emotional Disorders*. New York: International Universities Press.

Bowlby, J. (1953) *Child Care and the Growth of Love*. Harmondsworth: Penguin.

Bowlby, J. (1969) *Attachment and Loss, Vol. 1, Attachment*. London: Hogarth Press.

CACE (Central Advisory Council for Education (England)) (1967) *Children and their Primary Schools* (Plowden Report). London: HMSO.

Callaghan, J. (1976) Ruskin speech. http://education.guardian.co.uk/thegreatdebate/story/0,9860,574645,00.html (accessed 1 May 2012).

Cleave, S., Jowett, S. and Bate, M. (1982) *And So To School*. Windsor: NFER Publishing Company.

Consultative Committee on Education (1931) *The Primary School* (Hadow Report). London: HMSO.

Cowen, E. L., Pederson, A., Babigian, H., Izzo, L. D. and Trost, M. A. (1973) Long-term follow-up of early detected vulnerable children. *Journal of Consulting and Clinical Psychology*, 41: 438–46.

DCSF (Department for Children, Schools and Families) (2008) *Statutory Framework for the Early Years Foundation Stage: Setting the Standards for Learning, Development and Care for Children from Birth to Five*. Nottingham: DCSF Publications.

DES (Department of Education and Science) (1975) *A Language for Life* (Bullock Report). London HMSO.

DES (1990) *Starting with Quality: The Report of the Committee of Inquiry into the Quality of the Educational Experience Offered to 3 and 4 Year Olds*. London: HMSO.

DfE (Department for Education) (1998) *Desirable Outcomes for Children's Learning on Entering Compulsory Education*. London: QCA.

DfE (2012) *Statutory Framework for the Early Years Foundation Stage: Setting the Standards for Learning, Development and Care of Children from Birth to Five*. http://www.education.gov.uk/publications/standard/AllPublications/Page1/DFE-00023-2012 (accessed 27 March 2013).

Garmonsway, G.N. and Simpson, J. (1971) *The Penguin English Dictionary*. Middlesex: Penguin Books.

Gilmartin, B.G. (1987) Peer group antecedents of severe love-shyness in males. *Journal of Personality*, 55: 467–89.

Goldfarb, W. (1947) Variations in adolescent adjustment of institutionally reared children. *American Journal of Orthopsychiatry*, 17: 449–57.

GTC (General Teaching Council) (2010) *Professionalism and Pedagogy: A Contemporary Opportunity*. London: Teaching and Learning Research Programme.

van Ijzendoorn, M.H., Sagi, A. and Lambermon, M.W.E. (1992) The multiple caretaker paradox: data from Holland and Israel. *New Directions for Child and Adolescent Development*, 5–24.

Kochenderfer, B. and Ladd, G. (1996) Peer victimisation: Cause or consequence of school maladjustment? *Child Development*, 67: 1305–17.

Locke, J. (1996) *Some Thoughts Concerning Education and Of the Conduct of the Understanding*, edited by R.W. Grant and N. Tarcov. Indianapolis, In: Hackett Publishing Co.

Piaget, J. (1929) *The Child's Conception of the World*. New York: Harcourt Brace Jovanovich.

QCA (Qualifications and Curriculum Authority) (2008) *Early Years Foundation Stage: Profile Handbook*. London: QCA.

QCA (Qualifications and Curriculum Authority)/DfEE (Department for Education and Employment) (2000) *Curriculum Guidance for the Foundation Stage*. London: QCA/DfEE.

Siraj-Blatchford, I., Sylva, K., Muttock, S., Gilden, R. and Bell, D. (2002) *Researching Effective Pedagogy in the Early Years*. Norwich: HMSO.

Spitz, R.A. (1946) Hospitalism: a follow-up report. *Psychoanalytic Study of the Child*, 2: 113–18.

Sure Start (2002) *Birth to Three Matters: A Framework to Support Children in their Earliest years*. London: DfES.

## Further reading

Bruner, J.S. (1966) *Toward a Theory of Instruction*. Cambridge, MA: Harvard University Press.

Bruner, J.S. (1977) Early social interaction and language acquisition. In H.R. Schaffer (ed.) *Studies in Mother-Infant Interaction*. London: Academic Press.

Bruner, J.S., Caudill, E. and Ninio, A. (1977) Language and experience. In R.S. Peters (ed.) *John Dewey Reconsidered*. Routledge & Kegan Paul.

DCSF (Department for Children, Schools and Families) (2007) *KEEP: Key Elements of Effective Practice*. London: The Stationery Office.

Dewey, J. (1902) *The Child and the Curriculum*. Retrieved from http://books.google.com/books

Dewey, J. ([1916] 2009) *Democracy and Education: An Introduction to the Philosophy of Education*. New York: WLC Books.

DfES (Department for Education and Schools) (2007) *Practice Guidance for the Early Years Foundation Stage*. Nottingham: DfES.

DfES (2007) *Early Years Foundation Stage Framework*. London: DfES.

Freud, S. (1923) *Neurosis and Psychosis. The Standard Edition of the Complete Psychological Works of Sigmund Freud, Volume XIX (1923–1925): The Ego and the Id and Other Works*, 147–54.

Kohlberg, L. (1981) *Essays on Moral Development, Vol. I: The Philosophy of Moral Development*. San Francisco, CA: Harper & Row.

Locke, J. (1997) *An Essay Concerning Human Understanding*, edited by R. Woolhouse. New York: Penguin Books.

Maslow, A.H. (1943) A theory of human motivation. *Psychological Review*, 50(4), 370–96.

Palmer, J. (2001) *Fifty Modern Thinkers on Education: From Piaget to the Present*. London: Taylor & Francis.

Rousseau, J. (1979) *Emile, or On Education*. Trans. Allan Bloom. New York: Basic Books, 37.

Schacter, D.L., Gilbert, D.T and Wegner, D.M. (2011) *B.F Skinner: The role of reinforcement and Punishment Psychology*, 2nd edn. New York: Worth Incorporated.

Vygotsky, L. (1962) *Thought and Language*. Cambridge, MA: MIT Press.

Watson, J.B. and Rayner, R. (1920) Conditioned emotional reactions. *Journal of Experimental Psychology*, 3, 1: 1–14.

# 2

# The environment for learning
Jan Ashbridge

## Introduction

This chapter considers what is deemed appropriate for an early years setting and the different perspectives this might raise. Different styles, including play-based learning in an early years environment, are discussed. Physical and emotional aspects of the provision are explored. The use of the outdoor space is discussed with reflections on similarities between indoor and outdoor spaces as learning areas. Challenges to the provision of a child-centred environment for learning are reflected upon.

Consider the following questions:

What is the purpose of early childhood education?
What does society want our children to be doing and learning in our settings and classrooms?
How do children know what they are there for and what is expected of them?

The answers to these questions are many and varied. Different people in different times and places will have different opinions. These opinions and viewpoints will all be reflected in the learning environments that are created for children.

If we believe that early education is about childcare and enabling parents, especially mothers, to return to the workplace, we will create a homely, comfortable environment where children are relaxed and few expectations are made of them. If we believe that children need a compensatory environment away from impoverished social conditions our environment may have more structure. We may believe that this support and input could lead to better outcomes for children in the longer term and perhaps less need for them to work with other agencies later in life. Perhaps we believe that the early years are the time when children are prepared for school and that they need to start learning basic academic skills early in order to have success later in life. A learning environment created to support this could look quite formal indeed.

**Activity**

Read Pugh and Duffy (2006) page 6 and Dahlberg et al. (2007) page 76. What do you believe the purpose(s) of early years education to be? Look at the different ways people view early education and make a chart to show how each may impact on the environment that teachers and practitioners create.

## Looking back

In the early part of the twentieth century, the nursery environment was seen as being one which needed to be healthy, to provide good, nutritious food and medical care, to enable children to play outside in the fresh air and to compensate for the poverty and squalid home conditions faced by children in the industrial cities (Nutbrown et al., 2008: 6). This focus on play is pivotal for pioneers such as Rachel and Margaret McMillan who believed that children became whole people through play as it was through this that they applied and understood what they had learned. The McMillan sisters held that to do this effectively, 'ample space is almost as wanted as food and air – to move, to run, to find things out by new movement, to feel one's life in every limb, that is the life of a Nursery School' (McMillan, 1930). Space and the outdoors were also vital for Susan Isaacs who believed that 'the sanitised environment was not one where learning could happen' (Nutbrown et al., 2008: 104). An environment that reflected and included children's social realities was important. Isaacs also considered the emotional environment to be vital for children's development. She believed that parents are the first and most important educators of young children and that the provision of an environment that meets the emotional needs of children as they make the transition from home to school was vital (Nutbrown et al., 2008: 106).

Isaacs, and Johann Pestalozzi (1746–1827) before her, believed that an environment that supported children in discovering their world through activity was key to their ability to learn successfully. Motivation was all important and an environment that provided opportunities for meaningful play where children were able to pose their own questions, seek their own answers and satisfy their curiosity through the use of all their senses was the way to inspire this in children.

What is puzzling is that thinking such as this was widely known and discussed and yet for the most part did not make any significant impact on many children's early school experiences.

Forty years ago, I walked into a Reception class for the first time as a small child. It was bright, full of children (40 of us), it had a very big blackboard, a big carpet area and lots of little tables and chairs. The teacher had a big table which was right in the middle of the classroom. This is where she sat and where we all lined up for what seemed like forever to have our sums checked, or where we stood next to her big chair so she could listen to us read. We copied writing down off the big board into our books, wrote sums down off little cards and used our fingers to find the answers.

I knew I was there to listen, learn and to do what the teacher told me. School was about reading, writing, sums and sitting still. It was about being good and conforming; doing what you were told. How did I know? I was told so in lots of different ways. My parents said 'you have to do what you are told and work hard at big school!' and the teacher reinforced this by valuing and praising those of us who sat still and got on with our task. Those who made too much noise or were disruptive were sent down the corridor to see the headteacher or were made to sit on a chair in the corner. Perhaps the most important way was the classroom itself and what we were allowed to do in it. I recall tables, chairs and a big blackboard that we all looked at. Whatever was happening on that board was obviously very important. The teacher herself was obviously important – she had a very big table and chair. I felt very small indeed standing next to her. She checked your copying and your sums and made sure that it was done correctly and if not you were sent back to your table to do it again. Sometimes in the afternoon we would paint. We would come in to find every table was covered with newspaper and paper and paint were put out for us all. There were no other options. The environment created by the teacher dictated our activities and behaviour. School was serious. We were there to learn.

Despite all the work done in the late nineteenth and early twentieth centuries, my experience in the 1970s did not reflect this ethos at all. Why was this? Why was there such a focus on reading, writing and arithmetic? Why was the environment so structured and indeed regimented?

Expectations in early years classrooms are shaped by the agendas and policies of successive governments and the different ideas and ideologies that they embrace. The way that space is allocated and used reflects current ideas about pedagogy and curriculum. In 1975, Foucault noted that children had been traditionally expected to 'curtail and restrict their movement by sitting still and moving in regulated ways in environments such as schools' (McLaren et al., 2011: 101). Isaacs and McMillan had not made much of an impact by then!

We learned very specific things in an adult-controlled environment. There was no National Curriculum at the time so we were taught in a manner that suited our teacher, the school and its parents' expectations, all underpinned by the policy of the day. No room here for McMillan and Isaacs' outdoor, physical, risk-taking play, where the child's emotional needs are central. Indeed the 1970s saw a 'general disenchantment with education as a palliative for society's ills.' (Galton et al., 1980: 41). It was a time when much more emphasis was being placed on the assessment of children and the accountability of teachers and Callaghan's Ruskin speech in 1976 (Callaghan, 1976) ensured that this was to be a key priority for all political parties as the decade drew to a close.

The situation did not seem to have changed significantly in the ten years following, as in the 1980s the Conservative government had an education policy that wanted 'to see a return to traditional values in education and behaviour' (Baker, 1988 in Hustler et al., 1991: 107). It was in this climate that the National Curriculum was introduced in 1988. In terms of early childhood education, this emphasis on knowing things and factual and testable outcomes had quite an impact. Teachers were expected to teach a range of specific subjects from the Reception class. The different nature of learning and the development of children in the early years of school did not appear to be recognized.

A subject-based, outcome-driven curriculum creates a teacher that feels the need to pass on information in quite a didactic way. To accommodate this, the classroom they create will reflect the value they place on certain activities. Watching and listening to a teacher will need a classroom to be organized so that the children are all sitting down, each having a table and a seat.

Teacher training, following government policy, also had a part to play. Fisher (2002) claimed that, 'since the late 1980s, play and child development have been squeezed out of initial teacher training in favour of a more subject based approach' (p.124). This means, in effect, that there are teachers in the workforce today who do not know about or value play; do not know about integrated learning or how to create the environment required enabling this to happen.

**Reflections**

What have been the barriers to a play-based, child-centred learning environment? List them and the effects that these barriers have had.

## The present

Walking into a Reception or nursery setting today there is a very different atmosphere. Children walking in can see different areas of provision where they can choose to engage in a range of activities. If they want to paint, they can go to the workshop area; if they want to build they can go to the construction area. Role play areas ensure that imaginative play is available and cosy book corners invite children and adults in to share high quality books. Opportunities for learning are provided outside too and children can choose where to spend their time. Many children can plan their own learning and record what they want to do with their parents and carers so that bridges are made between home and school environments.

## What brought about these changes in approach?

By the time the *Curriculum Guidance for the Foundation Stage* (DFEE, 2000) was published, research had shown that children learned more effectively in an environment that reflected the holistic nature of their development. This framework and its successors have increasingly emphasized the importance of play as a primary way that children learn and make sense of the world (DCSF, 2009: 10; DfE, 2012: 6; DFEE, 2000: 7). These documents all agree that children learn in unique ways and that the adult's role is to identify these ways and provide for them within the learning environment. This focus on children's individual development and the role of play in that learning and development, which has been espoused by recent governments, has had a major impact on our concept of an appropriate learning environment. As the curriculum has altered, so have the expectations of Ofsted. Although we may wish it were otherwise, inspection is a powerful driver for change and the guidance and good practice case studies available on the Ofsted website are very useful for practitioners in developing an understanding of what an appropriate learning environment should actually look like. Settings are required to have an environment that is safe, stimulating, accessible to all children, uses the space efficiently and reflects the background of the children who use it (Ofsted, 2010). Good practice guidance tells us for example that an effective environment is one which can be altered to meet the children's needs and interests at a particular time (Ofsted, 2011: 4).

Initial teacher education now places much more importance on children's development and the kinds of environments where this can successfully happen. Links between learning through play and facilitating environments are forged early on in students' understandings and they are encouraged to go on placement actively looking for ways to develop and use the environment to support the learning of all children. In conjunction with the changing curriculum and the inspection framework, this deeper understanding of the nature of young children's learning has shaped and altered the environments that we provide for them to develop and learn in.

This fundamentally different way of viewing learning has much more in common with earlier ideas and ideals. It means that the environment we need to create must be fundamentally different also; not simply in the way it looks but in the way that we, the teachers, intend it to be used.

**Reflections**

Our recent frameworks (DCSF, 2009; DfE, 2012; DFEE, 2000), have given particular attention to the importance of the 'enabling' environment. What should the environment be enabling?

## Creating an enabling environment

The DfE recognizes three, key characteristics of effective learning in the EYFS: 'playing and exploring, active learning and creating and critical thinking' (2012: 7). An enabling environment needs to support and enable children to engage in activities that promote these kinds of behaviours and provide resources and adult involvement to develop and challenge their learning.

There are arguably two facets to the enabling environment – the physical and the emotional aspects. Each aspect is heavily dependent on the other. It is the adult who shapes and creates each through their values, beliefs and attitudes towards children, their learning and their needs. Fisher (2008) discusses 'rhetoric and reality', citing the work of Pascal (1990) and Bennett et al. (1997). Teachers reported that they valued play and that they had created child-initiated/play-based provision but when their practice was observed, they used largely teacher-directed strategies thus demonstrating that they had not really taken on board the importance of play or an environment that facilitates it. The environment looks wonderful – there are different areas of provision which look very appealing but they are not used or planned for in a way that supports learning. They are used for children's free play after their 'work' – the adult-directed learning. Dowling states that children spend their time in either controlling or informational contexts (2010: 21). Environments that are controlling are adult directed requiring children to comply; informational ones are those which 'encourage children to take responsibility for themselves by learning to plan their work, decide what resources to use and then have a part in assessing what has been achieved'. Guidance (DCSF, 2009: 5), tells us that the environment we create should ensure that children have a mixture of:

- Child-initiated play, actively supported by adults
- Focused learning, with adults guiding the learning
- Through playful, rich experiential activities

So the physical environment we create needs to be able to sustain child-initiated play and learning, adult-directed play and playful teaching in an environment which allows children to be active and hands on. In order for this learning to be successful and meaningful, children need to be able to plan and develop ideas independently. They need a well-organized environment in which they know where and how to access resources that are consistently available. This means they can get them when they need them and develop their skills in using them over time. They need to know that they can mix and match resources to solve problems they are involved in and be able to safely use and put away a range of equipment. These abilities will enable children to engage more fully in adult-directed play and learning independently but also develop their ability to plan their own autonomous learning as they become more confident and capable. Independence and autonomy are very important in helping children to develop positive attitudes towards themselves as learners and positive dispositions towards their learning.

**Activity**

Read Chapter 5 of Fisher (2008). This chapter provides a very sensible guide to the practicalities of setting up a physical learning environment that supports independent and autonomous learners. This is an environment where children have control and make choices. They are not simply passive recipients of 'someone else's decision making and control' (Fisher, 2002: 132).

Create two spider diagrams showing how the learning environment can be organized to support independence and autonomy and how these two aspects are intrinsically linked.

A truly enabling environment, however, needs more than this superficial knowledge about organization and resources – as important as this knowledge is. Johnston argues that an enabling environment is one which supports interactions on all levels and where children 'learn to relate to each other and become well rounded individuals, who are socially and emotionally able to interact with the world' (2012: 138). It is, she suggests, an enabling environment that should 'support children through transitions' providing continuity day to day as well as through more major transitions. It is a place where the adults from a range of disciplines are able to work together for the benefit of the child.

When looked at in this way the learning environment is less about a specific room but more about relationships and the attitudes of key people in the lives of young children. The early years classroom/setting is the place where very different worlds and sets of expectations come together (Hustler et al., 1991: 104). It is important, therefore, to understand these expectations and create an environment where everyone can recognize its purposes and its values. Parents may need clear explanations about the curriculum and the way that the environment is designed to support and enhance their children's learning. An environment that includes and welcomes parents and their contributions is one where the children will feel more comfortable and confident. This is easier to achieve if their backgrounds and cultures are obviously valued and celebrated – parents 'recognize' and share the ethos. Children bring their backgrounds and their culture into the setting with them. They come with a wealth of experiences from their home and their family; some good, some bad. They are usually eager to re-enact and discuss these experiences and this is a motivating factor that should not be overlooked. As children bring these different interests and experiences, it is the practitioner's role to take them and incorporate them into the routines, the physical environment and the activity that goes on within it. As this happens, children become more involved, more confident and more able to feel a sense of belonging to the setting. They are able to help shape the physical and emotional environment alongside the teacher, becoming more confident and more able to participate in the learning experiences on offer.

A learning environment that truly supports their play is a powerful motivator for children. It facilitates the development of positive learning dispositions and attitudes through providing opportunities for children to have choice and control. This motiva- tion comes from the excitement of exploring an environment where there are always new things to do, to discover and to learn. For this to be successful, the environment and the resources must be based on the children, their needs, their backgrounds, their interests, their concerns. Children are more interested in these than anything that we can plan for. Let's take these ideas that they bring and provide the flexibility in space and resources for them to explore them further, enhancing their play with sensitive interventions and specific resources. Motivation for children also comes from being able to choose who to play with and when and where to engage in that play. This independence and autonomy does not just 'happen'. It needs to be carefully sup- ported and built up by skilful practitioners. Children need to be guided round each area of provision and be shown how to care for the resources, how to use them safely, and to learn the boundaries and expectations in terms of behaviour, etc. In the same way, play does not come from nowhere. We need to provide children with stimuli, resources and ideas to model theirs on and freedom, space and time to develop their ideas.

The provision of space and time is an important consideration and one which often reveals more than we would like it to about our attitudes to children's play.

Giving children ownership and a sense of control over their learning involves changing the way that we view young children's capabilities. Do they need to have their day structured into work times and play times? If we are involved in a project and need to go for lunch or to stop for the day, we don't put everything away, we get our space tidy enough to leave and prepared for our next session. We don't want to have to begin all over again! Do we enable children to continue their learning from session to session in similar ways? We like to choose who to work with so we can match the skills of those around us to the problem in hand. We want to choose the most appropriate tools for the task and to choose where and when it's best to get the job done.

This ability to make choices and have those choices valued within a physical environment that has a wide range of open-ended resources, challenging, well-planned continuous provision and opportunities for children to change and adapt this environment to suit their needs enables children to truly participate in their learning environment. The more we enable children to participate and involve themselves in their learning, the better the quality of that learning (Wubie, 2011: 120).

## The importance of the outdoor environment

Much has already been written about the importance of the outdoors to the development and learning of young children. The outdoor environment is fundamentally different in nature and quality to the indoors. It is here that children can more freely create their own play agenda. Adults do not have the same control over this space as they do inside. This independence can engender excitement, motivation and self-esteem. It can also support the development of creativity as children use resources in their own way, creating and solving their own problems. The open-ended nature of the outdoor environment is well suited to the problem-solving nature of the EYFS which identifies the key characteristics of effective learning as – 'playing and exploring, active learning and creating and critical thinking' (DfE, 2012: 7). Where better to encourage exploration and active learning than in an environment where these things are truly possible?

The more physical nature of outdoor play can provide suitable conditions for play that involves risk-taking. Sometimes it is difficult for us as adults to let children engage in play of this nature but it is vital for their development. How will children know what they are physically capable of unless we let them find out in a safe and supportive environment? It is surely better to let them test out their 'risk monitor' (Canning, 2011: 97) and stretch themselves physically in the environment we create and monitor in order to develop their own understanding of what they are comfortable and capable of doing. Overcoming the challenges inherent in physical outdoor play is exciting! Children derive positive self-esteem by conquering their anxieties and fears.

Studies show that unrestricted movement is important for young children's well-being and learning and development. It is the dynamic immediacy of the interactions with the environment that enable children to learn and experience that learning in a deeper way (McLaren et al., 2011). Our understanding of young children's brain development adds to this argument. The multi-sensory nature of the outdoor environment enables children to gather so much more information about their world and the interactions that are possible. The act of movement itself enables more oxygen to get to the brain and therefore concentration is enhanced. These are the conditions under which children are able to become very deeply involved in their learning and as Laevers (2011) notes, are more likely to have an enhanced sense of wellbeing.

The prerequisite for all of this is once again the emotional environment – the values and attitudes of the teacher, and the way they translate this into the physical environment they create for the children. Are children encouraged to take risks? Are children supported sensitively through the outcomes of their risk-taking? Are children encouraged to be resilient and to persevere?

The emotional environment here is crucial: if children can take physical risks and know that they are supported and safe, they can then carry this confidence in to other aspects of their learning and development. Children need similar levels of self-esteem to approach a new activity confidently, to talk to unfamiliar adults and children, to make connections in their learning and take this from one area of provision to another gathering resources and inspiration along the way. 'The way in which the child engages with other people and their environment . . . underpin[s] learning and development . . . and supports the child to remain an effective and motivated learner' (Early Education, 2012: 4).

## Challenges

We have deeply rooted cultural and societal understandings of play, its purpose and the kinds of environment that our children should be cared for and educated in. Parents, senior managers, governors and indeed governments all have their own experiences of being in school and their understandings of what sort of environment should be expected.

We have a broad, balanced play-based curriculum framework which has been endorsed by two successive governments and a wide body of research that underpins this approach which requires a challenging, well-organized environment indoors and out where children have easy access to a range of natural and manmade resources.

This same curriculum framework also has specified outcomes for children at specific points which seem to necessitate that play is structured and organized and outcomes measurable. The temptation to over-structure and direct children's learning can come about through lack of training and lack of understanding of how to plan for the different areas of provision and how to monitor and evaluate the learning that is happening through play.

There is an interesting dynamic currently between the play-based curriculum framework which has been revised and reintroduced and some other messages from the government about children's education, such as the emphasis on daily, discrete systematic synthetic phonics and the recommendation from the Tickell review that a play-based curriculum 'should not preclude adult direction and teaching' (Tickell, 2012: 35). Add this to the target-driven system in which teachers in primary schools work and it is not surprising that some early years practitioners still feel the temptation to formalize the environment and the curriculum.

## References

Callaghan, J. (1976) Ruskin speech. http://education.guardian.co.uk/thegreatdebate/story/0,9860,574645,00.html (accessed 1 May 2012).

Canning, N. (ed.) (2011) *Play and Practice in the Early Years Foundation Stage*. London: Sage.

Dahlberg, G., Moss, P. and Pence, A. (2007) *Beyond Quality in Early Education and Care*, 2nd edn. London: Routledge Falmer.

DCSF (Department for Children, Schools and Families) (2008) *Early Years Foundation Stage*. Nottingham: DCSF Publications.

DCSF (2009) *Learning, Playing and Interacting*. Nottingham: DCSF Publications. www.foundationyears.org.uk (accessed 14 May 2012).

DfE (Department for Education) (2012) *Statutory Framework for the Early Years Foundation Stage: Setting the Standards for Learning, Development and Care of Children from Birth to Five*. www.education.gov.uk/publications/standard/AllPublications/Page1/DFE-00023-2012 (accessed 27 March 2013).

DFEE (Department for Education and Employment) (2000) *Curriculum Guidance for the Foundation Stage*. London: QCA.

Dowling, M. (2010) *Young Children's Personal, Social and Emotional Development*, 3rd edn. London: Sage.

Early Education (2012) *Development Matters in the Early Years Foundation Stage*. London: Early Education. www.media.education.gov.uk (accessed 14 May 2012).

Fisher, J. (2002) *Starting from the Child*, 2nd edn. Maidenhead: Open University Press.

Fisher, J. (2008) *Starting from the Child*, 3rd edn. Maidenhead: McGraw-Hill.

Galton, M., Simon, B. and Croll, P. (1980) *Inside the Primary Classroom* (The ORACLE Report). London: Routledge and Kegan Paul.

Hustler, D., Milroy, E. and Cockett, M. (1991) *Learning Environments for the Whole Curriculum*. London: Hyman.

Johnston, J. (2012) Enabling environments, in P. Beckley (ed.) *Learning in Early Childhood*. London: Sage.

Laevers, F. (2011) Experiential education: making care and education more effective through well-being and involvement, *Encyclopaedia on Early Childhood Development*. http://www.child-encyclopedia.com/pages/PDF/LaeversANGxp1.pdf (accessed 31 May 2012).

McLaren, C., Edwards, G., Ruddick, S., Zabjek, K. and McKeever, P. (2011) Kindergarten kids in motion: rethinking inclusive classrooms for optimal learning. *Educational & Child Psychology*, 28, 1: 100–13, Academic Search Complete, EBSCO*host* (accessed 26 March 2012).

McMillan, M. (1930) *The Nursery School*. London: Dent.

Nutbrown, C., Clough, P. and Selbie, P. (2008) *Early Childhood Education: History, Philosophy and Experience*. London: Sage.

Ofsted (2010) *Using the Early Years Evaluation Schedule: Guidance for Inspectors of Registered Early Years Settings Required to Deliver the EYFS*. Manchester: Ofsted. www.ofsted.gov.uk/resources (accessed 31 May 2012).

Ofsted (2011) *Effective Ways for Children to Succeed in the Early Years Foundation Stage: Throston Primary School*. Manchester: Ofsted. www.ofsted.gov.uk/resources (accessed 31 May 2012).

Pugh, G. and Duffy, B. (2006) *Contemporary Issues in the Early Years*, 4th edn. London: Sage.

Tickell, C. (2012) *The Early Years: Foundations for Life Health and Learning*. Crown Copyright. www.education.gov.uk (accessed 1 June 2012).

Wubie, B. (2011) Preschool children as co-curriculum developers. *National Social Science Journal*, 37, 1, 120–4 SocINDEX with Full Text EBSCO*host*, viewed 26 March 2012-05-14.

## Further reading

Ashbridge, J. and Josephidou, J. (2012) Classroom organisation and the learning environment, in H. Cooper (ed.) *Professional Studies in Primary Education.* London: Sage.

Cockburn, A. and Handscomb, G. (2012) *Teaching Children 3–11.* London: Sage.

Smidt, S. (2011) *Playing to Learn: The Role of Play in the Early Years.* Abingdon: Routledge.

# 3

## The adults around the child
### Julie Kitchen

### Introduction

The 2012 EYFS framework (DfE, 2012), with accompanying guidance material, re-states the principles of active learning and exploratory play; of child-initiated activity and personalized learning. It also outlines the role of the adult in the delivery of a play-based educational programme and the type of support that should, or could, be offered by early years practitioners. Some of the fundamental and underlying ideals of the framework are shared as central to the vision of what early years practice should look like but there is potential for varying interpretations of these interlinked principles and the debates which still exist around definitions and implementation. What does child-initiated activity really mean? Could the times when young children are led and directed by the adults around them restrict true creativity, independence and discovery learning in an inhibiting way? Is the environment provided by practitioners affected by their own understanding of how play, creative thinking and active learning should be embodied? These are questions which still merit discussion, even after the introduction of the new framework, and this chapter focuses on how a visit to the Kindergartens of Norway and research into children's independent writing challenged my view of the adult around the child and led to altered perceptions of what is possible.

### Activity

There are many adults involved in the development of young children, such as parents, carers, friends, relatives, members in the community and those at an early years setting. How can adults, particularly in a setting and perhaps as the Key Worker, promote appropriate interactions for children's learning and progress and foster positive self-images for the individuals as discussed in Chapter 1?

## A range of perspectives

The EYFS requires practitioners to implement learning and development through planned, purposeful play and a mix of adult-led and child-initiated activity (DfE, 2012). It is up to the practitioner to make a judgement about the balance of child-led and adult-led activity although 'it is expected that the balance will gradually shift towards more activities led by adults, to help children prepare for formal learning, ready for Year 1' (DfE, 2012: 6). This implies that it is more likely that children will achieve the aim of school readiness if an adult becomes more heavily involved in the direction and leading of learning. But what is 'school readiness' and can it be reached in different ways? Educationalists in other countries, or those basing provision on contrasting philosophies, appear to believe so. The age of starting school, for instance, is very different internationally and children under the jurisdiction of the EYFS are expected to begin formal schooling earlier than most of their European counterparts. With the exception of children in Northern Ireland (who start school at age 4) and Malta, the Netherlands, Wales and Scotland (who also begin at age 5), the rest of the 34 European countries who participate in the Eurydice information network (Eurydice, 2010), including Norway, start school at age 6 or 7. This has implications for the way that early childhood is perceived, the length of time the distinct phase of pre-school lasts and the impact that experiences in the early years have on academic standards in later years of schooling. While the 2012 EYFS framework recognizes the major impact of the birth to 5 years stage on future life chances and states that 'a secure, safe and happy childhood is important in its own right' (DfE, 2012: 2), there are opportunities for further exploration of what such a childhood should look like and whether it should change or stop when formal schooling begins. According to the principles of Steiner Waldorf education (which is practised to greater or lesser extents in many countries of the world) the first seven years are a time for children to experience childhood 'in a place where they can grow in peace and harmony, feeling safe and not under pressure to perform or compete' (Nicol, 2007: 2). This is a slightly more meaningful description of childhood than the brief statement supplied by the DfE (2012) and indicates the 'stress-free' nature of the Steiner approach. It is questionable whether practitioners and children in EYFS settings feel the same lack of pressure. The necessity to be ready and prepared for formal schooling is an early benchmark for achievement and the EYFS Profile demands assessment against defined criteria as a mark of performance and progress from birth. The Norwegian view is also that 'Childhood is a phase of life with intrinsic value' (Norwegian Ministry of Education and Research, 2012a) although their new 'Framework Plan' (Norwegian Ministry of Education and Research, 2012b) has seven learning areas which children should be acquainted with in Kindergartens. The Kindergartens should 'contribute to well-being and joy in play and learning' as their purpose is to 'safeguard children's need for care and play'.

In the 28 European countries whose children start school later than in England, the qualities and experiences of the pre-school stage are presumably deemed so valuable that they are extended for a significantly longer time. Does this also mean that children can learn though play for longer in these countries and that they are less directed by adults until formal schooling begins? It is very interesting to note that, despite the longer time spent in pre-school environments, Scandinavian children out-perform their English counterparts in international assessment tests in later years (OECD, 2009). This could indicate that it is more beneficial to wait a little longer for formal schooling (and consequently more adult-led activity) and for when the greater majority of children are truly ready for it. A study of the role of teachers in Finnish schools suggests that 'In addition to teacher support of active participation and friendly relationships we propose that the diversity of creative and imaginary activities in the preschool enriches children's curiosity, stimulates interest in the basics of literacy and nourishes their motivation for learning' (Hännikäinen and Rasku-Puttonen, 2010: 147). It is recognized that the opportunity to enjoy playfulness, before beginning formal schooling at the age of 6, could be beneficial. My visit to Norwegian Kindergartens was an opportunity to study a comparative view of early years practice and to find out how adults in pre-school settings there perceived their role.

## The early years in Norway

We thought we knew, before we boarded the plane to Norway, what a Forest School looked like. We had imagined, and eagerly anticipated, what it might be like to work without a statutory early years curriculum framework or restrictive health and safety regulations. We had heard about the very successful Scandinavian approach which led to Norway, Finland and Sweden being placed highly in international league tables in literacy, despite delaying formal education to the age of 6 or 7. What we found surpassed our expectations and allowed us to look at early years provision through very different eyes. Our party consisted of a group of PGCE students and lecturers from my university college. We visited two Kindergartens and a school near the town of Hedmark in Northern Norway and, while this could never be assumed to represent the whole of the country, Norwegian colleagues assured us that the provision we saw very much reflected what was likely to be found across the country in terms of ethos and general approach towards early years practice.

Our first experience of the Norwegian approach came as we walked to a small forest clearing by the edge of an ice-covered fjord. This was the children's usual expectation of their Kindergarten environment and it was breathtaking. Children were dressed appropriately for the cold weather and were allowed to move freely in the woodland environment. The fascinating part was the interaction which began to occur between the PGCE students and the children. It was quite natural for the students to begin talking to the children straight away, to join in with toasting the bread for lunch over an open fire and, after a time, to run through the trees with a pack of excited children in a game resembling 'Stuck in the Mud'. It was not until I noticed the rather bemused glances of the Norwegian practitioners that I thought anything could be different to the norm. 'We don't usually play *with* them like that' was the response when asked. The implication, which was borne out in other scenarios, was that the children are expected to explore their world freely and with each other, and that the adults usually stand back to observe and wait for times when intervention or facilitation is needed or asked for.

The images of the children examining piles of tiny stones against the backdrop of ice and sky embody the kind of self-absorption and concentration on self-initiated

**Figure 3.1** This is what interests us

**Figure 3.2** Splendid isolation

tasks to be found in an environment in which all activity of this kind is valued (Figures 3.1 and 3.2). Adult intervention in this context could more easily be seen as intrusion or interruption and, although there were times when an adult did step in to enhance learning, it was timely and well judged, requested or required. The Norwegian practitioners acknowledged their subsidiary and facilitating role but university colleagues who had been on a study visit to the UK told us they had been impressed by foundation stage practitioners and 'how hard they work'. We commented that the provision we had seen in Norway was wonderful to us (precisely because of its lack of intervention or prescription) and that the hard work they described could also be seen as overly bureaucratic and unnecessarily time consuming.

The group of Norwegian practitioners included what, for us, was the fairly rare sight of a male in an early years environment. In Norway, a man working in the early years sector is a far more common occurrence and it was immediately obvious that the Norwegian children were able to enjoy much closer interaction with all practitioners than they do in the UK, particularly in a physical sense. How strange and enlightening it was for us to watch the acceptable sight of several small boys and girls piling on top of a floored male practitioner with abandoned glee or to see them being lifted upside down, swung around, carried and dropped.

The second Kindergarten was in a forest on a snow-covered hillside and we were told that this was an extreme version of an outdoor nursery 'even for Norway'. There was a building for the children to go inside but this was rarely used – even when temperatures outside would be considered, by those accustomed to UK temperatures, to be bitterly cold. The environment was staggeringly beautiful and wild; a huge expanse of snow-covered hills with trees you couldn't see the top of and a sense of unlimited space. This was a Forest School in its most literal form, owned and run by a male entrepreneur who had built the school based on the Norwegian ideal that 'we are all one with nature'. We saw children climbing very high up those trees, warming themselves by an open fire and jumping on and off things without a second thought. We also saw how Norwegian children learn 'science': by experimenting with water and mud! (See Figures 3.3 and 3.4.)

Adults were obviously there but the way they interacted with the children was bound up with the central view that pre-school experience should be about free play (in response to young children's need for play) and that childhood has a value in itself which should be recognized and cherished. Strong cultural and traditional principles about the relationship of Norwegians with nature and the experience of childhood strongly influence the way that early years provision is made. I asked a Norwegian colleague what Kindergarten staff do if they don't have access to outdoor space (a position many UK practitioners can find themselves in). The reply was that a Kindergarten would never be set up in a place where it wasn't possible to play outdoors.

The children in the Kindergartens were constantly observed in their play and the practitioners knew them very well. There was no formal assessment, however, and the leader of the Kindergarten said that they would pass information 'stored in their head' to the teacher at primary school. Transition was seen as extremely important although, from what we saw, there was an immediate switch to formal schooling when the time came. There was a view that children were ready for it by this time and that they had learnt to love learning in preparation for later curriculum challenges.

**Figure 3.3** Discovery learning

**Figure 3.4** Norwegian independence

## Studying the role of the adult

The role of the adult practitioner in young children's learning has been perceived quite differently by a range of philosophers and educationalists over time. Colleagues in Norway told us that variances between the views of Piaget and Vygotsky were still debated as the fundamentally opposing views on the level or type of adult interaction offered to children. Although Piaget and Vygotsky both placed great emphasis on play, and still appear to influence current principles about active learning and child-centred planning, there is disparity in what they believed about adult intervention and involvement. As Rose (2007: 53) points out, the view of Piaget that children cannot progress developmentally until they are ready to discover it for themselves 'creates a dilemma for the adult in terms of how much children should be "left to themselves" and how much interaction or even acceleration an adult should provide'. This is in contrast to the view of Vygotsky that the zone of proximal development is 'the distance between the actual developmental level as determined by independent problem solving and the level of potential development as determined through problem-solving under adult guidance or in collaboration with more capable peers' (Vygotsky, 1978: 86). In Vygotsky's view there is a difference between what can be achieved if a child is left to his own devices and what he could achieve through adult intervention; a child will only reach his learning potential if an adult (or someone else) is there to make the difference. There is still the question of initial motivation and engagement in an activity, however, before such a scaffolding process can occur (Rose, 2007: 53). Vygostsky's belief is that 'if we ignore the child's needs, and the incentives which are effective in getting him to act, we will never be able to understand his advance from one developmental stage to the next' (1978: 92).

The philosophy of the world-famous Montessori approach shows some links to the Piagetian belief in that non-intervention by the adult is seen as key. As Montessori states, 'As long as teachers thrust their conclusions on the child . . . they will never attain the end, which is the child's spontaneous interest and application' (Montessori, 1948: 24). There appears to be concurrence between all three views that the greatest value lies in motivation by the child to act (i.e. to initiate their own activity) but disparity in how involved the adult should be after that. Although Montessori saw the teacher as a manager of the environment and an active facilitator (mostly in terms of classroom preparation), their role is essentially a passive one. She warns that interruption of a child's concentration may disturb a train of thought and undermine their efforts (Isaacs, 2007: 21). The High Scope approach also appears to be loosely based on Piagetian theory as children are expected to plan what they intend to do, carry out the plan and reflect on their accomplishments (Brock et al., 2009: 71). The approach does, however, view verbal interaction with the children as they play as a key feature. Similarly, advocates of the Reggio Emilia approach see themselves as partners in learning rather than directing or leading. As Thornton and Brunton (2007: 11) describe:

> The role of the adult is to plan starting points for the children to explore and to provide open ended resources that encourage the children to develop their own thinking and ways of learning. The adults watch and listen carefully to what the children do and say, and use their observations to guide and extend each child's learning.

This final statement may be the most helpful for those deciding how to provide for the child-initiated learning and purposeful play which is required by the EYFS framework. What is less clear, from consideration of other approaches, is why adult direction should play a significant part in any pre-school education.

**Reflections**

Consider your interactions with young children. How are you promoting their positive self-image and encouraging the development of their learning and understanding?

What do you think is the value of comparative studies considering differing approaches?

Does the knowledge of different approaches change your perceptions of appropriate practice? In what ways?

## Child-initiated activity and adult-led tasks in the development of writing

My own research focused on the potential tension between child-initiated activity and adult-led tasks. What really *was* the value of child-initiated activity and can two seemingly opposing approaches (teacher-directed learning and child-instigated activity) comfortably exist side by side in a balanced way? For a year, I observed contrasting approaches in my classroom to compare the response of children to the same area of development (writing); one with adult direction and one without.

I defined teacher-led writing activity as those times when children were asked to come and write in their books with an adult present to support. The following is a sample extract of conversation as this took place. The children were expected to complete the familiar task of drawing a picture and writing down something they had done at the weekend.

**Ch 3**  Have you writed it yet?

**Ch 1**  No! You're not meant to write first! You're meant to colour first!

**Ch 3**  I . . . went . . . to

**Ch 2**  I . . . c . . . u . . . r . . . car!

**Ch 2**  How do you do a 'd'?

**Ch 5**  (Draws shape on table and then in the air)

**Ch 1**  Down and round, up, down and *flick*

**Ch 2**  Up . . . down

**Ch 6**  No! . . . down . . . OK . . . do down . . . around (shows on table) . . . no, the other way! . . . around and flick.

There you go! There's a 'd'

**Ch 1** No – you're meant to do round first – you didn't make a 'd' properly

**Ch 6** That's not a mess – that's good!

**Ch 2** How do *you* do a 'd', L? . . . round, up, down and flick. Is that how you do it?

**Ch 6** Now you need a bit more stick . . . That's it! You've done it!

**Ch 6** (to Ch 1) You haven't done any writing yet

**Ch 1** I'm not meant to do writing yet

The pervading theme of this conversation is the need to use technical writing conventions and to do things correctly. There are 'rules' attached to the task (i.e. things you're 'meant to do') and an insistence that these must be adhered to. The purpose of the task has already been decided and, although the children later show a lot of interest and pride in what they, and each other, are doing, they do not have to make any decisions about the tools and equipment to use, the subject matter or the audience. Their phonic and handwriting skills are quite easy to assess (and link to EYFS Profile points for writing; DfE, 2013) as a result and there is a tangible record, stored in their books, to show development and progress over time. The type of writing which resulted is fairly predictable (see below) and the task is designed to show how particular (and previously determined) criteria are being met. I was able to tell from writing such as this, for example, that the child could:

- write some words from memory;
- hold a pencil and use it effectively to write recognizable letters, most of which are correctly formed;
- use phonic knowledge to write simple regular words and make phonetically plausible attempts at more complex words; and
- begin to form simple sentences.

The writing area was set up so that it could operate as an alternative 'adult-free zone' – a collection of resources and materials which were freely available and accessible to the children, whenever they wished to use them and for whatever purpose. This was intended as basic and constant provision which could be enhanced according to children's interests or to supplement whichever direction their learning took. The only stipulation was to look after the resources and make sure that they were stored properly at the end of each day. Initial interest was very high and there was great excitement about the opportunities on offer. Observations over time were fascinating and there was a group of children who spent a large part of 'choosing time' in that area. They explored the materials with gusto and relished the chance to produce things which were entirely of their own instigation (see Figures 3.5 and 3.6).

Projects ebbed and flowed. Party invitations were the vogue for a few days, followed by paper figures, school registers, books and sticky label creations. Sometimes a request would be made: for paper of a certain colour or type, for example, for gold and silver pens, glitter or a stapler. Within reason, these materials were supplied and the children could extend their original ideas in the particular ways they imagined.

**Figure 3.5** Personal choice

**Figure 3.6** No two the same

The children's efforts represented confidence, creativity, imagination, enjoyment and individual variation. It was an open-ended approach which could lead anywhere and frequently did. Conversations were more likely to be about the process of writing or creating something itself (see below); decisions were made and delight was taken in ownership.

**Ch 1** I need to make an invitation – it's nine weeks to my birthday

**Ch 2** What are you going to write?

**Ch 1** Lots of nice words. You can actually write to people – how many days it is. What do you think to that?

**Ch 2** What are you going to put?

**Ch 1** How many weeks until my birthday and then you write who it's for on the envelope and send it to them

**Ch 2** Is it a party invitation?

**Ch 1** Yes it is

**Ch 1** I'm going to have lots of nice food and things. That's what I'm going to write

I saw that the children were operating according to two contrasting sets of expectations. Table 3.1 summarizes these. It also demonstrates that there could be 'apparently conflicting pedagogical and linguistic positions in the pursuit of raising standards' (Cook, 2000: 74). Would the children be 'wrong', for example, if they wrote with a felt

**Table 3.1**

| Expectations from a prescribed and teacher-led writing task | Expectations from a child-initiated task in the independent writing area |
|---|---|
| Book/lined paper provided | Own materials chosen |
| Pencils (for writing) and coloured pencils (for drawing) provided | Own writing tools and equipment chosen |
| Task prescribed (i.e. expectation to finish satisfactorily) | Task initiated by child with no end product specified |
| Work to be collected and assessed | Product to be shared if so wished |
| Work saved at school in book or folder | Product to be taken home or given to who it was made/written for |
| Work shown to an adult | Product for a variety of purposes, reasons and audiences |
| Independence expected (in first attempts at writing) but evidence shown of progress towards skills in phonics | All attempts independent with no particular emphasis on the development of skills |
| Writing expected to be well formed and carefully presented | No particular emphasis on accuracy or presentation |
| Writing perceived as 'work' | Writing perceived as part of 'play', drawing and making things |
| Children sit with their ability group on their designated table | Children choose who to play with and where to sit |

pen in a prescribed writing situation, drew a picture in the wrong place or failed to meet a learning objective? Are these the kinds of dual expectations which make the transition from a play-based curriculum to a more formal and structured one more difficult? Did it matter that both approaches were existing side by side? The children appeared to accept that sometimes they wrote 'properly' and at other times no one was actually checking. This could have been because, in many ways, the two approaches were not as starkly different as those portrayed by the table. When 'directing' a writing task, for example, we would encourage the children to 'have a go' by themselves, particularly in the first instance. We certainly valued all their attempts and preferred them to write without too much support if possible. In the same way, there were times when children in the independent area came to ask me what the correct spelling of a word was and how to form a letter. From the evidence I collected, children tended to adapt their behaviour according to the context (and applicable set of expectations) they were participating in. When questioned, two-thirds of the children said they were, in fact, happy to write in either context although the open-ended nature of the writing area was acknowledged as a positive feature: 'you can make whatever you like', 'you can make all sorts of things' and 'I usually get to do lots of writing or make things'.

In terms of *writing* assessment, therefore, it was felt that children were far more likely to produce usable evidence towards individual targets for the development of phonic ability, handwriting and punctuation through teacher-led tasks. It was easier to collect documentary evidence of systematic progression in writing through tasks with specific objectives and outcomes and to keep samples of writing produced in this way as a record. It was obvious, however, that children using the writing area were regularly exhibiting something equally as valuable and perhaps even more so; they were constantly showing that their attitude towards learning was favourable. On a daily basis, in line with DfE (2013), they:

- showed an interest in classroom activities through observation or participation;
- displayed high levels of involvement in self-chosen activities;
- selected and used activities and resources independently;
- continued to be interested, motivated and excited to learn;
- were confident to try new activities, initiate ideas and speak in a familiar group; and
- maintained attention and concentrated.

In my view, they demonstrated these behaviours more emphatically because they knew no adult would intervene or take charge. Observations of children working in this way demonstrated the true value of child-initiated activity and the wealth of information about social interaction, independence, confidence and disposition meant that it was more than worthwhile.

As the children's technical writing skills matured some writing of very good quality *was* produced in the independent area. It seemed plausible that some of this developing skill was transferred from the more formal, adult-supported and planned writing tasks which were taking place alongside, when the children would be expected to write letters down on the line, leave spaces between words and select appropriate letters for the sounds they needed. The independent response, however, was more genuinely and flamboyantly representative of the children's developmental level and depth of understanding about writing as an enjoyable and creative process. As Fisher (2002: 3) concludes, 'herein lies the tension between the attainment of quantifiable outcomes and the recognition that there is more to being literate than can be measured'.

## Conclusion

The research appears to show that both teacher-led and child-initiated activity can complement each other as long as practitioners are aware of what each achieves and reflect carefully on their role. Even painting a picture cannot automatically be termed 'creative' just because it is in a creative media. If the child is led or directed, the task can quickly lose its spontaneity and sense of ownership. It becomes a test of a technical skill and the ability to follow instructions. There is a danger that, however much the value of child-initiated activity is demonstrated, the emphasis on school readiness by the current Government means that teacher-led activity becomes the more dominant approach. As Rogers (2007: 137) warns, 'Instead of actively exploring their world in whatever way and through whatever medium suits them best, young children in the UK have been encouraged to master the limited skills involved in learning to read and write.' Mindham (2005: 81) sees a similar danger and speaks of the damage which may later occur to children's amazing capacities for imagination, invention and creativity. There is no denying that, in some schools, where teachers follow a predominantly play-based curriculum in the foundation stage and a teacher-directed, prescriptive one in Year 1, the children's experience of transition can be quite harsh and disjointed (Fisher, 2009: 133). We do them no service at all to segment the two curriculum frameworks so that they are as far apart as possible. It is to be hoped that interpretation of the 2012 EYFS framework does not unnecessarily inhibit or limit our young children in this crucial and exciting stage and that the flourishing, enriched and ultimately beneficial experience of childhood, so appreciatively viewed in Norway, is more likely to be their lot. This could well be wishful thinking but is something to covet nonetheless.

## References

Brock, A., Dodds, S., Jarvis, P. and Olusoga, Y. (2009) *Perspectives on Play: Learning for Life*. London: Pearson Longman.

Cook, M. (2000) Writing and role play – a case for inclusion. *Reading*, 34, 74–8.

DfE (Department for Education) (2012) *Statutory Framework for the Early Years Foundation Stage: Setting the Standards for Learning, Development and Care of Children from Birth to Five*. http://www.education.gov.uk/publications/standard/AllPublications/Page1/DFE-00023-2012 (accessed 27 March 2013).

DfE (2013) *Early Years Foundation Stage Profile: Handbook*. http://www.education.gov.uk/schools/teachingandlearning/assessment/eyfs/a00217599/eyfs-handbook (accessed 7 May 2013).

Eurydice at National Foundation for Educational Research: Unit for England, Wales and Northern Ireland (2010) *Compulsory Age of Starting School in European Countries, 2010*. www.nfer.ac.uk (accessed 22 September 2012).

Fisher, J. (2009) 'We used to play in Foundation, it was more funner': investigating feelings about transition from Foundation Stage to Year 1. *Early Years*, 29(2): 131–45.

Fisher, R. (2002) *Inside the Literacy Hour: Learning from Classroom Experience*. London: Routledge Falmer.

Hännikäinen, M. and Rasku-Puttonen, H. (2010) Promoting children's participation: the role of teachers in preschool and primary learning sessions. *Early Years*, 30(2): 147–60.

Isaacs, B. (2007) *Bringing the Montessori Approach to your Early Years Practice*. London: Routledge.

Mindham, C. (2005) Creativity and the young child. *Early Years*, 25(1): 81–4.

Montessori, M. (1948) *To Educate the Human Potential*. Adyar, India: Kalakshetra Publications.

Nicol, J. (2007) *Bringing the Steiner Waldorf Approach to your Early Years Practice*. London: Routledge.

Norwegian Ministry of Education and Research (2012a) *Early Childhood Education and Care Policy*.http://www.regjeringen.no/en/dep/kd/Selected-topics/kindergarden/early-childhood-education-and-care-polic.html?id=491283 (accessed 22 September 2012).

Norwegian Ministry of Education and Research (2012b) *Framework Plan for the Content and Tasks of Kindergartens*. The Ministry of Education and Research.

OECD (2009) *PISA (2009) Key Findings*. http://www.oecd.org/pisa/pisaproducts/pisa2009 keyfindings.htm (accessed 30 September 2012).

Rogers, S. (2007) Supporting creativity. In J. Willan, R. Parker-Rees and J. Savage (eds) *Early Childhood Studies*, 2nd edn. Exeter: Learning Matters Ltd.

Rose, J. (2007) Helping young children to learn. In J. Willan, R. Parker-Rees and J. Savage (eds) *Early Childhood Studies*, 2 edn. Exeter: Learning Matters Ltd.

Thornton, L. and Brunton, P. (2007) *Bringing the Reggio Approach to your Early Years Practice*. London: Routledge.

Vygotsky, L.S. (1978) *Mind in Society: The Development of Higher Psychological Processes*. Cambridge, MA: Harvard University Press.

# Part 2
## The prime areas of learning and development

This section explores the prime areas of learning and development; that is personal, social and emotional development, physical development and communication and language. In Chapter 4 Anita Soni considers the development of personal, social and emotional development (PSED) as a governmental requirement as part of early years frameworks. Key points are raised concerning the 2012 EYFS framework, for example the importance of the Key Person in the organization and management of children's welfare and individual development. Challenges of this role are discussed. Anita formulates five challenges she feels concern the implementation of PSED within early years settings and offers pertinent suggestions to support those working with young children.

Chapter 5, based on physical development and written by Pat Beckley, considers the required aspects from the 2012 EYFS framework of moving and handling and health and self-care. The rationale for incorporating this element as a prime area of learning and development is discussed, highlighting the importance of this aspect in young children's lives. Practical suggestions for the implementation of the strand are provided and possible challenges for the practitioner involved in implementing the provision discussed.

Chapter 6 is also written by Pat and focuses on communication and language, covering the requirements of listening and attention and understanding and speaking, providing suggestions for implementation and the changes that fosters while addressing possible challenges that might arise.

The section opens with a consideration of PSED, from the perspective and insights of an educational psychologist, Anita Soni.

# 4

# Personal, social and emotional development
Anita Soni

## Introduction

This chapter gives an opportunity to consider and reflect upon the changes and challenges within PSED. In terms of changes I was interested to reflect on how PSED is viewed within English curricula and frameworks relative to the other areas of learning and development. I currently work as an educational psychologist (EP) and early years trainer. My role as an EP has led me to reflect on the role of the Key Person as part of promoting PSED in children and the challenges this brings. As a trainer I have been surprised by the way expectations of children within PSED may differ to other areas of learning and development. It is important to recognize that this chapter is not based on planned research, but instead on my experiences and reflections. Therefore the chapter will focus on the following questions within PSED:

- How has PSED changed over time in terms of its status within the curricula and frameworks for early years in England?
- How has the role of the Key Person developed and what are the challenges within it?
- What are the roles of expectations, difficulties and strengths in PSED?

## Has the status of PSED changed over time?

A statutory national curriculum for children under 5 in England is a relatively new phenomenon; it first came into being in 1996. The role of PSED can be traced back to the early versions of the curriculum through to the current day and the reformed EYFS framework (DfE, 2012).

The School Curriculum and Assessment Authority (SCAA) published a set of desirable outcomes for children's learning on entry to compulsory education alongside guidance on educational activities in 1996. This ran alongside the Childcare Voucher Scheme introduced by the Conservative Government at the time. All children in publicly funded, pre-school education were expected to follow a curriculum to enable them to make maximum progress towards these desirable learning outcomes published by the SCAA. The desirable learning outcomes were explicitly linked to the National Curriculum levels in Key Stage 1 and 'emphasized early literacy, numeracy, and the development of personal and social skills and contributed to children's knowledge, understanding and skills in other areas . . . to provide a foundation for later achievement' (DfEE, 1996: 1). This is the first mention of PSED and it is in the context of personal and social skills. It is interesting to note that early literacy and numeracy are placed first, although the three areas of early literacy, numeracy and personal and social skills are seen to form the core of the desirable learning outcomes and the foundations of other areas. This is similar to the role of PSED now within the reformed EYFS.

The desirable learning outcomes (DfEE, 1996) included 'personal and social development' as an area of learning. These outcomes were intended to cover personal, social, moral and spiritual development, the development of personal values and an understanding of the self and others.

The Qualifications and Curriculum Authority (QCA) went on to establish a foundation stage of education for children aged 3 to the end of the Reception year in 2000, resulting in the *Curriculum Guidance for the Foundation Stage* (QCA/DfEE, 2000). This became statutory guidance in 2002 and built upon the six areas of learning in the desirable learning outcomes and created stepping stones and early learning goals. The area of personal and social development in the desirable learning outcomes was expanded in the Curriculum Guidance to include emotional development and became 'personal, social and emotional development' (PSED). Within this guidance PSED was noted to be '. . . critical for very young children in all aspects of their lives and gives them the best opportunity for success in all other areas of learning' (QCA/DFEE, 2000: 28).

Here it can be argued that PSED was emphasized in comparison to the preceding Desirable Learning Outcomes framework which had placed it alongside early literacy and numeracy. This can be seen as a rise in importance of PSED as the priority area of learning. In addition it was presented as the first area of learning within the guidance, and the following was the first aim of the Foundation Stage: 'supporting, fostering, promoting and developing children's personal, social, emotional well-being' (QCA/DfEE, 2000: 8).

In 2003 the *Birth to Three Matters* framework ('Birth to Three framework' hereafter; Sure Start, 2003) was introduced and provided information for practitioners working with children under 3 on child development and effective practice to promote play and learning. While this was not statutory guidance, early years settings had to show regard for it when inspected by Ofsted. In the Birth to Three framework, there are four aspects which celebrated the skills and competencies of the babies and young children. A strong child was one of the four aspects and was seen as pivotal to the rest of the Birth to Three framework as it '. . . is one which runs throughout the Framework. We want all children to be strong, capable, confident and self-assured. The very early years are extremely important in this regard' (Sure Start, 2003: 8).

Although the Birth to Three framework (Sure Start, 2003) has a different label for PSED, the strong child, it would appear to contain many of the elements of PSED. The four components of a strong child were: 'me, myself and I'; 'being acknowledged and affirmed'; 'developing self-assurance'; and 'a sense of belonging' and these have similarities to the six aspects of the *Curriculum Guidance for the Foundation Stage* (QCA/DfEE, 2000): dispositions and attitudes, self-confidence and self-esteem, making relationships, behaviour and self-control, self-care, and sense of community. Both the Birth to Three framework and the *Curriculum Guidance for the Foundation Stage* placed a strong child and PSED as central, and as pivotal to other components or areas of learning.

The 2007 EYFS framework (DfES, 2007) brought together *Birth to Three Matters* and the *Curriculum Guidance for the Foundation Stage* and the *National Standards for Under 8s, Day Care and Child Minding* (DfES, 2003) in 2007. The revised version of the EYFS was published in May 2008 by the DCSF. This changed the role of PSED relative to other areas of learning and development by placing PSED as equal in status to the other areas of learning and development. It was stated within the learning and development requirements in the Statutory Framework for the EYFS (DCSF, 2008b) that 'None of these areas of Learning and Development can be delivered in isolation from the others. They are equally important and depend on each other to support a rounded approach to child development' (DCSF, 2008b: 11). However it is interesting to note that PSED was still the first area of learning and development shown in both the practice guidance for the EYFS (DCSF, 2008a) and the statutory framework for the EYFS (DCSF, 2008b).

The status of PSED seems to have come full circle, as with the arrival of the reformed EYFS (DfE, 2012), PSED is now a prime area alongside communication and language and physical development. The prime areas are described as '. . . particularly crucial for igniting children's curiosity and enthusiasm for learning, and for building their capacity to learn, form relationships and thrive' (DfE, 2012: 8). The other prime areas have changed from the desirable learning outcomes where personal and social skills were seen as crucial alongside literacy and numeracy. Personal, social and emotional development has changed and emotional development has come to be a part of it, but it has become crucial again! However it is interesting to note that it is shown first in *Development Matters in the Early Years Foundation Stage*, the non-statutory guidance for the EYFS ('Development Matters'; Early Education, 2012) but third within the 2012 EYFS framework (DfE, 2012), so maybe while it is agreed that it is crucial, there is still disagreement about how crucial. See Table 4.1 for a summary of the change in status of PSED since the mid-1990s.

**Reflections**

How important do you think a child's personal, social and emotional development is?

Do you think PSED should be:

- a prime area alongside other areas of learning and development
- underpinning the other areas of learning and development
- equal in status and value to the other areas of learning and development?

> **Why?**
>
> How important do you think parents think their child's personal, social and emotional development is?
>
> What about future educators of children further along the education system, such as in primary school, secondary school or in higher education? How important is a person's PSED to them?
>
> What about future employers of children? How important is a person's PSED to them?

## How has the role of the Key Person developed within PSED?

The Key Person approach was an aspect of practice I was unaware of until the Birth to Three framework in 2003 and then the EYFS in 2007. Once I learned of the approach, it seemed the most appropriate way of supporting children aged birth to 5 in PSED. However, over time I have come to feel it is the most beneficial way of working for all children of all ages in all parts of their learning. As an educational psychologist, when working with, assessing and supporting children, I always try to find the individuals who know a child best. Within an education or care setting these people are not always adults, as children are important too, but within this group there should be an adult. This person tends to be the key person for the child outside their family. I find I use this term a lot in my work!

Elfer et al. (2003) state that Elinor Goldschmied is the inspiration for the Key Person approach. They argue that '. . . even the youngest children need special kinds of relationships when they are cared for away from their parents, to "set them up" for life' (Elfer et al., 2003). The Key Person approach was described by Goldschmied and Selleck (1996) as a 'triangle of trust and communication' between the parent or carer, the child and the Key Person. The following list shows the main stakeholders within the Key Person approach and how they relate to each other. The main stakeholders are:

- the child;
- the parent (and this includes the significant adults in the child's life at home);
- the Key Person;
- the setting (including other staff and the manager).

Elfer et al. (2003) argue that unless there is a Key Person approach, there is a risk of 'multiple indiscriminate care' (Bain and Barnett, 1986) and an increased risk that special relationships with children might never occur. They describe the Key Person approach as:

> a way of working . . . in which the whole focus and organisation is aimed at enabling and supporting close attachments between individual children and

**Table 4.1**

| Date | Curriculum or framework | Label for PSED within the curriculum/ framework | Role of PSED relative to other areas of learning | Sections within PSED |
|---|---|---|---|---|
| 1996–2000 | Desirable learning outcomes (DfEE, 1996) | Personal and social development | Central alongside early literacy and numeracy and contributing to other areas of learning | |
| 2000–2007 | Curriculum Guidance for the Foundation Stage (QCA/DfEE, 2000) | Personal, social and emotional development | Critical to young children and underpinning other areas of learning | Dispositions and attitudes, self-confidence and self-esteem, making relationships, behaviour and self-control, self-care and sense of community |
| 2003–2007 | Birth to Three Matters Framework (Sure Start, 2003) | A strong child | Runs throughout the framework | Me, myself and I, being acknowledged and affirmed, developing self-assurance, a sense of belonging |
| 2007–2012 | Early Years Foundation Stage (DfES, 2007) (DCSF, 2008b) | Personal, social and emotional development | Equally important to other areas of learning and development | Dispositions and attitudes, self-confidence and self-esteem, making relationships, behaviour and self-control, self-care and sense of community |
| 2012 | Reformed Early Years Foundation Stage (DfE, 2012) | Personal, social and emotional development | A prime area of learning and development alongside communication and language and physical development | Self-confidence and self-awareness, managing feelings and behaviour, making relationships |

individual . . . staff. The Key Person approach is an involvement, an individual and reciprocal commitment between a member of staff and a family.

(Elfer et al., 2003: 8)

This quote emphasizes that it is 'a way of working' for the whole setting and therefore must be a philosophical approach that the whole setting understands, agrees on and embraces. The guidance to settings has changed to reflect this.

The statutory guidance for the 2012 EYFS has developed and built on the previous statutory guidance for the EYFS (DCSF, 2008a) which had stated the following as a specific legal requirement: 'Each child must be assigned a key person. In childminding settings, the childminder is the key person' (DCSF, 2008a: 37). There was additional statutory guidance to which providers must have regard:

> The key person should help the baby or child to become familiar with the provision and to feel confident and safe within it, developing a genuine bond with the child (and the child's parents) and offering a settled, close relationship.
>
> The key person should meet the needs of each child in their care and respond sensitively to their feelings, ideas and behaviour, talking to parents to make sure that the child is being cared for appropriately for each family.
>
> (DCSF, 2008a: 37)

According to the 2012 EYFS framework (DfE, 2012), it is a safeguarding and welfare requirement that:

> Each child must be assigned a key person . . . Providers must inform parents and/or carers of the name of the key person, and explain their role, when a child starts attending a setting. The key person must help ensure that every child's learning and care is tailored to meet their individual needs. The key person must seek to engage and support parents and/or carers in guiding their child's development at home. They should also help families engage with more specialist support if appropriate.
>
> (DfE, 2012: 7)

The role of the Key Person is more clearly defined in the reformed EYFS, where it is seen as going beyond being assigned. A Key Person approach does not occur by simply allocating children to practitioners, and the reformed EYFS shows the Key Person role to be an ongoing one throughout the child's time at the setting, and that there is a second strengthened role in terms of parents.

However, as Elfer et al. (2003) argue the Key Person approach is not without its challenges, and it is important to consider them. Elfer et al. (2003) highlighted five main challenges:

- It brings staff too close to a parental role and they risk becoming over-involved in the child.
- It encourages children to get too close to a member of staff, so it is painful for them when the member of staff is unavailable.

- It is threatening for parents if a special relationship is built between their child and another adult.
- The Key Person approach is complicated and can prevent staff working as a team.
- The Key Person approach undermines opportunities for children to build relationships with all staff.

These are important challenges, and I would add from my experiences of training on this approach that there are other challenges too. However, these are not insurmountable and simply require some creative thinking and the recognition of the value of the approach. Other challenges I have come across include:

- The child is only with us for a short time, either a few hours a week or a short number of weeks, and so doesn't need a Key Person.
- The child spends longer hours in our setting than any staff member and so can't have the same Key Person all day.
- The child attends another setting and has a Key Person there and would be confused by having another Key Person here.
- The child is happy to go to anyone and doesn't need a Key Person.
- The child is a challenge and is exhausting for anyone to have as a Key Person.
- The parent wants a different Key Person to the child's allocated Key Person.
- Practitioners finding it upsetting that the child clings and needs them so much as a Key Person.
- Practitioners can become over-attached to children.
- Practitioners can have different levels of closeness with children, and therefore may privilege some relative to others in terms of time and energy.

These issues and others are valid, but reflect that this is an approach that is not fully understood and supported by all those who are part of the setting. Therefore there are a number of principles that must be in place for the Key Person approach to work effectively for all. We will now look at each of these in turn.

## 1 Everyone needs to have a shared understanding of the Key Person approach in their setting

It is essential that all members of an early years setting – staff including leaders/managers and assistants, parents and children – understand the Key Person approach and how it works in their setting. This means staff must have a common understanding of the role of the Key Person, and of the importance of building a close relationship with the child and their family. Elfer et al. term this: 'ensuring that all the children and their families had an entitlement to a special attachment relationship with one member of staff – a designated person to support the mental, health, well-being, care and learning of each children enrolled . . .' (Elfer et al., 2003: 36). Similarly parents need to have regular opportunities to understand the role through discussion and information-sharing through displays and leaflets. This needs to be communicated appropriately in language that parents understand and are comfortable with.

Developing a shared understanding of the Key Person approach can be done through staff discussion on the key responsibilities of a Key Person in the setting, and how to support other staff members in their Key Person role. This needs to be done by each setting in order to tackle the issues in a way that works for all the staff within the setting. Within training, there are often discussions about the role of the Key Person in relation to greeting, feeding, eating, drinking, toileting and changing, and how this works when staff are engaged in other activities.

## 2 There need to be systems to support the Key Person approach in the setting

It is essential that there is systematic support for the Key Person approach. Many of the concerns listed above result from practitioners having insufficient time to discuss the emotional content of their role with children. This means that practitioners all need regular opportunities to talk about how they are feeling about the children and their families. This is best supported through an effective system of supervision. Although supervision is a mechanism used to support and challenge those in what are termed the 'helping professions' (Hawkins and Shohet, 2006), it has not been a common feature of practice in early years settings and schools: 'Supervision is a concept that is widely accepted and valued in the social service and nursing sectors, and evidence suggests that the educational field could benefit from adopting it' (Steel, 2001: 96).

The reformed EYFS has recognized the value of supervision as shown in the following quote from the Statutory Framework:

> 3.19 Providers must put appropriate arrangements in place for the supervision of staff who have contact with children and families. Effective supervision provides support, coaching and training for the practitioner and promotes the interests of children. Supervision should foster a culture of mutual support, teamwork and continuous improvement which encourages the confidential discussion of sensitive issues.

> 3.20 Supervision should provide opportunities for staff to:

> *   discuss any issues – particularly concerning children's development or well-being;
> *   identify solutions to address issues as they arise; and
> *   receive coaching to improve their personal effectiveness.
>
> (DfE, 2012: 17)

This shows recognition of the value of supervision; however, it is critical that supervision is recognized to have more than managerial and educative functions, but to be an opportunity for staff to explore how they are feeling, particularly in relation to their key children and families, and to gain support.

In addition there needs to be a buddy system where the Key Person has a second person in place who also knows the child and can take the place of the Key Person when needed. This is stated within Development Matters in the EYFS (Early Education, 2012) within PSED as guidance for babies aged 0–11 months: 'Ensure the key person is paired with a "buddy" who knows the baby and family as well, and can step in when necessary' (Early Education, 2012: 8).

## 3 There needs to be an acceptance of the need to invest time in building relationships and the development of the Key Person approach

It takes time to build relationships, and Elfer et al. (2003) identify that the Key Person needs to take a proactive approach. At the individual level, this means investing time in getting to know the child and family prior to the child starting at the setting, to ensuring that time is spent with the child and family on a regular basis to know when to step in and provide security and closeness and when to step back and give opportunities to explore.

Time needs to be spent understanding the Key Person approach, why it is needed and the implications for the approach in the setting. There also needs to be time to continuously support staff in managing the issues that arise from the Key Person approach including practical issues alongside having emotional needs met. As stated previously this can come through high quality supervision, as well as regular open discussions about how the Key Person approach is working within the setting.

## 4 There needs to be honesty in the setting about the Key Person approach

For the Key Person approach to work best, there needs to be an honest approach so that staff can discuss how they are feeling in relation to children and families, and equally other staff can share observations of how the children and families seem to be responding. This is not easy! It requires all those involved to be honest about sharing issues as they arise, to be reflective about the Key Person approach and to take a child-centred view of practice.

During training, there were frequently conversations in terms of considering whether the allocated Key Person was the most appropriate choice, and whether the child or family was better suited to a different Key Person. Elfer et al. (2003) state: 'We believe this key person "switching" should be very much a last resort' (Elfer et al., 2003: 46). The reason they state this is that building relationships as a Key Person is sophisticated and will include challenges, and that one should not switch at the earliest challenge. They see the challenge as a professional development opportunity that should be addressed and worked at. However there are also practical reasons for change, such as a child changing their attendance pattern or staff members moving and then there needs to be an open and honest discussion about the best Key Person for the child. Nevertheless it is very important to be aware of the number of changes of Key Person a child experiences in their time at the setting and if these are frequent, they are likely to have a negative impact on the child, family and the Key Person too.

## 5 The Key Person approach requires staff who are reflective, flexible and responsive to working on challenges

This final point is one that encompasses all the previous points in that the staff in the setting need to take a reflective approach to their work. This means allowing time and space for reflection on action, not simply reflection in action (Schön, 1987).

> **Reflections**
>
> How do you know if there is a shared understanding of the Key Person approach in your setting?
>
> What are the systems in place in your setting that support the Key Person approach?
>
> When is quality time given to the different aspects of the Key Person approach: time with children, time with families, time in staff groups, time with managers, times as a management group? Are any aspects being neglected?
>
> How is honesty promoted within the setting in discussing how the Key Person approach is developing and sustained?
>
> How is reflection upon the Key Person approach promoted?

## What are the roles of expectations and the understanding of children's difficulties and strengths in PSED?

As a trainer, I have run a number of short courses on understanding child development, and as part of this training have asked practitioners when they would expect children to achieve certain ages and stages. Initially I ran this training across all areas of learning and development, and found that as would be expected child development is recognized to be unique to the child, but that there was a broad understanding and expectation of when children would achieve certain aspects of development in some areas of learning and development more than others.

It could be argued that the child development framework I was using was flawed, and there is no single universal view of what children achieve at different ages as this is mediated by things such as the child's culture, experiences, family and preferences amongst other factors. However, books such as Mary Sheridan's *From Birth to Five Years* (first published in 1960) have been used by a wide range of professionals to 'appreciate the range of normal development in order to facilitate the identification of developmental differences' (Sheridan, 1997: ix).

Rather than using Sheridan, I used the Development Matters statements and early learning goals within the EYFS (DCSF, 2008b), as this was the current national framework, to see whether practitioners were aware of approximately when children achieve certain aspects of their development. I was surprised to see that many practitioners would be unsure when children achieved the following:

- seek to be looked at and approved of;
- can be caring towards each other;
- work as part of a group, taking turns and sharing fairly;
- begin to accept the needs of others, with support.

It was interesting to see patterns in that some practitioners over-estimated when the first two statements would occur and under-estimated when the second two statements occurred. This led to a lively, reflective discussion about expectations of children and how these are formed for practitioners. From practitioners' comments it would appear that experience seemed to play a large part in the process, but also the abilities of other children within the group. As would be expected, practitioners pointed out (correctly) that they had children of a certain age capable of a certain Development Matters statement at a significantly earlier age, particularly in relation to statements in 'Making relationships' and 'Behaviour and self-control' (DCSF, 2008b).

This led me to reflect with the practitioners on what we term children who have particular strengths and talents in PSED, and how easy it is to recognize that these children have these strengths. It seemed from discussion that as practitioners we tended to see these children who were able to do things earlier than many other children as 'nice' or 'good', and potentially see other children who were maybe developing at the typical level as underperforming. I feel it is rare to be told that a child is particularly talented in PSED!

**Reflections**

What do you term children who are performing well above expectations in PSED for their chronological age?

How do these children affect your expectations of other children within the group?

How easy is it to know expectations for each age and stage in PSED?

## Conclusion

This chapter began by considering how the status of PSED within the curriculum has changed over time, and is now recognized again as a 'prime area of learning and development' in the reformed EYFS (DfE, 2012). The chapter then went on to reflect on the challenges that come with implementing the Key Person approach as an essential part of promoting children's PSED. Five principles were offered to identify how these challenges can be addressed within settings. The chapter concluded with a brief consideration of expectations of children within PSED, and how the fact that children who display strengths in PSED are sometimes labelled can, at times, have a detrimental impact on what is expected from other children.

## References

Bain, A. and Barnett, L. (1986) *The Design of a Day Care System in a Nursery Setting for Children under Five.* London: TIHR Occasional Paper No. 8.

DCSF (Department for Children, Schools and Families) (2008a) *Practice Guidance for the Early Years Foundation Stage.* Nottingham: DCSF.

DCSF (2008b) *Statutory Framework for the Early Years Foundation Stage: Setting the Standards for Learning, Development and Care for Children from Birth to Five.* Nottingham: DCSF.

DfE (Department for Education) (2012) *Statutory Framework for the Early Years Foundation Stage: Setting the Standards for Learning, Development and Care of Children from Birth to Five.* www.education.gov.uk/publications/standard/AllPublications/Page1/DfE-00023-2012 (accessed 27 March 2013).

DfEE (Department for Education and Employment) (1996) *Nursery Education: Desirable Outcomes for Children's Learning on Entering Compulsory Education.* London: HMSO. (Accessed from QCA Archive website http://www.qca.org.uk 26 July 2007).

DfES (Department for Education and Skills) (2003) *National Standards for Under 8s, Day Care and Child Minding.* Nottingham: DfES.

DfES (2007) *Statutory Framework for the Early Years Foundation Stage: Setting the Standards for Learning, Development and Care for Children from Birth to Five.* Nottingham: DfES.

Early Education (2012) *Development Matters in the Early Years Foundation Stage (EYFS).* London: DfE.

Elfer, P., Goldschmied, E. and Selleck, D. (2003) *Key Persons in the Nursery.* Oxford: David Fulton.

Goldschmied, E. and Selleck, D. (1996) *Communication Between Babies in their First Year.* London: National Children's Bureau Early Childhood Unit.

Hawkins P., and Shohet, R. (2006) *Supervision in the Helping Professions,* 3rd edn. Maidenhead: Open University Press/McGraw-Hill.

QCA (Qualifications and Curriculum Authority)/DfEE (Department for Education and Employment) (2000) *Curriculum Guidance for the Foundation Stage.* London: QCA/DfEE.

Schön, D. (1987) *Educating the Reflective Practitioner.* San Francisco, CA: Jossey-Bass.

Sheridan, M. (1997) *From Birth to Five: Children's Developmental Progress.* London: Routledge.

Steel, L. (2001) Staff support through supervision, *Emotional and Behavioural Difficulties,* 6(2): 91–101.

Sure Start (2003) *Birth to Three Matters: An Introduction to the Framework.* London: DfES.

# 5

# Physical development
Pat Beckley

## Introduction

This chapter explores issues involved with the implementation of the EYFS prime area of learning and development concerning physical development. It discusses the two elements of the area: moving and handling and health and self-care. Consideration is given to the rationale for this aspect as a crucial element in children's development and practical suggestions of strategies to use are provided.

## Rationale for the inclusion of physical development as a prime area

Children given access to opportunities to participate in physical development at the earliest ages can develop their potential at their own pace. Failure to have these opportunities could pose serious risks to an individual child's development at a crucial time, when they may not be able to recover from the omission of appropriate experiences.

The 2012 EYFS framework (DfE, 2012) outlines the two elements of physical development: moving and handling and health and self-care. It is expected that strategies underpinning the area of learning and development are implemented through playing and exploring, active learning and thinking critically. Both elements of physical development follow the framework pattern and address issues from birth to 60+ months. Recommendations cover the guiding principles of a unique child, positive relationships and enabling environments. Time spans are given but they might not necessarily be followed in a sequential timeframe. Some aspects may be experienced by individual children and secured readily while others may require further experience to secure the aspect of development. The framework supports practitioners to draw on children's prior learning through enabling them to identify achievements by observing what a child can do. Helpful examples of ways adults could help are given. Strategies to support practitioners consider their environment for learning, through such examples as the use of space, resources and activities are given. The exemplar development is provided in age phases, for example birth–11 months, to provide practitioners with a knowledge and understanding of how children might progress, culminating in the appropriate early learning goal.

Many factors influence a child's physical development, for example the environment the child has access to, resources available, space, genetic issues, personality and experience (Doherty and Brennan, 2008). Children enjoy movement – it might even be painful for them not to move for any length of time – and can experience the joy of practising movements from the earliest age. A baby's movement in the womb and subsequent stretching and flexing of toes and fingers at birth testify to their desire for movement.

Children's gross physical development can be encouraged through providing an appropriate environment for them to be able to move freely, enabling them to practise such skills as walking, running, hopping, skipping and balancing. They can assess their own skills and limitations, building on their knowledge of their abilities to practise the next steps in their learning and acquiring an understanding of their achievements and personal safety. Equipment and apparatus can be provided to support the enjoyment of discovering these skills, for example balls, hoops or skittles, bicycles, tricycles and shared riding apparatus and large equipment for climbing, sliding or balancing. Children enjoy devising their own games and activities as well as those facilitated by adults. Making dens, participation in road safety role play such as pretending to be riding an ambulance or as lollipop adults can foster positive attitudes to physical movement and play. Children might move using various levels of involvement. It could be simply as a way to 'let off steam' or involve highly complex games which require high levels of intellectual as well as physical involvement.

Fine motor skills can also be developed through an appropriate environment. Babies and young children enjoy flexing their muscles and observing and practising what their fingers and toes do. They explore textures around them and learn about materials and resources that are safe and unsafe. Activities which promote handling and fine motor skills may be incorporated while children's play is directed in a variety of areas. For example a group of children building a train track or roadway may also be practising their arm and hand movements pushing toy cars or trains along the tracks, which may later become relevant movements for letter formation when handwriting. Painting, drawing and mark making can develop into useful manipulative tools for gaining practice in using resources which require careful control such as pencils or pens.

Ongoing, formative assessments can provide useful insights into possible further support needed for children. This might take the form of confidence building in their own ability, overcoming fear of resources and materials or be part of a carefully devised programme of physical activity. This could be a programme for a disability such as cerebral palsy, where a child might need to access certain physical movements to ensure joints and muscles remain supple. The Key Person or early years leader would need training from the child's health visitor to ensure the correct movements were accessed and supported at regular and specific times each day. Failure to do so could result in stiffness and possible lack of later use therefore such aspects are a crucial consideration in early years practice. Policies need to be carefully written so that all adults involved with the welfare of the child can follow appropriate and agreed procedures. This includes any specific needs for children, for example asthma or diabetes.

**Case study**

Peter had cerebral palsy which had resulted in tightening of the muscles in his ankles. He had a prescribed programme of movements to his legs and feet to encourage the continued movement of his ankles and to enable him to walk and run with ease. Peter did not like to miss aspects of practice in the early years setting so his Key Person worked hard to build a strong, positive relationship where he was encouraged to be successful. His participation and eagerness to do the necessary activities varied. Sometimes he happily participated and undertook the tasks required while at other times he needed encouragement. Progress was shared between parents, staff and outside agencies and his progress was satisfactory.

## Physical development as part of the learning environment

The physical development area of learning and development as a prime area is woven into other areas. It covers aspects which are essential for children's learning, progress and wellbeing. This is discussed in Chapter 1 where Liz emphasizes the importance of emotional development, in Chapter 4 where Anita considers the prime area of personal, social and emotional development and in Chapter 13 where Jackie discusses children's wellbeing. The expectations for physical development can link to Maslow's theory (1943), which describes basic human needs as physiological (food, drink, sleep, shelter, care). These aspects need to be addressed before children are able to learn and thrive. Instances of a child's failure to thrive in such circumstances could range from severe, where a child might feel suicidal, to less severe, for example when a change has unsettled a child but they are beginning to adjust. Naturally staff can be vigilant to observe any changes in a child's behaviour and consider steps to support or address any issues that may have arisen. Such issues can have a profound impact on a child's ability to thrive and therefore be motivated to explore their surroundings and be excited by their experiences.

**Case study**

A child regularly came to an early years setting unwashed and with badly fitting and dirty clothing. Often he had some of his clothing missing. His Key Worker ensured he was not hungry and gave him clothing to ensure he was sufficiently warm. He had little interest in his surroundings, although he did follow a friend who sympathetically helped him during the day. This was monitored for a while and the situation did not improve so the early years leader discussed the situation with his parents. It was agreed that the local social services department should be contacted to access support. A health visitor visited the family and supported them in gaining access to further help, in turn helping their son.

The learning environment can promote children's physical learning and development. The area will depend on the environment the setting is able to access. If a child is at home or with a small group of children in a childminder's home setting, physical activities can be wide ranging and varied. The home can provide access to physical activities and movements when playing and engaging with activities such as drawing, painting, using malleable materials, crafts, sewing, cutting, pasting or making objects. Gross motor activities can be accessed as part of everyday tasks such as visiting the shops.

In an early years setting care should be taken to ensure areas of learning and development of the 2012 EYFS framework are evident, wherever possible, in the learning areas within the setting. For example mark-making materials can be provided in all areas to enable children to have access to them if they can be incorporated into their play. If the children feel safe and secure within the setting they are able to access the available areas independently and be willing to attempt areas new to them within the facility. In this way, areas within the setting can promote physical activity, for example independently choosing the areas and movements between them, accessing and returning resources for their play, using resources in an active manner, such as moving freely when building using blocks, cloths and planks. Monitoring children's choices can help aid an understanding of children's preferences of activities and their growing strengths and interests. Sometimes it might be useful to encourage individuals to 'have a go' in areas that may seem difficult or challenging.

**Case study**

Wayne was reluctant to attempt any activities such as painting or drawing. It was felt he would gain confidence after a few days in the setting, observing others accessing the resources, but he did not. His Key Person attempted to encourage him but he remained reluctant. When asked why he did not wish to draw, paint or make marks he said his parents did not want him to use these resources as he might make a mess at home and had been told he could not. He was told he could use them in the early years settings and he was given a crayon. Initially he hesitated and gently put a dot on the paper. This was followed by a small mark then his frustration at being unable to use drawing materials surfaced and he scribbled furiously over the paper and onto the table. He was shown the parameters of the paper and had another go, this time carefully drawing on the paper. This was swiftly followed by numerous paintings and drawings using a variety of mark-making implements.

## Health and self-care

The environment for children in the early years should be welcoming to all who enter and be a stimulating and exciting place for children to explore experiences in their learning through play. All aspects of health and safety should be considered, including the cleanliness of the environment and procedures for keeping it and the resources stored there clean. This involves cleaning routines performed by children, practitioners and cleaning services.

To promote children's health and develop their ability to independently have self-care requires an understanding of what this entails. There has been much media attention concerning obesity in children but care needs to be taken to ensure they receive an appropriate well-balanced diet to support their developing bodies and bones. A variety of fruit or vegetables can be on offer at snack times. Water should be freely available for children to access. There are a number of ways food times can be successfully managed in a setting. This may entail a child's independent access to food available, perhaps through a 'ticket' or name system to identify when a child has taken their share. It could be a more formal arrangement where groups have staggered times to eat their snacks during a specific part of the day where everyone has the option to have a snack as part of a mealtime. Whatever the arrangement it is useful to have interactions between peers or with adults and children to make the time a pleasant, stress-free social occasion. Adults should be aware of the food intake of the children in their care, ensuring a well-balanced meal is eaten. Note should be taken of any reluctance to eat or of overeating and consideration given to possible causes and solutions to rectify or resolve this.

Children can be encouraged to become aware of healthy choices through their participation in preparing food or setting a table for mealtimes, where they are involved in the aspects needing consideration in the readiness for eating. Most children seem to enjoy cooking and baking and can gain an in-depth knowledge of a variety of food and where it comes from. This can lead to exciting wider developments in their learning, through gaining an understanding of how plants and animals grow and what this entails. Visits or having visitors to the setting can promote their wider interests and knowledge of different work and lifestyles. Compiling shopping lists, visiting supermarkets and shops, reading recipes, devising role play of shops and mealtimes and involvement in making food to share, as well as having responsibility for the sharing of snacks in the setting, can enhance children's understanding of the importance of healthy eating and ways to achieve this. Other agencies can be accessed to promote awareness of relevant issues and perhaps provide visitors to support children's understandings, for example health visitors, nurses or dentists may visit.

Promoting healthy eating and physical development incorporates consideration of allergies, cultural preferences and support from adults working in the setting. These aspects need to be taken into account when planning for activities based on healthy eating, such as food eaten in the setting and baking activities, and discussed with parents or carers at the meeting prior to the child starting the provision. Following this meeting care can be taken to adhere to parental/carer advice, ensuring children remain safe when accessing the resources prepared.

**Case study**

Parents approached a setting to gain a place for their son, who had a severe reaction to peanuts or any products containing peanuts. They described how other people became anxious when he visited other groups and were concerned that he might be excluded from activities because of his allergic reaction. As the parents had been so proactive in describing their son's condition and working with relevant agencies, staff were able to access training to become aware of what it entailed and actions to be taken in the event of an anaphylactic shock. The son subsequently entered the setting and it was evident he was well aware of how to deal with situations where he might be in difficulty. A situation did not occur during his time in the setting but staff took great care to ensure the environment was appropriate for him, choosing ingredients in baking time which did not contain peanuts, for example types of margarine, and generally maintaining vigilance for the welfare of the boy in their care. This enhanced all the children's awareness of themselves as individuals and promoted their care of each other and their variety of specific needs.

## Diversity

Diversity issues need to be considered when planning for topics such as healthy eating. Personal circumstances and individual needs should be taken into account to help individuals within the setting. Children will have different experiences of food and what constitutes health. It might be necessary to introduce children to a variety of foods, following parental permission to support their participation in talking about aspects of their resources, for example fruit from other countries. Possible allergies should have been checked before children enter the setting but it is worth double checking with parents/carers to ensure all children can safely participate in such activities.

**Case study**

When children in a family from Bangladesh entered a setting care was taken to welcome them, for example through bilingual signs around the learning environment, particularly in the entrance. Other aspects were considered, such as inclusion of saris in the role play clothes shop. A particularly successful experience incorporated the inclusion of Bangladesh-style sweets with the biscuits and buns made in the setting or brought by parents for an end of term celebration. Parents and carers, including those who had recently arrived in the country, shared their recipes with each other and staff and much interest was aroused by the variety of food.

**Reflections**

What are the aims for physical development?

How can we promote this aspect for the children as individuals?

How can we incorporate these areas of learning and development throughout the framework?

How can we support progression in these areas?

How can we support children who require additional help, including possibly working with other agencies?

## Conclusion

It is evident that the aspects moving and handling and health and self-care play a crucial part in a young child's learning and development. Those responsible for the development of the children in their care have numerous issues to consider when devising an appropriate environment for them to promote physical learning. This crucial area in the framework can have significant impact on their future lives, where the foundations of a healthy lifestyle are made.

## References

DfE (Department for Education) (2012) *Statutory Framework for the Early Years Foundation Stage: Setting the Standards for Learning, Development and Care of Children from Birth to Five*. www.education.gov.uk/publications/standard/AllPublications/Page1/DfE-00023-2012 (accessed 27 March 2013).

Doherty, J. and Brennan, P. (2008) *Physical Education and Development 3–11: A Guide for Teachers*. London: David Fulton.

Maslow, A. (1943) A theory of human motivation, *Psychological Review*. 50: 370–96.

## Further reading

Beckley, P., Elvidge, K. and Hendry, H. (2009) *Implementing the Early Years Foundation Stage: A Handbook*. Maidenhead: Open University Press.

Bilton, H. (1999) *Outdoor Play in the Early Years*. London: David Fulton.

Bowlby, J. (1953) *Child Care and the Growth of Love*. Harmondsworth: Penguin.

Burnett, G. (2002) *Learning to Learn*. Carmarthen: Crown House Publishing Ltd.

Dalhberg, G., Moss, P. and Pence, A. (1999) *Beyond Quality in Early Childhood Education and Care*. London: RoutledgeFalmer.

Miller, P. and Pound, L. (2011) *Theories and Approaches to Learning in the Early Years*. London: Sage.

Moyles, J. (ed.) (2010) *Thinking about Play: Developing a Reflective Approach*. Maidenhead: Open University Press.

# 6

# Communication and language
Pat Beckley

## Introduction

This chapter emphasizes the importance of this area of learning and development. The strands within this area are discussed; that is listening and attention, understanding, and speaking. Inclusion issues are considered, including strategies for children with English as an additional language (EAL).

## A crucial Area of Learning and Development

The ability to communicate and use language forms a crucial aspect of our lives. It is part of virtually all other areas of learning and development and forms the basis of other aspects, for example becoming literate. It is also necessary to learn this ability at a young age as it is difficult to acquire later, when our brains have already formed to respond to certain stimuli. Therefore it is vital that practitioners provide opportunities for babies and young children in the early years to have opportunities to develop their communication and language experiences in interactions with their peers and through adult conversations. Chapter 3 discusses ways this can be promoted in more depth. The enabling environment should be considered for the opportunities it provides to facilitate children's confidence in communicating with others in stimulating, motivating surroundings which will ensure their engagement with the range and variety of activities they devise and participate in. Partnerships with parents and carers can provide readily available knowledge of children's prior knowledge and abilities before they enter early years settings. Any aspect which may require support from other agencies can be discussed before the child enters the setting to enable appropriate support to be available from the outset. Observations of children's activities can identify the development children have achieved. The 2012 EYFS framework (DfE, 2012) identifies three elements in the communication and language area of learning and development; that is listening and attention, understanding, and speaking. This area of the framework is underpinned by the characteristics of effective learning and early years principles.

## Listening and attention

Children can be encouraged to listen with attention and engagement throughout all areas of learning and development in the 2012 EYFS framework. The early years goals (ELGs) described in the documentation for this element state that children should 'listen attentively in a range of situations'. They emphasize the importance of building on stories to promote listening, anticipation of events and responding with 'comments, questions or answers'. The final point in this section of ELGs describes 'how children should give their attention to what others say and respond appropriately, while engaged in another activity'. This highlights the need to ensure listening and attention are incorporated into all areas of learning and should be valued as crucial in the child's development. The framework supports practitioners with suggestions for the identification of achievements, for example 'turns towards a familiar sound' at birth to 11 months or listens to others in small groups at 30–50 months. The age span indicated provides guidelines for practitioners although timings will depend on the individual child's progress and development.

Research in the learning and development of babies and young children indicates that children respond to sounds at the earliest age, and are possibly able to hear sounds before they are born, for example the mother's heartbeat, music, familiar voices or whistling. Babies respond to the sights around them listening intently to voices and demonstrating an awareness of familiar voices, often being comforted by them. Children attempt sounds and copy movements appearing to 'talk' to those who are in conversation with them. In this way they can learn about speech patterns and forms of language which are apparent in the culture in which they are brought up. They learn the cultural norms and expectations through listening to adults around them. They learn the boundaries and rules of the culture they are growing in. It is important for staff to agree on possible procedures and routines within settings as they form the background for children to learn about appropriate language and provide role models for their language development.

In order for children to listen and demonstrate attention it is relevant to show that these elements have their importance in the home and setting. Promoting listening through such activities as reading stories and discussions and questions based on them, can show the value placed on listening. Hearing others' views can be considered, for example discussing other children's ideas and building on them can also be useful. Experiences children have in the home or setting can be encouraged, discussed and their importance valued, particularly those which incorporate children's involvement and engagement. These experiences can stimulate children's thinking and lead to the development of an understanding of relevant concepts through play.

Developing children's interest in stories and rhymes encourages their knowledge of language patterns and sequences and their comprehension of how language works.

**Case study**

In a Reception class circle time session children shared their experiences of a visit to the local shops. They later recalled and shared their own experiences. They discussed this with a friend and later recounted their friend's favourite part

> of the visit to a wider group. This encouraged careful attention to the friend's ideas, a growing understanding of and empathy for the friend and thought and planning in speaking about another's ideas.

## Understanding

The ELG for the understanding element states 'Children follow instructions involving several ideas or actions. They answer "how" and "why" questions about their experiences and in response to stories or events'. This aspect ranges from the child stopping and looking when he/she hears their own name at birth–11 months, to addressing complex tasks such as responding to instructions involving a two-part sequence at 40–60+ months.

Children can develop this element through a variety of experiences, for example a small world activity could promote children's discussions about how to organize and plan a farm, discussing and naming animals, collaborating to plan areas of the farm while sorting animals to do this. In this way children can imagine and recreate experiences to talk about with their friends and adults by sharing experiences, and learning from them is heightened through the interactions. Common greetings and exchanges can be learned formally and informally through these conversations, for example a greeting at the start of the day or saying please or thank you when appropriate.

Care can be taken to encourage children's understanding, particularly if a child finds this aspect challenging. Language can be built from an emphasis on one word to two and three words. Some children may find attempting to understand three or four instructions within a conversation confusing and difficult to follow. This can result in a child following the final word uttered with the previous words blurring into incomprehension. However, a child may also understand the first or middle part of the instructions and be unable to understand the rest. It may appear that a child is behaving badly when in fact they are simply unable to follow complex instructions.

Children can explore their surroundings, developing their understanding in their play. The setting can provide a rich enabling environment where babies and young children can investigate natural and made resources indoors and outdoors. They can begin to develop their own complex understandings of their environment through questioning and finding out about how things work and what they are made of, and what can be planned and devised through the understanding they develop in their interactions with others.

## Speaking

The ELG for this element states 'Children express themselves effectively, showing awareness of listeners' needs. They use past, present and future forms accurately when talking about events that have happened or are to happen in the

**Reflections**

How do you help children to understand their surroundings and the world they live in?

Think about how you share stories. Do you interact with children, share ideas and discuss the story read?

Do you vary your voice to identify different characters in the story when you are reading it?

Do you show your enthusiasm for the story?

future. They develop their own narratives and explanations by connecting ideas or events.'

Children's opinions should be valued and respected. This can be encouraged through their interests and achievements. This aspect is further considered in Chapter 3 'The adults around the child' where mutual respect is observed as a means to foster children's communication and language through enquiry and motivation. In such an environment children can feel safe and valued. Positive relationships between children and adults and between children and their peers can promote learning and development through a sense of positive self-esteem and self-worth. Behaviour issues can be dealt with in an environment where children know they are valued. This is explored further in Chapter 11.

Aspects of communication and language and other issues in the early years are interwoven. Misunderstandings can result in a child being frightened or appearing to misbehave when in reality they do not understand what is happening around them, the reasons why it is happening and how they should respond. If a child transfers settings or moves from home to a setting they may have to respond rapidly to a change in expectations. Many providers seek to lessen this impact and successfully liaise to ensure transferring is as smooth a transition as possible for the child. Documentation for the new EYFS supports the transition, enabling providers to access a framework which has a common structure.

Care can be taken throughout the early years provision to ensure elements of the communication and language element are promoted. This can be fostered through the interactions with the adults and peers around the child, including formal, adult-led and adult-initiated and children's independent and free flow activities. In the learning environment each area should be considered to ensure this crucial aspect is covered. This can include a mark-making area, mathematics, small world, construction, book corner, role play areas, music corner, art and craft areas, malleable tables, IT and outdoor area. In a home setting ongoing activities can be used to promote communication and language while time can be allocated for example, for sharing a book chosen to reflect an idea brought up in conversations or one chosen by the child.

In a setting the areas can be considered by adults to ensure all aspects of communication and language are included. For example in the construction area resources can be stored and labelled with words and pictures so that children can discuss what equipment they might need for the task they have devised. Writing materials can be accessed to provide opportunities for ideas to be noted and plans made. In this way groups of young children can discuss their models, made either in a group or as individuals, sharing and communicating the strengths of their ideas and any difficulties they might have had. Models can be displayed to encourage children to reflect on their work.

---

**Reflections**

How are children welcomed to the setting?

Are personalized needs shared between staff team members?

Do displays celebrate the work of all children?

---

## Inclusion

Learning for individuals should be personalized, particularly in this crucial area, to ensure all make progress and that provision for each individual as a unique child is able to meet their needs. The 2012 EYFS framework provides a consistent basis for children's development and can be used to help children when they transfer to different providers or settings. Through gaining a knowledge of the child as unique practitioners are able to respond appropriately, supporting children where necessary through further help or possible contact with other agencies. The two year review should make these procedures more readily accessible to ensure that whatever setting children attend they can have a smooth transition and continuous progress through their learning and development. If a child has been identified as having special educational needs (SEN) particular attention might be necessary to ensure the child's needs are carefully planned for and settings are prepared with the knowledge and resources to support the child before they start the provision. Children have the legal right to be treated fairly, regardless of race or religion or any other aspect of their life. Children should be able to communicate in their first language and parents can choose settings where they feel they are able to do this. Some parents may have a mistrust of settings as a result of their own negative experiences and may have difficulty communicating with the setting. Staff can encourage parents to participate in activities and get to know their child's Key Person to overcome this anxiety. Some children may enter the setting as gifted and talented individuals and again their development can be supported in an environment where all children are accepted as individuals and allowed to flourish at their own level of ability.

Connor had been identified as partially deaf before he started the nursery provision. Liaison had already been in place through contact with his childminder and parents who informed the nursery of Connor's achievements through communication and what were deemed to be his next steps. The nursery was therefore well prepared to meet Connor's needs before he arrived. The lead teacher had discussed Connor in the staff team meeting and his Key Person had been identified. Connor readily settled into nursery and through his previous positive experiences with other children played happily with his new friends. His Key Person ensured Connor was sitting near her and facing her during small group sessions. She took care to face him directly when talking to him, to help him lip-read. The children quickly learned the technique and followed the adult's example.

Communication and partnerships were highly important in identifying how Connor's needs could be best met and to ensure he settled happily. The Key Person played a vital role in preparing for his arrival, observing his progress and development and liaising and sharing his achievements with those connected with his welfare. Ongoing informal meetings at the beginning and end of session, and at such events as open days or fairs, ensured Connor maintained his confidence in his abilities and knowledge that he was well supported when he required it. It also raised children's awareness of empathy towards others through their consideration for their friend.

## Diversity

Children come to settings with different experiences and skills. Children from some backgrounds may need further support in communicating with others, while children from a home environment where English is not their first language may need help to develop their bilingual achievements. The setting should reflect the lives of children using it so care will need to be taken to provide an enabling environment reflecting the diverse nature of the community it serves. Resources and bilingual books can promote a sense of diversity. These should be carefully chosen so that a stereotypical view is not given. Resources where children can use their imagination to develop their knowledge can be used, for example a sari or large piece of material in the role play area. The Key Person can prove to be an important link to developing partnerships with parents/carers to build on individual children's knowledge of language. The family can be encouraged to use their first language at home with the child's bilingual abilities celebrated in the early years setting. The Key Person can provide a buddy system with a friend to support a child who is unsure of English. Bilingual books can encourage and stimulate children with possible help from colleagues who may have knowledge of different languages or the parents themselves may like to help.

**Case study**

Saima began the nursery the day after she and her family had arrived from Bangladesh. A member of staff met the mother but she had to go back home with her other children while her husband had begun his new job. The Key Person welcomed Saima and introduced her to a buddy. Saima went with her friend to the sand tray. She watched the other children quietly but did not speak. For a few days Saima continued not to speak to others but watched them intently. When she felt confident she began to speak a few words with others and after a few weeks could speak key words in English and be easily understood. She helped her mother interpret what others were saying. Staff at the nursery encouraged her mother to become involved in the mother and toddler group that had been arranged by parents and carers and she began to participate in community activities.

Saima quickly became part of the nursery group but it required a great deal of effort on her part to keep up with her peers through their spoken English. Besides having to adjust to a different climate, housing, clothes to keep warm, routines and new friends Saima had to learn a new language in addition to the one she was proficient in, to maintain her progress and participate with others.

**Reflections**

Does the setting have a visual timetable to support an understanding of routines during the day?

Does the setting have a rich, diverse environment that reflects our diverse society?

## Conclusion

The professional can use their skill to encourage all children, including those with SEN, the gifted and talented and those who come from diverse backgrounds to communicate and use language. Boundaries can be set in the provision to help the children feel safe through appropriate language and use of voice from the practitioner. All children like to be praised for their achievements and when careful effort has been made on their part. These aspects can be shared between adults and children to celebrate good work and consider the behaviour expected in a setting. This can be modelled and demonstrated by the practitioner in the role as a leader of good practice and fairness.

Communication and language are the key to children's development as individuals and as members of the wider community. The ability to communicate and have

*Handwritten annotation: on enviroment +
parents view*

knowledge of langua... ...d awareness of those around us, both in the local ... ...of the wider world. Individuals are at a huge disadva... ...ve difficulty accessing the ability to communicate in ... ...unity, through interactions in their everyday lives and accessing modern ... ...ical networks. Communication and language transcends other areas of life and is crucial in the early years as a foundation for children's growth and happiness.

## Reference

DfE (Department for Education) (2012) *Statutory Framework for the Early Years Foundation Stage: Setting the Standards for Learning, Development and Care of Children from Birth to Five*. http://www.education.gov.uk/publications/standard/AllPublications/Page1/DfE-00023-2012 (accessed 27 March 2013).

## Further reading

Alexander, R. (ed.) (2010) *Children, their World, their Education: Final Report and Recommendations of the Cambridge Review*. London: Routledge.

Gopnik, A., Meltzoff, A. and Kuhl, P. (1999a) *How Babies Think*. London: Weidenfeld and Nicholson.

Keenan, T. and Evans, S. (2002) *An Introduction to Child Development*, 2nd edn. London: Sage.

Nutbrown, C. (2011) *Threads of Thinking: Schemas and Young Children's Thinking*, 4th edn. London: Sage.

Nutbrown, C. and Page, J. (2008) *Working with Babies and Young Children*. London: Sage.

Pugh, G. and Duffy, B. (2010) *Contemporary Issues in the Early Years*. London: Sage.

Siraj-Blatchford, I. and Clarke, P. (2000) *Supporting Identity, Diversity and Language in the Early Years*. Maidenhead: Open University Press.

# Part 3

# The specific areas of learning and development

Part 3 explores issues concerning the specific areas of learning and development that are: literacy, mathematics, understanding the world and expressive arts and design. These areas are deemed no less important than the prime areas but are felt to be less age crucial. Awareness of the knowledge and understanding of the specific areas can be developed by children and adults as part of lifelong learning.

The renowned researcher Kathy Ring has written Chapter 7 based on literacy. It includes findings from her recent research and Kathy poses insightful reflections on literacy in the early years from her findings. She argues for a broad-based approach to literacy for young children, linked to other areas of learning within the 2012 EYFS framework.

Chapter 8 focuses on mathematics and is co-authored by Elizabeth Carruthers who has written a number of books on early years mathematical theory and practice using her expertise from her role as headteacher at Redcliffe Children's Centre, Nursery School and Research and Development Base in Bristol. Emma Butcher has collaborated with Elizabeth and they kindly share their experienced insights of mathematics with early years children in this chapter.

Rachel Sparks Linfield shares her expertise of the specific area of learning and development, namely understanding the world, in Chapter 9. Rachel's observation of an incident in an early years setting gives much pause for thought and promotes the questioning of personal values and views concerning play-based learning. The three aspects covered in understanding the world that are people and communities, the world and technology are thoroughly discussed in turn and implications for practitioners highlighted.

Chapter 10 completes the specific areas of learning and development with Estelle Martin's work on expressive arts and design. She discusses this element within the framework covering: exploring and using materials and media and being imaginative. These aspects link to strands such as design and technology, art, music, dance, role play and stories.

The section opens with Chapter 7 and Kathy's research on literacy based on Maisie, a child case study.

# 7

# Literacy: a broad understanding of what it means to be literate
Kathy Ring

## Introduction

The aim of this chapter is for readers to gain a broader understanding of what can be termed literacy practice within EYFS settings. I will argue that the ELGs (DfE, 2012) for communication and language and for literacy are too narrowly focused and will maintain the blinkered view of the young child's literacy capabilities currently held by many parents and practitioners, as well as many of those involved in monitoring literacy standards at school, local authority and national levels. Instead such goals should be age appropriate and should support all concerned in recognizing the breadth, richness and possibilities of young children's multimodal, interwoven responses to their experiences. Combining perspectives from social semiotics and the idea of language and literacy learning as social practice, I will use an episode of meaning making observed in a nursery context to show how one 'almost 3'-year-old girl's behaviours, supported in literacy practice by the affordances of her nursery environment, exemplify a broader understanding of literacy. My analysis is a celebration of the child's competency as a multimodal text maker engrossed in socially situated literacy practice.

## The research project

This episode of meaning making, recorded on videotape, was part of data collection for a small-scale, longitudinal research project 'Supporting a Playful Approach to Drawing' (2004–2010). Taking a sociocultural approach, the project focused upon early years practitioners' development of strategies for supporting and valuing drawing within their settings. Previous research (Ring, 2003) had reported the teachers' misconceptions about drawing and the way these misconceptions influenced their practice to the detriment of the child's experience. Provision for drawing was seen to be limited and adult interaction with children who were drawing was over-directed and focused on what was meaningful to adults, i.e. people drawing and name writing. There was a lack of praise and recognition for creativity and originality. Data collection, as part of this subsequent research project, recognized the need to reflect both the integration of drawing within children's multimodal ways of making sense of their worlds and the situated nature of drawing within what Dyson (1993) terms 'a continuum of symbolic systems', where drawing is seen to have a close relationship to gesture, body movement, speech and the eventual emergence of writing. A three-day course was designed where training and action research were intertwined to address both theoretical understanding and pedagogical practices. Sixty early years teachers (three cohorts of twenty) took part in an interweaving of training, debate and analysis focusing upon data collected as a first phase of action research within their own educational setting. My own role was as trainer-researcher. A second longer phase of in-depth study took place with a smaller number of self-chosen practitioners. In the final third phase of the project I videotaped episodes of meaning making in three of the most visited settings, the focus being children or children and practitioners engaged in drawing activity or interaction in relation to drawing activity (Ring, 2010).

An intended outcome of the research project was that practitioners would have a better understanding of drawing as a tool for learning. This outcome was achieved, with practitioners in the first phase of the project gaining a broader understanding of drawing as theorized by Kress (1997) and Dyson (1993). The collection of visual data, alongside verbal and written narrative, focused upon and extended knowledge of social practice in relation to children's multimodal activity, within which drawing was situated, highlighting key aspects of adults' support for such activity. A further outcome of the project was access to children's responses to an environment where everyday provision was made for children to access drawing in a child-appropriate way. Ring (2010) noted that this provision had improved the children's opportunities to:

- develop an enthusiasm for and love of drawing;
- use whole body action when drawing;
- observe, draw alongside and collaborate with their peers;
- use drawing tools that move fluently across the page or space or material and leave a strong visible impact;
- explore drawing, make their own choices, become engrossed;
- feel secure enough to experiment and take risks with drawing, build up their drawing skills and behaviours pleasurably within safe, secure, unpressurized conditions.

The sharing of this data across a small group of practitioners led to a group analysis that highlighted strong elements of communication, language and literacy, as put forward in the EYFS statutory guidance (DCSF, 2008), within children's drawing events. It also led to discussion about the diversity and complexity of literacy practices and events (Genishi and Dyson, 2009), with drawing being recognized as significant in terms of supporting or indeed being part of literacy practice but seemingly being located most strongly within the EYFS area of learning classified as creative development (DCSF, 2008). The practitioners felt that the statutory division of children's activity into areas of learning within documentation (DCSF, 2008) influenced the structuring of observation proforma. This in turn impacted upon the focus of practitioner observations and what they looked for, and therefore collected, as the child's significant activity. This structuring of practitioner thinking through documentation was internalized and influenced their subsequent thinking and planning for the next steps of learning.

One unexpected outcome came with the wider perspective video data brought to the project. It proved to be a powerful tool in allowing an event to be re-visited and re-viewed with a new focus, in this case the multimodal, interwoven nature of young children's literacy practice. Within this chapter I focus upon: Maisie, almost 3 years old; Leah, her just-4-year-old play partner; and the supportive environment provided by their very experienced nursery teacher, a teacher researcher within the above research project.

## Contrasting understandings of literacy

There are currently many interpretations of the term literacy, reflecting its dynamic and ever-evolving nature (Moll, 1994). A clear division can be seen, however, between those who view literacy as an essentially linear process of 'mastery and control of the systems and processes of written language' (Siegal, 2006: 66), and those who believe that literacy is not in isolated bits of knowledge but is part of children's rich, multimodal ways of making meaning within their world (Dyson, 1993; Kress, 1997; Pahl, 1999) crucial for their construction of self-identity (Halliday, 1975).

## A traditional understanding: early learning goals (DfE, 2012)

Traditionally, early literacy has involved:

* learning to read the meanings conveyed by a combination of words and images found in picture books (Flewitt, 2008);
* drawing pictures to supplement early writing (Flewitt, 2008);
* writing as a linear progression from 'making scribbles, to lines, to letter strings to invented, and finally, conventional spellings on paper' (Fang, 1999).

This focus upon spoken, printed and written language is still predominant in the early literacy policies of many countries. Indeed, since the early 2000s there has been a movement towards more prescriptive literacy policies in some countries, for example the particular focus in England (DfES, 2006) on the teaching of phonics (Flewitt, 2008).

Within the reformed 2012 EYFS framework (DfE, 2012), the ELGs for the *prime* area of communication and language and the *specific* area of literacy (see Table 7.1), emphasize the traditional skills and expression of literacy through speaking, reading and writing. It is notable, however, that with the translation of this area of learning into an ELG it is only 'speaking', a narrow understanding of the term communication, that becomes the focus for practitioners when assessing children's ability

**Figure 7.1** Writing from a teacher-led activity

to 'express themselves effectively' and 'develop their own narratives and explanations by connecting ideas or events' (DfE, 2012: 8). It is also notable that the specific area of literacy is, in its translation to ELGs, broken down into the two sub-headings of reading and writing and within both these goals there is an emphasis placed upon phonic knowledge (see Figure 7.1).

While achievement of these skills is of crucial importance, the sharp focus upon *only* these skills within the ELGs for communication, language and literacy means children's broader multimodal achievements are rendered invisible and forgettable. Within 'Development Matters' (Early Education, 2012), material produced to support statutory documentation, helpful messages are given throughout about the need for: flexibility in regard to the use of developmental statements; recognition of individuality; and cross-referencing across the areas of learning. However, as in the material relating to the previous statutory framework (DCSF, 2008), communication through symbolic representation is located within the area of expressive arts and design. Recognition of a wide range of early literacy behaviours will therefore be dependent upon practitioners' wider and contextualized understanding and interpretation of communication, language and literacy, i.e. being able to recognize early literacy behaviours within other areas of learning.

**Table 7.1** Communications, language and literacy within the 2012 EYFS framework

| | Area of learning and development | Early learning goals |
|---|---|---|
| **Communication and language** | Involves giving children opportunities to experience a rich language environment; to develop their confidence and skills in expressing themselves; and to speak and listen in a range of situations | *Listening and attention:* children listen attentively in a range of situations. They listen to stories, accurately anticipating key events and respond to what they hear with relevant comments, questions and actions. They give their attention to what others say and respond appropriately, while engaged in another activity. <br><br> *Understanding:* children follow instructions involving several ideas or actions. They answer 'how' and 'why' questions about their experiences and in response to stories or events. <br><br> *Speaking:* children express themselves effectively, showing awareness of listeners' needs. They use past, present and future forms accurately when talking about events that have happened or are to happen in the future. They develop their own narratives and explanations by connecting ideas or events. |
| **Literacy** | Involves encouraging children to link sounds and letters and to begin to read and write. Children must be given access to a wide range of reading materials (books, poems, and other written materials) to ignite their interest. | *Reading:* children read and understand simple sentences. They use phonic knowledge to decode regular words and read them aloud accurately. They also read some common irregular words. They demonstrate understanding when talking with others about what they have read. <br><br> *Writing:* children use their phonic knowledge to write words in ways which match their spoken sounds. They also write some irregular common words. They write simple sentences which can be read by themselves and others. Some words are spelt correctly and others are phonetically plausible. |

As has been recognized in relation to practitioners' understanding of the role of drawing as a tool for young children's meaning making, where practitioners are overly reliant on narrow outcomes or goals, there is a tendency for over-direction by practitioners. Children are often fitted into a narrow form of behaviour as soon as possible in a race to achieve the requirements of top-down policy initiatives (Ring, 2010). As recognized by Fuller (2007), policy initiatives frequently emphasize a universal childhood, and often one that is based on white, middle-class notions of what it means to be a child in neo-liberal times. It must be noted that the isolation of reading and writing skills and movement away from young children's highly contextualized ways of expressing meaning within school settings has been considered a major factor when accounting for children's successes and failures in American schools (Dudley-Marling and Paugh, 2005; Taylor, 1993).

## A broader understanding of literacy: socially situated, multimodal practice

Social semiotic theories of communication recognize that children become literate in many ways, not just through language. Their use of different modes is shaped by the social and cultural worlds of which they are part. These are worlds that are saturated with visual and graphic information where being literate includes being able to use computers and mobile phones alongside their more conventional encounters with storybooks (Kress, 1997; Kress, 2001; Kress and van Leeuwen, 1996; Marsh, 2010; Taylor, 1993). Flewitt (2008) recognizes that reading can mean following a linear sequence, reading each page from top to bottom, from left to right, one page after another. It can also, however, mean learning to read an on-screen text where there are 'diverse spatial arrangements of meanings' which require interpretation of a 'medley of visual images, symbols and layout'. Writing can be holding a pen and forming letters and words, but it can also be 'learning to control a computer mouse, manipulating a cursor through the mouse, and identifying, finding and pressing the keys of a traditional keyboard to create letters and words on screens' (Flewitt, 2008: 124) (see Figure 7.2). Flewitt uses the plural term 'literacies' to capture how, within a

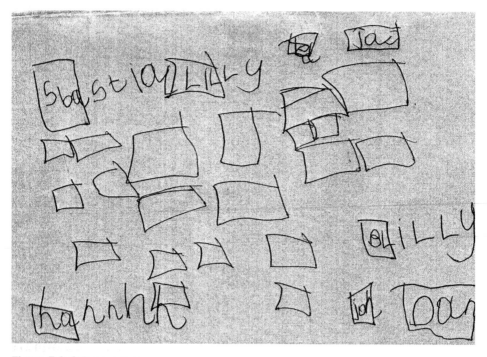

**Figure 7.2** School register

broader perspective on literacy as social practice, children build and express their understandings in diverse ways according to context and purpose. She emphasizes the importance of practitioners reflecting on their own practice in order to better support children's understanding and competence in 'diverse forms of visual, printed and digital literacies', within meaningful contexts (Flewitt, 2008: 122).

Kabut (2009), considering the meaning making of the child before the age of 2, draws attention to children entering school as emerging makers of pictorial and written representations, reflecting their working models of written language and the ways that they use those models to mediate their activities. In arguing that learning to read and write entails more than what is usually addressed in the traditional literacy curricula, she recognizes the significance of the young child who uses markers, pencils or crayons to make marks on a piece of paper and then gives it to their parents as a personal letter. Kabuto identifies classroom routines and the way that materials are organized as having a direct impact on children's sign-making processes, stating that children's sign-making is directly related to their interest and to the resources and tools that are immediately available to them. Her findings are corroborated in the work of Kress (1997) and Anning and Ring (2004).

Dyson's approach to literacy has been influential since the 1980s and is grounded in Vygotsky's understanding of literacy as a meaning construction process (Whitmore et al., 2005). She sees learning how to mean, i.e. 'learning what to say and how to say it across endlessly diverse situations and where the "saying" could be verbal or nonverbal', as fundamental to becoming literate (Genishi and Dyson, 2009: 9). Dyson has developed Vygotsky's (1978) observation that writing development is related to both playing and drawing and that literacy learning requires acts of meaning making which involve multiple symbol systems. Within a continuum of children's use of symbol systems she highlights the interrelationship of gesture, speech, play, drawing and writing for the young child. She recognizes the importance of speech in allowing children to represent meaning, to share their ideas with other people and to engage in increasingly more deliberate, better planned and more playful activity (Dyson, 1993). Rather than a uniform linear progression, however, for Dyson (1990) no two paths to literacy are seen as looking the same. She recognizes a young child's journey through literacy as a 'messy, noisy, and colourful process' (1986: 407–8). Literacy is not acquired merely through the mastery of conventional letters, words, and sentences but is present in all forms of young children's meaning making: talking, drawing, playing, building, singing, acting and more (Barrett, 2011; Dyson, 1986; Gallas, 1994). In emphasizing that young children make meaning by moving fluidly among various symbol systems, Dyson recognizes the need to

> unhinge writing development from its narrow linear path and to portray its developmental links to the whole of children's symbolic repertoires and the breadth of their textual landscapes. These developmental links foreground our key human strengths – social and symbolic flexibility and adaptiveness – as key also to children's growth as skilful users of written symbols.
>
> (Dyson, 2001: 127)

Dyson sees the role of practitioners as helping young children to 'weave literacy from the rich diversity of resources they bring to school with them' (Dyson, 1990: 211). For Pahl, (2008: 144) drawing on ideas from the New Literacy Studies (Street, 2000), the use of the term 'text making' is used to refer to 'drawings, writing or mixtures of the two, or can be realized in other modes such as moving-image media, sound and gesture'. She describes observable moments, when the creative processes of these texts are observable to practitioners or parents, as 'literacy events' (Street, 2000).

The decision-making of a knowledgeable, skilled and reflective practitioner is key to ensuring that children have opportunities for extension and development, while maintaining a strong sense of self-identity (see Figure 7.3). Pahl (2008: 144) understands literacy practices as being bound up with everyday life and the importance of links being made between 'out-of-school literacy practices that they experience in the

**Figure 7.3** This is how a secretary writes

home, and their literacy learning at school'. As recognized by Claxton and Carr (2004), the child's disposition to learn is closely associated with their sense of who they are and what they can do. Crucial to this are the routines and rituals surrounding how the child learns to mean (Ring, 2006). Within early childhood settings children's sense-making and actions are heavily dependent upon the social practices of their community for what is possible and expected. Frequent participation in shared activity is recognized as creating a powerful context for learning. Within such strategies as 'sustained shared thinking' (Siraj-Blatchford and Sylva, 2004), there needs to be recognition of the child's interests, preoccupations and, most importantly, ways of acting. The child's initial manipulation of symbols/signs in their emotional communications with adults and peers, their engagement in significant gestures, and their gradual use of symbols and signs in pretend play are all seen to be part of the young child's progression towards significant learning dispositions (Siraj-Blatchford, 2007).

### Reflections

What are your views of how children become literate?

How are communication and language encouraged in your setting or with the young child or children you are supporting?

In your experience do different approaches work best for different children? What are the factors involved?

## Maisie's story: a literacy event

### Background

Maisie is nearly 3. She has just been allocated a morning place at a nursery school, which she attends sporadically. She has a loving and caring home life. The children in Maisie's class are supported by a warm and responsive qualified teacher who is very aware of her role in providing opportunities for playful meaning making in a rich and rewarding environment. The emphasis is on Maisie feeling she belongs to the classroom community without pressure for her to fit into over-demanding routines and rituals.

I focus on Maisie because when I arrive and seat myself unobtrusively to watch and record children's activity with a still and video camera she comes and stands between my legs. We are both silent and she has her back turned to me, surveying the range of activity ongoing in the room. (All children are inside at this point, a practice that will change over the coming year as children gain free access to both indoor and outdoor provision.) I peep at her face. It is solemn, intent in her observation of what is happening around her. After some time she departs. What follows is an observation of Maisie in interaction with an older girl, Leah, focusing on their involvement with mark-making materials, the purpose of my visit. I do not spend the morning following Maisie; it is her involvement in a mark-making event which means she is captured on video.

## The event

There are two long pieces of paper on the floor, torn from a roll and spread across the width of the room. The teacher is kneeling on the floor with one girl to her right and two boys facing her. The teacher has used the width of a pastel to make some non-representative marks on the paper, demonstrating the effect of tool use. She is now quietly joining in with the children's conversation, following their lead and occasionally pulling the pastel in her hand across the paper. The two boys are busily drawing, highly involved in a self-chosen activity using the available pastels. Their drawing is purposeful, no content prescribed by others. One boy uses the side of the pastel to create a smudgy wide line.

Maisie approaches and watches the ongoing activity; she is dressed in a voluminous pink silk and net gown from her previous activity. The teacher encourages her to take part by indicating the space next to Leah, an almost-4-year-old girl at her side. Leah moves up a little and puts a handful of pastels on the floor next to Maisie. Maisie picks up one of the pastels and spreads her body out full length on the floor. As she begins to make a mark the older girl also stretches out and curves her body towards Maisie, watching what Maisie is doing.

## Line drawings of the involved children

Maisie slowly makes a line on the paper curving it around and joining it up so that it resembles a racetrack. Leah, the older girl, makes a small mark on top of a part of Maisie's drawing. Maisie looks at her intently. She speaks 'Di, da, didaaa', pointing to the mark Leah has made. Leah, in response draws a bold line down the middle of Maisie's shape. Maisie makes a curved shape in the space above her previous drawing. Leah places a line across her previous line, making a cross within the boundaries of Maisie's original shape. Both girls are watching each other intently. Maisie repeats her spoken rhythmic phrase, addressed to Leah who listens carefully.

From this early joint communication develops a many times repeated turn-taking pattern in which Maisie takes the leading role and Leah supports. As Maisie makes a semi-circular mark she sounds 'da'. Leah responds by drawing a short straight line across Maisie's semi-circle and Maisie sounds 'didaaa'. There is a pause and Maisie sounds out rhythmically 'da, da, didaaa'. Maisie then further develops the sequence of actions. As she makes her sounds she now accompanies them by rhythmically nodding her head and thumping her feet on the floor. While Maisie intensifies her multimodal actions, Leah, the follower, enjoys Maisie's performance and her own small part in it, lying in a relaxed position across the paper. Maisie, her sounds getting louder and her actions stronger, moves onto all fours, and together the girls cover a section of the paper with marks as part of their meaning making. There is another pause. Leah draws an oval shape on the paper and Maisie responds with sounds formed in a sentence-like structure. Both girls are now subdued, the older child puts her pastel down and leaves the activity. Maisie makes no move to follow her but sits back on her heels, looks thoughtful and then leaves the activity.

## Interpretation/discussion

When Maisie makes a mark on paper this triggers an emotional response from her. She demonstrates that the creation of the mark is meaningful in that it symbolizes some internalized memory. Leah supports her in the role of a more experienced other (Vygotsky, 1978) and is both a willing audience, and a participant in shared text making. Maisie, with Leah's support, shows evidence of being an expert communicator and 'symbol weaver' (Dyson, 1986). She creates her patterned story through the intermingling of her channels of communication, i.e. a combination of eye gaze, facial expression, physical proximity, gestures, vocalizations and body language is used to supplement her inscribing of pastel marks on paper. As recognized by Dyson (1993), she is using what she knows to support what is new. In this case her well-practised rhythmical sound making and body movements are incorporated into her playful exploration of sign making through mark making – a relatively new form for expressing ideas. Maisie enjoys her initial communication with Leah and Leah's response and therefore repeats it and builds upon it, wanting it to happen again and again. At the end of the episode of interaction between Maisie and Leah there is left behind a shared text of marks on paper, telling part of the story of the event. It can be anticipated, drawing upon Dyson's (1993) understanding of a symbolic continuum, that over time her use of movement, talk and mark making will become more complex and more practised. There is the potential for her texts to become a complex interweaving of oral narrative, drawing and writing (Dyson, 1986).

Maisie and Leah are successful readers of each others signs, as they engage in interaction around the ongoing development of a text. Leah is skilful in her support of Maisie for as an older child she has spent more time at the nursery and has internalized an understanding of the routines and rituals of the learning context. Throughout the time they spend together Leah does not say a word and her silence forms part of the communication, giving space for Maisie's responses. She positions her body so that it curves in a relaxed position across the paper towards Maisie. This is a non-threatening pose, accepting and protective of the younger child. She watches intently letting Maisie's strong movements dominate but keeping the interaction going through the minimal action of adding a mark to the text as a stimulus for a further response from Maisie. Leah enjoys the rhythmical and word-like use of sound, which takes a strong place in Maisie's performance. She matches Maisie's pace as her actions start slowly, build to a crescendo and die back. This seemingly simple, playful interaction draws upon a multiplicity of forms of communication that we take for granted as everyday behaviour. The possible combinations for each sequence vary with different cultural conditions but also because of the people involved; they create their own unique mix.

The practitioner responsible for creating an environment within which Maisie will thrive as a learner recognizes the importance of children developing a positive view of themselves as a learner and as a member of a learning community. She has made changes to her environment in order to ensure children have access to drawing activity which is child appropriate and is constantly available. Within this environment children understand that drawing activity is recognized as significant by adults. Maisie is showing increasing confidence in her use of marks on paper as a tool for story building and internalizing. Leah has been using drawing regularly as a tool for representing meaning for some time. Her willingness to spend time with Maisie affirms for Maisie her inclusion within the nursery routines and rituals and her developing sense of belonging. Leah is taking on the caring and supportive role she has experienced so often when interacting with her class teacher. Just as her teacher has behaved towards her over time, so Leah allows Maisie to demonstrate that she can take the lead and can control her actions sufficiently to fit in with another in order to maintain the interaction.

## Conclusion

The broad understanding of literacy, emphasized within this chapter, is exemplified in Maisie's weaving of multimodal behaviours in playful interaction and text making with her peer. She shows through her gesturing, sound making, dramatizing and drawing how literacy is re-presented through, rather than separate from, her meaning making. As Maisie and Leah interact through their use of materials within the rules and rituals of their environment, their playful social practice is seen to be complex, multilayered and dynamic. They are engaging in a 'literacy event' (Street, 2000) in which their creation of a shared, meaningful and multimodal text is one of many momentary building blocks within their overall literacy development. Within this educational learning environment the importance of *making* meaning, as a process of building upon what children know and can do, is recognized and children are importantly afforded the time, space, resources and understanding needed to retain their natural integration of multiple modes of literacy as they engage in new experiences.

Through their everyday structuring of environments, their routines and rituals and the detail of their interventions, practitioners can show a commitment to exploring, with children, the breadth of creative possibilities within a broader understanding and use of the term literacy. Working within this 'messy, noisy, colourful process' (Dyson, 1986: 407–8) they are recognizing and working with, not against, children's inherent flexibility and adaptiveness.

## References

Anning, A. and Ring, K. (2004) *Making Sense of Children's Drawings*. Maidenhead: Open University Press.

Barrett, M.K. (2011) 'Educating Teachers about the Complex Writing Processes of Preschool Students (Project)'. *Honorable Mentions*. Paper 1. http://scholarworks.gvsu.edu/coeawardhonor/1 (accessed November 2012).

Claxton, G. and Carr, M. (2004) A framework for teaching learning: the dynamics of disposition. *Early Years*, 24(1): 87–97. (TACTYC ISSN 0957-5146)

DCSF (Department for Children, Schools and Families) (2008) *Statutory Framework for the Early Years Foundation Stage: Setting the Standards for Learning, Development and Care for Children from Birth to Five*. Nottingham: DCSF Publications.

DfE (Department for Education) (2012) *Statutory Framework for the Early Years Foundation Stage: Setting the Standards for Learning, Development and Care for Children from Birth to Five.* www.education.gov.uk/publications/standard/AllPublications/Page1/DFE-00023-2012 (accessed 27 March 2013).

DfES (Department for Education and Skills) (2006) *Independent Review of the Teaching of Early Reading. Final Report, Jim Rose (The Rose Review).* London: DfES Publications.

Dudley-Marling, C., and Paugh, P. (2005) The rich get richer; the poor get direct instruction. In B. Altwerger (ed.) *Reading for Profit: How the Bottom Line Leaves Kids Behind.* Portsmouth, NH: Heinemann.

Dyson, A.H. (1986) Transitions and tensions: interrelationships between the drawing, talking, and dictating of young children. *Research in the Teaching of English*, 20(4): 379–409.

Dyson, A.H. (1990) Weaving possibilities: rethinking metaphors for early literacy development. *The Reading Teacher*, 44(3): 202–213.

Dyson, A.H. (1993) From prop to mediator: the changing role of written language in children's symbolic repertoires. *Language and Literacy in Early Childhood Education*, 4: 21–41.

Dyson, A.H. (2001) Writing and children's symbolic repertoires: development unhinged. In S.B. Neuman and D. Dickinson (eds) *Handbook of Early Literacy Research.* New York: Guilford.

Early Education (2012) *Development Matters in the Family Years Foundation Stage (EYFS).* London: DfE.

Fang, Z. (1999) Expanding the vista of emergent writing research: implications for early childhood educators. *Early Childhood Education Journal*, 26(3): 179–82.

Flewitt, R. (2008) Multimodal literacies. In J. Marsh and E. Hallet (eds) *Desirable Literacies: Approaches to Language and Literacy in the Early Years*, 2nd edn. London: Sage.

Fuller, B. with Bridges, M. and Pai, S. (2007) *Standardized Childhood: The Political and Cultural Struggle Over Early Education.* Stanford, CA: Stanford University Press.

Gallas, K. (1994) *The Languages of Learning: How Children Talk, Write, Dance, Draw, and Sing their Understanding of the World.* New York: Teachers College Press.

Genishi, C. and Dyson, A.H. (2009) *Children, Language, and Literacy: Diverse Learners in Diverse Times.* New York: Teachers College Press.

Halliday, M.A.K. (1975) *Leaning How to Mean: Explorations in the Development of Language.* London: Edward Arnold.

Kabut, B. (2009) Colour as a semiotic resource in early sign-making. *Early Childhood Research and Practice*, 11:2.

Kress, G. (1997) *Before Writing: Rethinking the Paths to Literacy.* London: Routledge.

Kress, G. (2001) Visual and verbal modes of representation in electronically mediated communications: the potentials of new forms of text. In I. Snyder (ed.) *Page to Screen: Taking Literacy into the Electronic Era.* New York: Routledge.

Kress, G. and van Leeuwen, T. (1996) *Reading Images: The Grammar of Visual Design.* London: Routledge.

Marsh, J. (2010) *Childhood, Culture and Creativity: A Literature Review.* Newcastle: Creativity, Culture and Education.

Moll, L. (1994) Literacy research in community and classrooms: a sociocultural approach. In R. B. Ruddell, M. P. Ruddell and H. Singer *Theoretical Models and Processes of Reading*, 4th edn. Newark, DE: International Reading Association.

Pahl, K. (1999) *Transformations: Children's Meaning Making in a Nursery.* Stoke on Trent: Trentham Books.

Pahl, K. (2008) Looking with a different eye: creativity and literacy in the early years. In J. Marsh and E. Hallet (eds) *Desirable Literacies: Approaches to Language and Literacy in the Early Years*, 2nd edn. London: Sage.

Ring, K. (2003) Young children drawing at home, pre-school and school: the influence of the socio-cultural context. Unpublished doctoral dissertation, School of Education, University of Leeds.

Ring, K. (2006) What mothers do: everyday routines and rituals and their impact upon young children's use of drawing for meaning making. *International Journal of Early Years Education*, 14(1): 63–84.

Ring, K. (2010) Supporting a playful approach to drawing. In P. Broadhead, J. Howard and E. Wood (eds) *Play and Learning in the Early Years*. London: Sage.

Siegal, M. (2006) Rereading the signs: multimodal transformations in the field of literacy education. *Language Arts*, 84(1): 65–77.

Siraj-Blatchford, I. and Sylva, K. (2004) Researching pedagogy in English pre-schools. *British Educational Research Journal*, 30(5): 713–30.

Siraj-Blatchford, I. (2007) Creativity, communication and collaboration: the identification of pedagogic progression in sustained shared thinking. *Asia-Pacific Journal of Research in Early Childhood Education*, 1 (2): 3–23.

Street, B.V. (2000) Literacy events and literacy practices: theory and practice in the New Literacy Studies. In M. Martin-Jones and K. Jones (eds) *Multilingual Literacies: Reading and Writing Different Worlds*. Amsterdam/Philadelphia: John Benjamins Publishing Company.

Taylor, D. (1993) *From the Child's Point of View*. Portsmouth, NH: Heinemann.

Vygotsky, L.S. (1978) *Mind in Society: Development of Higher Psychological Processes*. Cambridge, MA: Harvard University Press.

Whitmore, K.F., Martens, P., Goodman, Y.M. and Owocki, G. (2005) Remembering critical lessons in early literacy research: a transactional perspective. *Language Arts*, 82(5): 296–300.

# 8

# Mathematics: young children co-construct their mathematical enquiries

## Elizabeth Carruthers and Emma Butcher

## Introduction

This chapter emphasizes that young children are natural problem solvers. They are born with a sense of curiosity and want to find out about their world. They strive to understand how things work and are persistent in their concerns. Tizard and Hughes (1984) in their study of nursery children were surprised by the wealth of inter-actions that happened between their case study children and their parents, in particular the everyday family mathematical interchange and this resulted in a further study focusing on mathematics (Hughes, 1986). This raised questions: if chil-dren at 4 years of age were tuned into understanding mathematics then what happens in schools? The mathematics of schools is different and Hughes' seminal work, *Young Children and Number* (1986) found that although many young children could mechanically do the algorithms taught to them, most had no understanding of school mathematics and therefore could not transfer that knowledge to different situations. Yet writers such as Cobb and Bauersfeld (1995) and Boaler (2009) high-light the need for children to understand mathematics in school.

The chapter draws upon two case studies of one nursery group and their Key Person, a qualified teacher, and illustrates children as natural problem solvers. It is set in an inner city, multicultural nursery and a children's centre. Emma, the teacher, is also co-author of this chapter. The case studies put forward are just a glimpse of the many and complex interactions that happen throughout the course of a year. The children are 3 and 4 years old.

## Practical mathematics?

The answer to embedding context and purpose in mathematics, especially in early childhood, has a tradition of using practical items that children can manipulate to work out problems. This is usually adult directed and precise. It is an attempt to simplify mathematics for young children. It can be predictable and task orientated. The resources are usually set apparatus used for calculating, for example plastic cubes, elephants and teddy bears. Even when the apparatus appear to be more imaginative the questions are still adult focused and adult constructed. Carruthers and Worthington's (2006) research uncovered that early years teachers placed a great emphasis on the apparatus.

The materials, it appears, become the main focus of the mathematics pedagogy not the children's thinking. Practical mathematics is seen as the answer to bridge the gap between the concrete and the abstract. However, Askew and William (1995) advise that results from their and other studies (for example Hughes, 1986; Walkerdine, 1988) show that practical work does not necessarily lead to understanding abstract concepts so needed in mathematical learning. It is not simply a case of rejecting equipment and materials but also of moving the emphasis on to abstract thinking which is much more complex and high level. It is about supporting children as problem solvers and thinkers and the resources need to be carefully thought through. In this chapter the case studies use what may be termed 'intelligent resources' and 'intelligent experiences' which are culturally appropriate and relevant to the children.

Children will make sense of their experiences if they are their own and they are leading them. Problems that are set by the classroom teacher will not have the same meaning or interest to the child because they are not personal or situated in meaningful contexts for the child. It could be argued that problems set can be meaningful in the context of the real world, for example setting a problem about money or even having real money available for children to handle and explore. However, if this is done without previous connections then it can be arbitrary to the young child and the struggle for meaning ensues.

Teachers valuing and understanding children's home experience helps children build upon existing knowledge. The case studies in this chapter exemplify children's own mathematical enquiries. The teacher in the case studies listens to children's current areas of interest and concern. This is through everyday conversation and when ideas arise. It is not in set lessons. The teacher seizes opportunities that support children's natural enquiries.

## The relationship between learner and teacher

Schrimsher and Trudge (2003) and Fleer (2010) discuss the important relationship from a Vygotskian root of the interplay between teacher and child. They describe the Russian word *obucherie* as meaning teaching and learning; therefore teaching and learning are not seen as isolated units. This view of teaching and learning as connected is in opposition to the teacher as giver of knowledge and directly instructing pupils. Schrimsher and Trudge (2003) explain the importance of the word *obucherie*: 'The more accurate interpretation of the word (obucherie) as teaching *and* learning connotes highly interactive relations involving all participants in creative activity and growth' (Schrimsher and Trudge, 2003: 298, original emphasis).

Indeed Siraj-Blatchford and Sylva (2004) identified that one of the most important pedagogical strategies in the nurseries in her research project was 'sustained shared thinking'. This involved the teacher and child in shared dialogue that arose naturally from some enquiry the child had. Stephens (2010, cited in Deakin-Crick et al., 2004) places high importance on co-construction where the adult and child share equal power in the conversation and they build understanding together taking part in 'a mutual bridge of meaning'.

The teacher in this chapter describing her case studies has a deeply important relationship with these children. She knows their family and home culture and she really wants to understand the children and what they want to explore. She is their Key Person and the children feel secure to talk to her. They are eager to bring in their ideas to discuss every day because they know she will be listening to them. She knows children's own knowledge is important and she says she learns so much from them. A lifelong learning study identified that the quality of the learning relationship between teacher and child was the most important factor to enhance children's learning ability (Deakin-Crick et al., 2004).

Schrimsher and Trudge (2003) explain that individual factors, for example children's interests and background histories, should be interwoven with teacher's motivations and together in democratic practice they make not a zone but zones of proximal development. This is far removed from many writers' conceptions where they see (e.g. Daniels 2007) only the child as being in the zone of proximal develop-ment. Indeed that view could be assumed to be lessening the child's agency and sense of self-empowerment. The relationship between learner and teacher seems pivotal in promoting the self of the learner and advancing the child's learning. There does seem to be a vital connection between teacher and child and also the interconnectedness between teaching and learning.

## What do we believe about children?

Fleer (2010) writes it is how we perceive children that determines how we teach them. If we view them as having simple reasoning then we will teach them simple concepts and use materials that are carefully graded. However, if we view children as dynamic individualized thinkers then we will strive to make sure that we listen and respond and provide intellectual experiences that not only match but challenge their growing awareness of the world around them.

> **Reflections**
>
> Consider your views of the children's learning and abilities you are working with. Does this affect how and what is taught?
>
> What approach to learning do you feel children should have access to?

## Children's agency

In the examples of children's play and mathematics in this chapter the children's sense of identity is strong; they believe in their own ideas and solutions. They are confident to try out new things. They are not waiting for the teacher's command but to work sometimes in cooperation with her through unfolding conversations that lead to much deeper thinking. The mathematics is broad, not isolated but connected to their thoughts and they use mathematics as needed. It is a democratic process where children have sense of ownership and agency.

## Case study 1

### Listening to Alfie and his parents

*Emma writes:*

I visited Alfie at home and talked and played with him. In conversation with his mum, I discuss Alfie's interests in fantasy play, Pirates, Dr Who, books and Christmas. His family experiences included camping, festivals and pantomimes. As he settled into nursery in the autumn term his interest in Christmas and Santa surfaced again. His parents shared that he still talked about Christmas at home and this increased as Christmas drew nearer.

### Supporting Alfie's enquiry

I put out a variety of advent calendars in his group's area in the morning as the children came into the nursery. The different types of calendar I felt would stimulate discussion. To further enhance the countdown to Christmas I wrote on the little child-height whiteboard '11 more sleeps to Christmas'.

### What happened

*Emma's observation:*

Alfie's mum read the message on the whiteboard to him when they arrived at nursery.

**Alfie:** No, it's three more sleeps (knowing this is fewer than 11 and three is a good number because he is 3).

**Barley:** We already opened number 8 and ate the chocolate . . . I'll be the chocolate maker.

**Alfie:** I'll be one of the elves making the chocolate.

**Barley:** We just need to make it all hot so it melts, will you do a job, get a spoon. (Alfie continued to mix the 'chocolate'.)

**Alfie:** All the people want chocolate. (Alfie used the whiteboard to denote the orders of people wanting chocolate.)

**Alfie:** Look, all these people want chocolate calendars. (He wiped off my writing on the whiteboard first and then made lines all over the board. Each line represented a person who wanted a chocolate calendar. Other children had also joined this play.)

**Barley:** This needed to go in the oven.

**Alfie:** This is to melt the chocolate for the calendars until they are all full to down there (pointing to the calendar from top to bottom). My next job is to sprinkle the stars on to the fairy dust makers, no one else is allowed in the chocolate factory it's full up. (Alfie pretended to talk over a tanoy, similar to a supermarket.)

**Alfie:** Excuse me, we are closing the chocolate factory in three minutes so every one of my workers can go home. . . . open the chocolate factory. (Christvie joined the play using the whiteboard next to Alfie making 8s all over the board.)

**Christvie:** Only 8 left over it's all the chocolate gone. The calendars are all finished. (Alfie watched Christvie writing.)

**Alfie:** The chocolate takes five months to make we're making lots and lots of chocolate in three days for Christmas, we're making it all nice for the children.

*Emma reflects:*

In this short space of time children were drawing on their home and nursery experiences to play in their imaginary worlds where the possibilities are endless. Moll et al. (1992) write about the bank of experiences children draw on from home as 'funds of knowledge' and they build on this knowledge in school as they make connections. Children, at the same time, were also using mathematics in appropriate contexts the way they understood it.

Responding to children's interests is highlighted in the 2012 EYFS framework (DfE, 2012). We cannot presume we know children's interests unless we know them, their background and their current lines of enquiry. Tizard and Hughes (1984) emphasized the importance of children searching for meaning. They called this 'passages of intellectual search' where children are digging deep to find out more about something they find interesting. Alfie, in this episode, was doing exactly this; mixed up with his recent viewing of 'Charlie and the Chocolate factory' and his enquiry into Christmas he played out his understanding in many different ways.

## The whiteboard

The whiteboard is a negotiated space and children and adults use it for their thinking. Emma used it as a model and a communication point to the children. It was purposefully used for writing and mathematics.

Alfie's mum read Emma's message to Alfie and in doing so read it to the children standing by. The parent felt comfortable, understanding the open culture of the nursery, to take part in the morning session. Parents also feel they can share information with Emma who is keen to listen and uses the knowledge to plan experiences that the children will make connections with and build upon.

## The mathematics

The mathematics was integrated within children's ideas of Christmas, fairy dust and making chocolate. The mathematics used was quantity, number recognition, data

**Figure 8.1** Case study 1

handling, ideas of time in minutes, months and days. Quantity was also used in terms of being full up, linked to ideas of open and closed. There was also the flow of mathematical graphics expressed on the whiteboard giving children another way to communicate their mathematical ideas. Children were free to write and draw in their own way and they did so. Carruthers and Worthington (2006) state that when children are not hampered by correct procedures and their graphics are valued then this develops into children using their own graphics as a tool to help them think through *their* mathematics.

## Pedagogical points

Emma put out the calendars and wrote on the whiteboard as a stimulus; she did not know what would happen and therefore the space she created between herself and the children had democratic principles. Gooche (2010) states it is a risky undertaking for a teacher to just see what happens and work in ways that they are not sure of the outcome. Emma knew this may not work but she would try something else if not. For this episode of play Emma did not speak, the children took over. However, Emma was listening and they knew she valued what they were saying. In an environment that encourages children's own thinking socially inclusive relationships are part of the ethos (Lancaster, 2003).

Isaacs (1967: 62), a pioneer of early childhood education, said that within her nursery she wanted 'to stimulate the active inquiry of the children themselves rather than to teach them . . . We wanted to bring within their immediate experience every range of facts to which their interests reached out'. Emma responded to the children's enquiries through taking part in equitable conversations and providing materials that would stimulate further enquiry.

## What next?

*Emma writes:*

Over Christmas, I managed to find an illustrated copy of the book (*Charlie and the Chocolate Factory*) and put it out for the children to select if they wished. Alfie noticed this book and asked me to read it, other children joined in and spent a long time understanding different parts such as the glass elevator, Augustas being sucked into the pipe and Mike shrinking. The children had so many questions to ask such as, 'What is an elevator?' For many days the children asked to be read different parts of the book. One day, Alfie declared himself 'Willy Wonka'. Luke had been aware of Alfie's and other children's growing enthusiasm over the story but he was not familiar with *Charlie and the Chocolate Factory* himself. However, he brought over a large wooden truck to deliver Afie's chocolates to the 'big green shop'. He was joining in because he was interested to take part in this play. Play becomes the magic space where anybody can join in and everbody can have ownership.

*Emma further reflects:*

Alfie incorporated so many things into this play including signing reports, real factories, smoke chimneys, and Doctor Who. He looked at how he could exploit blocks which was a new medium in his imaginary play. He had not really accessed blocks much prior to this and he chose to use these. Alfie and the other children were freed from thinking concepts are separate; they were free to make their own inter-linking connections between experiences and this is highly complex. This high level of thinking would not have occurred if the children had been denied their freedom to think. It is difficult for adults to keep up with the speed of children's links because it can suddenly move on so quickly to something totally different. Egan (1992: 22) states 'It is hard to get a grasp on what imagination is, it doesn't seem to lend itself to practical methods and techniques that teachers can easily employ'.

## Parents

*Emma reflects:*

Parents, I believe are children's first and most valued play companions. Children's experience, theory and freedom of play derive from home experiences; parents see their children as players and play with them. There are many wonderful things that parents and extended family members naturally do to support their children. Each family will do this differently but in natural, loving ways without the backdrop of any curriculum guidance. Respecting and sharing with parents the children's play and the way they incorporate the things that children draw upon that have been influenced from home, reflects parents' natural competency. This is in opposition to a view that parents need to be educated in how to play with their children or professional guidance about 'how to play' with your child, which is more likely to instil anxiety in parents, threatening the joy and rich interactions they already share. These surround very diverse themes from family to family but help to create a vibe within a group, where children can influence each other through their varied knowledge and experiences rather than striving to be as similar as possible. This has been the strength of the group: that the children all have different things to bring to each other and to me.

## Case Study 2

### Radiators and heating

The following case study is about a group interest which started as a conversation at lunch time. This conversation was initiated by the children who were sharing their understandings of heating, radiators and fires. This conversation influenced the play of other children who were listening.

**Tilly:** We have to put the heat on when it's frosty.

**Luke:** When Mummy and Daddy put heating on in our home it gets warmer.

**Barley:** I got a radiator and a fireplace, I got four radiators.

**Luke:** I got lots of radiators, like this (holds up all his fingers). I got one in my room and three downstairs.

**Tallan:** I got a radio and a fire but Nanny hasn't got either, she keeps warm in the bath.

**Tilly:** I got a radiator in my red room.

**Barley:** My radiator comes on in the morning, you have to be careful, it can get very hot.

**Emma (teacher):** One of my radiators at home is broken, the dial is stuck on the hottest setting 8 and it gets too hot so I have to keep it switched off.

**Barley:** Or you might get a burn.

**Emma (teacher):** You might do, but it makes the room too hot and heating is expensive.

**Luke:** Has the nursery got any radiators? I don't think it has. I can't see any, but it's not cold in here.

(Luke goes off to look in the large room, no radiators, but in the smaller rooms are overhead heaters or radiators.)

**Barley:** The nursery might not have radiators cos they get too hot and that's not safe for children.

**Emma (teacher):** That might be true but I know there are some radiators. (I showed them those in smaller rooms with safety guards and heat coming from the top.)

## The following day's play

Luke was trying to shut the door in the room with a radiator using blocks as an emergency measure because he said there might be a fire.

**Luke:** Someone put the heating on and it's getting hotter and hotter.

**Emma (teacher):** Oh no! That sounds dangerous, can the heating be turned down?

**Luke:** We can turn it down, we need a hose and we need a sign to say stop, how can I get a sign?

**Emma (teacher):** You could make one.
(Luke volunteers to make a sign and writes on it 'Stop' in his own writing. He then attached his stop sign to the top shelf before the entrance of the room. Luke noticed children about to go in the room.)

**Luke:** Stop, no you can't go in, you need to play somewhere else! I need to draw another sign. (Luke takes a pen to his sign and adds more writing to it.)

**Luke:** That says stop we can't go in it, too hot. (Luke is joined by Christvie and Tallan who latch onto his play with excitement. Christvie talks about becoming Fireman Sam and putting the fire out, going into the room pretending to wear an oxygen mask.)

**Luke:** We need to get everybody out, they can't come in it . . . too hot.

**Christvie:** I am Fireman Sam I get everybody out; I can't see it is too smoky.
(Luke becomes increasingly excited by this play. Luke and Christvie ran into and out of the room pretending to get people out of the room. This continued for some time.)

The conversation continued on the minibus a day later about car heaters and frost. Tilly was interested in the frost and the frozen windows explaining that her mum had to put the engine on to clear the ice so they could get to nursery. Serena wondered why her car window did not have ice. Conversations ensued between Barley, Taog and Christvie about steam and frost on the windows of the minibus. Emma then discussed condensation with the children.

### Emma explained:

The children had been re-thinking and sharing their insights from their current shared happenings at home of putting on heating in the winter, something the children would be aware of from conversations and the physical warmth of heating in their homes. They were making new shared meanings out of the conversations in the nursery and supporting each other. Children use the adult and other children in social times such as lunch to raise conversational topics of their interest, sharing their ideas and adding new insights. This was also a serious topic for the children and part of their home experience.

## What next?

Knowing that the children had this shared understanding and similar experience, it seemed like an ideal opportunity to introduce or bring to the children a different piece of equipment. I was able to collect a number of thermometers for the children to see and handle at the beginning of the session; this generated talk and further shared experience of the children's experience of having their temperatures taken by their parents or doctors. Most of the thermometers were not for oral use but for room temperatures or food temperature; this introduced many of the children to different temperatures that can be taken and the idea was added to their bank of experience.

Alfie wanted to make the colours of the numbers on the thermometer change. He took it outside and asked what the bottom number -5 meant and how this number could be achieved. Putting the thermometer on the wall in our group space provoked children to ask 'What's the temperature?' The children incorporated this into their repertoire of enquiry. The children's conversations about heating prompted me to expand their repertoire of experience through finding thermometers as a form of measure of different temperatures. Observing and listening to children enables adults to uncover their interests and find new possibilities for extending these in meaningful and contextual ways.

**Figure 8.2** Case study 2

In addition to thermometers, I put some photos and diagrams of how heaters and radiators work, knowing some children would be curious about the different pipes and the cyclical nature of heating, like other discoveries they had uncovered; for example, sewage, waterworks, transportation, recycling and waste disposal. This served as a further source of conversation for the children. I made sure basic resources such as tubes, wires, switches and road cones were available to the children. I also asked parents and other practitioners about how this could be supported.

## Reflections on case study 2

The above episode highlights the complex role of a nursery teacher who is attuned to the children's thinking and this cannot be underestimated. Rose and Rogers (2012: 73) write that 'authentic listening shows the child we are interested in them and value their ideas'. In doing this the children will feel confident to share their ideas again and again. In the episode Emma described above, she was providing opportunities for children to go as far as they could in their own thinking. Jordan (2010) states that teachers should be addressing the complex understandings that are within the subject itself. She goes on to say:

> Unfortunately, in the absence for many teachers of sufficient knowledge, or interest in learning more, children are exposed to their teachers reinforcement of lower level concepts such as colour, counting and shape, even when such reinforcement is inappropriate or unnecessary.
>
> (Jordan, 2010: 99)

Children in nurseries and Reception classes are often restricted to numbers 5 or 10 to count and this is usually out of context. When children's own enquiries are followed they are challenged intellectually. For example, in the conversations above Alfie was enquiring about negative numbers and how they worked in the context of temperature. It is this important subject knowledge that teachers of young children need to know or find out about to support the children's intellectual enquiries.

## The importance of conversation

In both case studies the space for conversation was crucial. Askew (2012: 154) promotes talk as the 'primary means through which learners construct mathematical meaning'. He goes on to say talk is a major means of extending and reflecting on our direct experiences. The conversations were real and anybody could start the conversation not just the teacher. The conversations became the backbone of the children's mathematical enquiries. The topic of conversation also went on through a day or even a week or weeks and this was interwoven with the children's play.

## The mathematics

The mathematics arose naturally during their temperature enquiry; it was not isolated. This means that the children will make sense of this experience because it will be connected to their own thinking and they will have thought through the ideas involved. Mathematical concepts of measures of heat and increase and decrease in temperature evolved through conversation and real experiences. Alfie brought in the interest of negative numbers. Children thought through and mentally counted the number of radiators in their house. Gelman and Gallistel's (1978) research found that young children can count objects or anything that is in front of them but they stress they can also count objects or items they cannot see. They hold these objects in their mind and can think abstractly. It is important that they are given opportunities to do so.

The children were in an open, enquiring culture that encouraged counting to be more than adult-directed number rhymes or objects in front of them. They were applying and using their knowledge of counting to help their enquiry. Emma (teacher) used numbers in natural contexts, for example to explain the numbers on her radiator. In doing so she may have brought new knowledge to the children.

## Spontaneous play episodes

The children engaged in spontaneous imaginary play. Van Oers (1996) connects imaginary play to the beginning of abstract thinking and mathematics. The play episodes described in this chapter were genuine child-initiated play where the children decided the theme, content and resources. It is this kind of imaginary play that Vygotsky (1978) claimed is when children operate at their highest intellectual level. It is in opposition to the set-up role play which can be found in most Reception classes in England where the teachers decide the theme and choose children to play in the area.

The children in the play episodes were exploring and communicating complex meanings that reveal their understanding of how mathematics works. There is no set time for this genuine play as children go in and out of what Emma calls 'a magic space' any time in the day.

## A culture of mathematical enquiry

There is no doubt that the psychological environment is paramount to encouraging children's own mathematics where they have ownership of their learning. Therefore it would be reasonable to say, as expressed at the beginning of the chapter, that the mathematics that involves children's own mathematical enquiries cannot be planned for in a set lesson.

Shuard (1983) said it is not about 'doing an investigation', it is working investigatively; that is the crucial matter. Children need to be encouraged to thrive in a culture that supports mathematical enquiry. Carruthers and Worthington (2011) express the need for mathematics to be woven throughout the day and that children can revisit their enquiries time and time again. Relationships are vital and it is crucial that adults understand how to share power so that children can take part fully in their own play and are able to access opportunities and real choices. Intelligent resources and experiences open up the mathematics. However, it is the children's thinking that is the most useful resource. If teachers observe and value children's knowledge both from home, nursery and school and use this to plan mathematical experiences this will be the vital step that will enhance the breadth and depth of mathematics education in schools and nurseries.

## References

Askew, M. (2012) Talk: the key to mathematical understanding. In M. McAteer (ed.) *Improving Primary Mathematics Teaching*. Maidenhead: Open University.

Askew, M. and William, D. (1995) *Recent Research in Mathematics Education*. London: HMSO.

Boaler, J. (2009) *The Elephant in the Classroom: Helping Children Learn and Love Mathematics*. London: Souvenir Press.

Carruthers, E. and Worthington, M. (2006) *Children's Mathematics: Making Marks, Making Meaning*, 2nd edn. London: Sage.

Carruthers, E. and Worthington, M. (2011) *Understanding Children's Mathematical Graphics: Beginnings in Play*. Maidenhead: Open University Press.

Cobb, P. and Bauersfeld, H. (1995) *The Emergence of Mathematical Meaning*. Hillsdale, NJ: Lawrence Erlbaum Associates.

Daniels, H. (2007) Pedagogy. In H. Daniels, M. Cole and J. V. Wertsch (eds) *The Cambridge Companion to Vygotsky*. Cambridge: Cambridge University Press.

Deakin-Crick, R., Broadfoot, P. and Claxton, G. (2004) Developing an effective life long learning inventory. The ELLI Project. *Assessment in Education*, 11: 248–72.

DfE (Department for Education) (2012) *Statutory Framework for the Early Years Foundation Stage: Setting the Standards for Learning, Development and Care for Children from Birth to Five*. www.education.gov.uk/publications/standard/ALLPublications/Page1/DFE-00023-2012 (accessed 27 March 2013).

Egan, K. (1992) *Imagination in Teaching and Learning*. London: Routledge.

Fleer, M. (2010) *Early Learning and Development: Cultural-Historical Concepts in Play*. Melbourne, VIC: Cambridge University.

Gelman, R. and Gallistel, C.R. (1978) *The Child's Understanding of Number*. Cambridge, MA: Harvard University Press.

Gooche, K. (2010) *Towards Excellence in Early Years Education: Exploring Narratives of Experience*. Abingdon: Routledge.

Hughes, M. (1986) *Young Children and Number: Difficulties in Learning Mathematics*. London: Blackwell.

Isaacs, S. (1967) *Social Development in Young Children*. London: Routledge and Kegan Paul Ltd.

Jordan, B. (2010) Co-constructing knowledge: children, teachers and families engage in a science rich curriculum. In L. Brooker and S. Edwards (eds) *Engaging Play*. Maidenhead: Open University Press.

Lancaster, L. (2003) Moving into literacy: how it all begins. In N. Hall, J. Larson and J. Marsh (eds) *Handbook of Early Childhood Literacy*. London: Sage.

Moll, L., Amanti, C., Neff, D. and Gonzalez, N. (1992) Funds of knowledge for teaching: using a qualitative approach to connect homes and classrooms. *Theory into Practice*, 31(2): 132–41.

Rose, J. and Rogers, S. (2012) *The Role of the Adult in Early Years Settings*. Maidenhead: Open University Press.

Schrimsher, S. and Trudge, J. (2003) The teaching/learning relationship in the first years of school: some revolutionary implications of Vygotsky's Theory. *Early Education and Development*, 14(3): 293–312.

Shuard, H. (1983) Discussion and the teaching of mathematics. *Educational Analysis,* 5(3): 15–32.

Siraj-Blatchford, I. and Sylva, K. (2004) Researching pedagogy in English pre-schools. *British Educational Research Journal,* 30(5): 713–30.

Tizard, B. and Hughes, M. (1984) *Young Children Learning.* London: Fontana.

Van Oers, B. (1996) Are you sure? Stimulating mathematical thinking during young children's play. *European Early Childhood Education Research Journal,* 4(1): 71–87.

Vygotsky, L. S. (1978) Mind in Society: The Development of Higher Psychological Processes. Cambridge, MA: Harvard University Press.

Walkerdine, V. (1988) *The Mastery of Reason.* London: Routledge.

# 9

# Understanding the world: 'When did they paint the trees green?'
## Rachel Sparks Linfield

## Introduction

Some years ago I visited a nursery where children, in an area labelled 'Our world', were making collages. Each child had a square of paper to cover with materials for a given property such as shiny, soft or rough. One girl, however, had found a large piece of shiny card and was using it as a mirror while she covered her hands with PVA glue, and dabbed spots on her cheeks to be 'like Mummy when she goes out'. While I watched in horror, concerned with safety issues such as glue near eyes, the nursery teacher in charge did nothing to stop the child but simply observed discretely. She later told me that she was delighted that Poppy had had the opportunity to engage in imaginative play. She commented 'Wasn't that wonderful! Poppy was pretending the glue was body lotion and she now knows it's wet and very sticky.' My views were, though, slightly different. I wished that Poppy had shown understanding of how glue should be used. I also wondered whether the teacher would have felt similar pleasure if Poppy had attempted to drink green paint as apple juice, or decided to eat a cake of clay. Yet despite these concerns this memory of child initiation, and learning through play to develop understanding of the world, has remained with me.

Within the revised EYFS (DfE, 2012), 'understanding the world' presents practitioners with both challenges and opportunities. The breadth of subject areas that underpin understanding the world give practitioners a real opportunity to cover material that will interest children, develop key skills and place child-centred learning at the heart of their practice. At the same time, however, it presents challenges with ensuring that learning is centred on a child's experience of the everyday world, and not on adult perceptions of what the focus should be. In this chapter, the themes specified within the curriculum documentation for understanding the world (people and communities, the world and technology) are outlined. Within each theme the challenges and opportunities of a child-centred learning approach are discussed.

## Recent developments in the early years curriculum

The observations of Poppy took place at a time when the early years curriculum tended to be dominated by adult planning, and focus on half term topics.

Understanding the world, or 'knowledge and understanding of the world' as it was then titled, came through topics such as Ourselves, Autumn, Colour, Food and Winter. The value of child initiation was not always recognized and areas of learning were often taught in isolation. Indeed many nursery and Reception class settings were divided into labelled areas that implied activities for literacy, numeracy and knowledge and understanding of the world were discrete. Poppy's teacher though recognized the value of children learning through play and having opportunity to follow their own explorations. She did not insist that Poppy make a collage but allowed her to investigate properties of materials through imaginative play. She observed with sensitivity and, when the time came to clean up, provided valuable assistance in removing the glue. She also, at this point, ensured Poppy knew that glue was not body lotion. She discussed what could be used safely if Poppy wanted in the future to be her mother getting ready to go out. It made me question my own practice. How often did I let the children guide their own learning? Did the activities that I planned to develop children's understanding actually inhibit what they wanted to discover? In addition, it illustrated the complexities of the EYFS where there is often a fine balance for practitioners of knowing when to allow child-initiated activity and when to intervene.

Since Poppy was in a nursery there have been many changes to the early years curriculum. The importance of planning for a balance of child-initiated play and adult-led activity, the use of the out of doors environment and the benefits of having close partnership between early years practitioners and a child's carers, which were key features of the 2008 EYFS (DfES, 2008) have been re-emphasized within the 2012 EYFS framework (DfE, 2012). This framework promotes a climate where children can have the freedom to investigate, explore and understand their world. Indeed the new EYFS highlights that: 'Children are born ready, able and eager to learn. They actively reach out to interact with other people, and in the world around them' (Early Education, 2012: 2).

At birth children use their senses as they look towards noises, recognize smells and develop preferences for textures. For many young children there is an innate desire to explore. Who will come if I cry louder? What happens if I rattle this ball? Yet it must also be recognized that: 'Development is not an automatic process . . . It depends on each unique child having opportunities to interact in positive relationships and enabling environments' (Early Education, 2012: 2). For children to gain maximum benefit from the understanding the world area of learning the role of the practitioner is key. Practitioners need to be able to listen and observe children, to work in partnership with parents and carers, to respond to children's desires but also to be knowledgeable about what understanding the world entails. At Key Stage 1 to understand the world involves children learning about geography, history, science, religion and information communication technology (ICT). It requires the use of subject-specific skills and general enquiry and investigation. Within the EYFS, however, pleasingly these subject areas are linked through three themes. This chapter aims to help practitioners understand the themes encompassed within the understanding the world area of learning. It considers the role that each child should play in shaping what and how they learn and the resources and environments that can enable this to happen.

**Reflections**

How do you feel young children should learn about the world around them and the wider community?

How could this knowledge and understanding be encouraged?

## What is understanding the world?

The *Collins Dictionary* (Harper Collins, 2009) offers 'the ability to learn, judge, or make decisions' and 'personal opinion or interpretation of a subject' as two possible definitions of 'understanding'. For 'world' suggestions include: 'the earth as a planet'; 'the human race'; 'the total circumstances and experience of a person that make up his or her life'; and 'an area, sphere or realm considered as a complete environment'. Combining these definitions illustrates both the importance of 'understanding the world' and the enormity of 'our world'.

Learning to understand is a valuable, lifelong skill. It involves using what we know to make informed opinions. Understanding is not simply having knowledge. It is about using the knowledge, exploring and coming to informed opinions. Understanding the world is vital if children are to develop and to progress. It involves so many aspects including the natural and the man-made world. It is concerned with people, other animals, plants, objects and technology. It involves facts and opinions, views on the utilitarian and the aesthetically pleasing. In the words of Stan, aged 3 years: 'It's all about me. It's really int'resting.'

Within Development Matters (Early Education, 2012) understanding the world is outlined as a specific area of learning. It encompasses three aspects:

- people and communities
- the world
- technology.

Although this chapter will initially consider each one individually it is also worth remembering that in the same way each area of learning links, so do the three aspects. In many respects, the names are of most use for organization, planning and assessing. Through spending time on understanding the world children should have the opportunity to consider who they are, where they live, how things work and why things happen. They should be able to gain a sense of time and place.

## People and communities

The ELG for people and communities states: 'Children talk about past and present events in their own lives and in the lives of family members. They know that other children don't always enjoy the same things, and are sensitive to this. They know

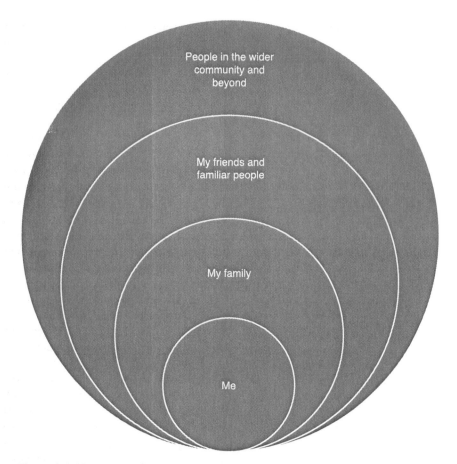

People in the wider community and beyond

My friends and familiar people

My family

Me

**Figure 9.1** Illustration of components within people and communities

about similarities and differences between themselves and others, and among families, communities and traditions.'

Figure 9.1 illustrates the aspects that children should have the opportunity to explore starting with the child. As children become more aware of themselves as individuals they also have the opportunity to discover the many ways in which they are similar to family members and children around them. This balance of similarities and differences for some children will be a challenge. At times children are delighted that their eye or hair colour is the same as their friend's. At other times feelings of despair come as they realize they cannot ride a bike like their brother or catch a ball. Helping children at an early age to appreciate both similarities and differences will be of immense importance later in life.

Practitioners will need sensitivity and knowledge of children's circumstances to help the children to make sense of peoples and communities. The use of resources such as quality photos will be invaluable in helping children to become aware of traditions within cultures that are not their own. Care needs to be taken to avoid negative stereotypes. It is also, however, important to realize that for many children being different is fine and that often children do not focus on aspects that for an adult are obvious. For example, when Lucy, aged 3, who attended a nursery where the children were predominantly white, wanted to describe her new friend she told her father that he needed to look out for a quite tall boy with black curly hair. For Lucy, the fact that Suraj was the only black-skinned child within her group was irrelevant.

When considering 'me and my family' and special occasions such as birthdays, seasons and festivals children start to appreciate the passage of time. The importance of language and developing key vocabulary associated with time cannot be under-estimated. Frequently in everyday life children are required to 'Wait a moment' or are told that something will happen 'in a second/minute' and yet the minute or second may not be accurate representations of these units of time. How then, are they to gain a true sense of what time is? There are so many concepts associated with time: years, months, fortnights, weeks, days, hours, minutes, seconds, today, yesterday, tomorrow, next, early, late, seasons . . . the list is endless. Gaining understanding of time requires experience, the chance to use vocabulary associated with time and also appreciation that acquiring concepts of time requires time! For many children building concepts of the future, such as 'tomorrow', may be difficult. The role of practitioners in listening to how children use words and helping them to understand will be vital, rather than attempting to impose an instant adult definition.

Edmund, aged 4 years, regularly asked his Key Worker 'When is it tomorrow?' Monica showed him the class calendar which was changed each day and explained 'Today it is Tuesday. Tomorrow is Wednesday, that's the day after today.' The next day Edmund came beaming into the classroom, looked at the calendar and announced, 'It's Wednesday today. You said Wednesday was tomorrow. It's tomorrow now isn't it? Wednesday's tomorrow.' Sadly, the concept of 'tomorrow' and the future was extremely difficult for Edmund to understand fully. Why could he live in each day such as Monday and Friday, with their own names, but not tomorrow? Why did the day that was tomorrow change? Why was it always today? Thinking about the number of sleeps helped Edmund to understand the passage of time; understanding of the future required more concrete examples that were pertinent to him. Edmund's Key Worker and family helped him to look forward to important events such as birthdays, the Christmas play, holidays and the school fete. Gradually he gained a concept of the future, and in turn, 'tomorrow'.

Concepts of the past are perhaps easier to adopt although for many children grandparents lived with dinosaurs. Some nurseries use memory boxes to inspire interest in the past. A memory box is a box with a lid that children use to collect memories of *their* own choosing. These might be a sock they wore when they were younger, a handprint at a given age, photos, a card for a celebration or a wrapper from a favourite food item. The boxes can be used to show change over time and help to develop a concept of the past. Children can also talk about the future, by considering items that will be included after future key events happen.

## The world

Understanding the world requires an immense amount of knowledge as well as time to process and explore the information. A trainee teacher recently enquired 'Is anything not in the world? Is there anything I shouldn't be thinking about?' While for some practitioners the enormity of the world may be a challenge, for others the wide variety of people, places, materials, objects and phenomena that could be considered as part of the world makes understanding the world such a stimulating and exciting area of learning for children.

The ELG for the world explains: 'Children know about similarities and differences in relation to places, objects, materials and living things. They talk about the features of their own immediate environment and how environments might vary from one another. They make observations of animals and plants and explain why some things occur, and talk about changes.' As with people and communities the starting point is the child (Figure 9.2). As children explore their worlds they then are able to make comparisons and appreciate the similarities and differences they observe.

For children there are a wide variety of worlds. A 'world' might be a hiding place, a home, the immediate environment, the park or a small toy in a plastic world. It might include where they live and the places they have visited. For some children there will be a series of worlds. Each one will house a place where they have stayed or perhaps

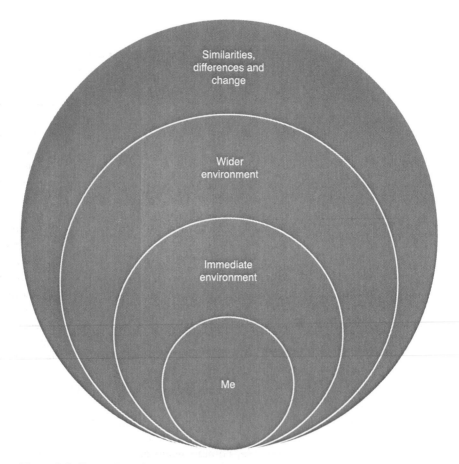

**Figure 9.2** Illustration of components within 'the world'

**Figure 9.3** Connie's world

be where a relation lives. Connie (aged 3 years) when asked to draw the world did a circle ('because the world is round'), her house, Mummy and Daddy. It is interesting to see that her two brothers do not feature (see Figure 9.3)!

In addition, resources such as television programmes, films and books may have created for some children a complex picture that combines reality and imaginary worlds. Thus the key to helping children develop understanding of the world is to start with the child, their interests, their current understanding and most importantly, their own questions. What is 'their world'? What is in their world? What do they currently want to explore in their world? Practitioners are likely to find that answers to such questions differ significantly from the ones they would give!

One autumn, when Rosie (aged 4 years) looked at black and white photos of her uncle as a baby she asked 'Why are the trees grey?' Her mother replied 'That's how it was when Uncle Alan was a boy.' The mother meant that photos often were black and white in the 1960s. Rosie, however, considered the photos and then asked 'So when did they paint the trees green? Will they ever just be grey again?' Rosie assumed that her uncle had been born in a black and white world and that colour had only been introduced at a later stage. Her mother then found some colour photos to show that the world had had colour in the 1960s, it was just some of the photos that were black and white. Despite being shown the colour photos Rosie still felt that colour changes involved paint. Her thoughts were strengthened by autumn. When walking to school Rosie then started to look intently at the trees. Throughout October she noticed that each day someone appeared to have 'painted the trees'. She spotted leaves that one day were green, gradually turned orange then brown.

In school Rosie asked her teacher whether she could have some green paint to cover some brown leaves that she had gathered on the way to school. Intently, Rosie tried to paint her leaves but was disappointed when some were so dry that they disintegrated. The few leaves on which paint stuck still did not look like 'real leaves'.

The teacher spent time talking to Rosie about 'Uncle's grey days', the autumnal tree colours and realized that despite looking at the photos, talking to her mother and observing the trees Rosie still felt that someone painted the world. This thought had been further reinforced by the painters painting the outside of a nearby house. Luckily for Rosie she had a teacher and family who were willing to listen to her ideas. Through looking at more photos, doing investigations with paint and making observations of trees, Rosie's understanding progressed. This episode in Rosie's life demonstrates that children may hold firm ideas of what their world is and how it works. It also illustrates that their conceptions of the world may be very different to those of an adult and are particularly personal to them. Helping children to observe, to question and to reflect is critical to helping them develop understanding.

When children consider geographical aspects of the world, it is helpful to have appropriate language to further their understanding. Leanne (aged 3 years) knows that she lives in Weetwood. But, Weetwood is in Leeds. Leeds is in West Yorkshire. West Yorkshire is in England. England is part of the United Kingdom. The United Kingdom is part of Europe. Europe is part of the Earth. The Earth is a planet within the Milky Way. The Milky Way is a galaxy within the universe. The universe is . . . This list of words to name places, starting with Leanne's home area, illustrates the vast nature of the world. While the EYFS documentation does not stipulate precisely the environments that children should explore, many will be fascinated to explore much further than their immediate environments. Some of the words describing places will be familiar to children through personal experiences of visits or through programmes on television but concepts such as a village or county can be hard to comprehend for children even when they have had concrete experience. Do I live in a village? Is Leeds a village? Is Leeds in England? Is England in Yorkshire? Where is Toyland? What is land? Yet again we see a need to help children develop their understanding of the world by finding out what they already know and what they might wish to find out next.

## Technology

The word technology often conjures up images of computers, industry, skill and expertise. Many parents though, while concerned that their children want to spend time playing computer games or watching the television, will also appreciate that advances in technology are frequent and being technologically minded will probably be of benefit to their children.

The ELG for technology requires that children 'recognise that a range of technology is used in places such as homes and schools' and 'select and use technology for particular purposes' (Early Education, 2012: 42). Siraj-Blatchford (2008) discusses the need to provide children with 'essential early experiences' in order 'that they are to understand and be empowered by technology in their later lives' (p. 347). This reinforces the fact that within the early years to 'understand technology' does not require detailed knowledge of how things are made or work. It is more about knowing why technology is used and being able to select the appropriate resource. 'Technology' includes a wide variety of resources many of which children use or see in everyday life. Figure 9.4 illustrates some aspects of technology which children are likely to experience.

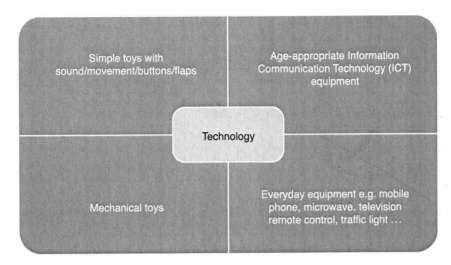

**Figure 9.4** Illustration of components within technology

While some aspects of technology may require adult planning others will be child initiated. Children in role play as a parent using a mobile phone, a shop assistant scanning food labels, a doctor's receptionist making appointments on a computer or a person in the weather station doing a forecast have the opportunity to select and use technology and to develop understanding of how it plays a part in their lives. When Fraser (aged 3 years) outside in a pedal car, says his 'Sit Nav' (Sat Nav) does not work and asks for directions to the nearest garage it is evident that children's awareness of technology is wide. Through play, and in particular role play, much technology can be appreciated. In addition trips within the local environment, perhaps to a shop, fire station or library, can also develop understanding of how and where technology is used. The challenge for practitioners is to build on these episodes through questions, comments or finding additional resources, and to use the technology to access other areas of the curriculum such as people and communities. Fraser's 'Sit Nav' was taken to the 'Sat Nav mender'. While at the mender Fraser used his mobile phone (a box from a packet of jelly) to text queries for directions from his friend who apparently worked for the BBC (Fraser's name for the RAC).

It is when selecting age appropriate ICT equipment and applications for settings that practitioners will have the greatest input. But, they need to keep in mind the unique needs of the children and what will engage them. Catalogues are full of suggestions for ICT in the EYFS but what will be beneficial and which parts will help to develop children's understanding of the world?

When considering how practitioners should make choices and plan for the use of ICT within the early years Price (2009) summarizes John and Iram Siraj-Blatchford's eight key identifiers:

- Applications should be educational
- Encouraging collaboration

.ttegration and play through ICT
The child should be in control

- Applications should be transparent and intuitive
- Applications should not contain violence or stereotyping
- Awareness of health and safety issues
- Educational involvement of parents

(Price, 2009: 2)

When choosing ICT for understanding the world the key identifier is perhaps that children are in control in the sense that they are aware of the value of the technology within their lives. Thus they do not simply enjoy using the technology, they also talk and appreciate its purpose.

Ball (2003 cited in Ward, 2008: 159) when considering the role of ICT for aiding learning suggested it should be viewed as:

- a tool;
- a reference source;
- a means of communication;
- a means for exploration.

For understanding the world the role of ICT also applies to technology as a whole. Digital cameras have many uses in recording observations both outside and in. Computers may be used to search for pictures and information and to provide labels and records. Keyboards might help children to explore sound. When using programmable toys such as 'Beebots' children can explore simple programming, use the Beebots to pull objects and enjoy learning about technology through play.

Catering for technology within an EYFS setting will have resource implications. While vast sums of money may be spent on interactive SMART boards, digital cameras, programmable toys and word processors children can also have good experiences of technology through role play and less expensive equipment. The key is for practitioners to ensure that the technology within a setting helps children to develop their understanding. Clearly there will be times when technology activities are teacher led but also, technology must offer scope for child-initiated learning.

## Questions, challenges and opportunities

Throughout this chapter the role of the practitioner in ascertaining what a child currently knows and the importance of being led by the child have been stressed. In order to know what children need there clearly has to be observation and interaction. Early years practitioners tend to be good observers, and also experts at asking questions which help children to move on in their actions and thinking. It is also though important to give children the opportunity to formulate their own questions.

Children's questions can help them to clarify their own knowledge as well as show practitioners a child's current understanding and desires. Harlen (2000: 119) suggested that children's questions were 'very important to teachers since they help to indicate the boundary between where children feel they can and cannot make sense of something'. This was demonstrated by Sam (aged 4 years) when I visited his nursery setting. His group were greatly enjoying investigating moving toys. As they explored it became clear that the ladybird hanging from a spring was a source of intrigue. The children were keen to know how the spring worked and what happened to the ladybird if the spring was pulled harder. The following week when I visited again Sam eagerly greeted me. 'Guess what Mrs Linfield?' he asked. 'My nose is a lot springier than Huw's.' I looked at his runny nose wondering what a 'springy nose' was. I then watched fascinated as he picked his nose, pressed his finger and showed me the springy contents. He then invited Huw to demonstrate that his nose mucus was indeed less springy. 'But do you know,' Sam then asked, 'if I roll it into a ball and flick it, it don't go so far as his. Why do you think that is?' I had no answer but together, after we had washed our hands(!), we explored what happened if we flicked balls, made from a selection of materials in a variety of sizes.

This investigation of 'springy noses' clearly was a major source of interest to Sam. He was fascinated that things which could appear so similar behaved differently. His questions showed what he knew but also what he could not yet understand. Why did the balls not all travel the same distance? Did it matter what the ball was made from or was it the size that mattered? Sam's questions led to many investigations. He also displayed surprising aspects of fair testing as he insisted that he and Huw used similar amounts of 'springy nose stuff' and tried to ensure they both moved their hands in the same way.

Understanding the world thus brings many challenges and opportunities for children and for practitioners. Good understanding for children comes from the opportunities they have to play, gather knowledge, make discoveries, explore, investigate, ask questions, and search for answers. When practitioners are aware of the knowledge the children currently have and the skills and attitudes they possess hopefully they can then help develop children's understanding the world. They can encourage children to realize the relevance of their discoveries and be excited to continue learning. Understanding the world involves a vast knowledge base and also many skills that are useful, not only within the early years but throughout life.

It can be seen that a child-initiated learning agenda gives incredible opportunities for the practitioner to develop knowledge on an individual basis. One wonders whether this opportunity should simply be confined to an early years setting, or in fact be the central strand through the whole of a child's education.

## References

DfE (Department for Education) (2012) *Statutory Framework for the Early Years Foundation Stage: Setting the Standards for Learning, Development and Care for Children from Birth to Five*. www.education.gov.uk/Publications/standard/AllPublications/Page1/DFE-00023-2012 (accessed 27 March 2013).

DfES (Department for Education and Skills) (2008) *Statutory Framework for the Early Year Foundation Stage: Setting the Standards for Learning, Development and Care for Children from Birth to Five*. Nottingham DfES Publications.

Early Education (2012) *Development Matters in the Early Years Foundation Stage.* London: Early Education.

Harlen, W. (2000) *The Teaching of Science in Primary Schools,* 3rd edn. London: David Fulton.

Harper Collins (2009) *Collins Dictionary.* Glasgow: Harper Collins.

Price, H. (ed.) (2009) *The Really Useful Book of ICT in the Early Years.* London: Routledge.

Siraj-Blatchford, J. (2008) 'Please can we have another bit?' Information and Communication Technology in the early years: an emergent approach. In D. Whitebread, and C. Coltman (eds) *Teaching and Learning in the Early Years.* London: Routledge.

Ward, H. (2008) The use and abuse of ICT. In H. Ward, J. Roden, C. Hewlett and J. Foreman *Teaching Science in the Primary Classroom.* London: Sage.

## Websites

http://ictearlyyears.e2bn.org/

Site featuring useful advice on using technology from the Homerton Children's Centre

http://www.datec.org.uk/curricguide.htm

Site featuring advice on Developmentally Appropriate Technology for Early Childhood

# 10

## Expressive arts and design
Estelle Martin

### Introduction

This chapter will explore the expressive arts and design (EAD) area of learning and development of the 2012 EYFS framework (DfE, 2012). The significance of EAD continues to be emphasized as a cross-subjects range of learning experiences and opportunities. The opportunity for babies and young children to develop their creativity is considered. The importance of babies and young children experiencing high-quality play and learning activities is advocated through the EYFS and how this translates into practice is of interest in this chapter.

### Rationale for EAD

The importance of practitioner creativity can be established and reviewed through reflective practice and dialogue. In order to be creative and express oneself the opportunity to explore and engage one's imagination is essential. In this way it means that all adults, whether parents or practitioners, can create the conditions to support young children's expressive identities through a range of media and creative activities. Hope (2004: 70) highlights in planning experiences in design and technology, that for Foundation Stage children, opportunities for free exploration of materials and techniques are essential to allow children to be in charge of their own learning and to make their own connections from one area of learning to another. Foundation Stage teachers need to clearly articulate the importance of child-initiated learning of *process* rather than *product* and of the way in which such experimentation contributes towards children's knowledge of material properties and mechanical systems.

### Multimedia

Children in contemporary childhood are required to become increasingly technologically literate in known and novel ways as the use of multimodal media continues with the digital applications in learning in our digital age. These include the use of personal computers, mobile phones, digital cameras, camcorders and games that require use of electronic media. Even very young children are familiar with screen-based images and digital texts, which present new challenges and opportunities to the development of literacy alongside the range of experiences teachers provide for expressive arts and design. This includes considering the modes of communication that children may find most relevant and meaningful in their play and experience of multimedia at school, early years settings and also at home.

Children become skilled at using and interpreting a diverse repertoire of representational modes. Remember we can recognize the role of popular culture and children's social worlds in their literacy, learning and play (Marsh, 2005). The children have more choice in terms of how they represent meaning and make sense of their experiences with the addition of new technologies available to them. So in this way early years practitioners can be challenged by and challenge the changes in reflecting with colleagues and parents about how children's opportunities and use of multimodal media may enhance or limit children's holistic development.

## Play as a creative process for EAD

Play empowers a child to be in tune with the whole self and the creative self. Opportunities for self-directed play support the development of the imagination through which children can explore, investigate and realize the properties of materials they use and their potential through experimentation and cause and effect.

The process of experimentation becomes more complex when children are able to express their intentions and motivations in order to create layers of understanding through communication with others. Play facilitates this understanding through social relationships and imitation of lived and imagined experiences. The role of language supports this dynamic and thus enables children to express their ideas and creative potential. Children in the EYFS can be enabled to Represent their thoughts, ideas and creativity through opportunities to communicate through a wide range of modes in addition to speaking and writing. This early years pedagogy is promoted clearly by (Bruce, 1991: 117) in the following paragraph:

> Dance, drama, painting, sculpture, music, facial expression, body language, mathematical symbols, eye contact, and touch, are all important ways of representing and communicating, and are often just as precise as spoken words.

Further to this in terms of expressive arts and design, Bruce continues to argue that free-flow play creates the conditions for rich representation by the children. This type of play is important as the role of the imagination is a powerful influence in the process of play and learning in young children's lives. The potential for a range of possibilities can be created in children's thinking and social worlds when they develop their play scenarios as their imaginative capacities are extended as part of their cognitive development. For role play, studies from a child's perspective (Rogers and Evans, 2008) revealed that 4-year-old children in Reception classes, when asked for their perceptions, valued role play highly in relation to interaction on a social level with their peers. Children's meaning making and understanding of the world are supported by playful experiences which are relevant to their interests and patterns of development.

This can be observed in children's role play as the children introduce characters as well as animals who 'tell and show the story' as the sequence is co-constructed with their peers. The children may make decisions and solve problems if the social rules allow or demand types of behaviour in the scenario. In her research Broadhead (2004) shows the capabilities of young children in resolving conflicts in play scenarios and how they learn how to represent their ideas through play and the social processes involved. In my own research (Martin, 2005) children in Reception classes were able to write narratives about their stories and draw their lived experiences that represented their thinking and knowledge about their friendships and the friends they played with and what they wanted to express about their experiences and emotions. The children were able to combine their drawing and writing to represent their worlds and use their creative endeavours – including how they designed their pictures and chose colours and movements – to express characterization and personalities in the drawings. My research concurs with the argument that drawing can provide the tools for thinking, modelling and communicating ideas, concepts, understanding and emotion (Hope, 2004: 174–5; Hope, 2008).

## Music making, movement and dance

Babies and young children can experience a range of enjoyable and satisfying activities through music making. Music involves the abilities of listening, use of voice, singing, expression of emotions and learning rhythms. Music can be a superb holistic and creative influence on children's development and learning throughout their lives. Music making can be seen as essential to a child's education and creative identity. Through music children can learn about culture, the stories and narratives of others, and references to their own lives through lyrics – the spoken word set to music (singing). Children can become knowledgeable about instruments, the sounds they make and the diversity of instruments that make music, alongside learning what instruments can be used to accompany singing, story telling, drama, role play, movement and dance. In this way, early years practitioners can promote and create the conditions and opportunities for children to experience the different ways in which the diversity of music making is integral to their education and imagination. Children can be enriched by:

- listening to music;
- reflecting about music (responses and sharing ideas, feelings);
- making music.

So music can also be viewed as an integrating mechanism that intersects with all areas of learning and development in the EYFS.

Reception classes, nurseries and early years settings can engender musical experience through a range of activities:

- Real instruments can be made available for experimentation.
- Children can listen to classical, popular and children's music, songs both traditional and multicultural, and modern rhymes.

- Children can experiment with making musical instruments.
- Electronic technologies can be used to listen to and to make music.
- Games (rhymes and songs) with whiteboard applications can be used by children and adults in an interactive way, following the sequence on screen by learning to look, listen and touch to produce an effect and make changes.
- It can be quite exciting for children to move or dance while following the visual journey or story on screen.

Movement and dance can be wonderful ways for young children to express themselves and become aware of their bodies in using new and different movements that are connected to the feel of the music and their imaginations.

The connection between movement and learning is strong so opportunities for dance and movement are essential to stimulate creative development and support physical competencies and coordination (Davies, 2003). Music and movement provide opportunities for physical, social, emotional and cognitive aspects to come together. Movement and dance encourage cooperation between children in the social aspects and communication skills that include listening and taking turns and concentration! This element of EAD is cross-curricular and intersects across the areas of learning and development in children at their own level of ability and interest, promoting children's awareness of their own coordination and sense of control and independence. It is a powerful source of emotional and physical release and feelings of joy and fun! Remember that it is a multi-sensory experience.

Music can evoke feelings that can find release and public expression in combination with movements or dance that represent their interpretation, feelings and imagination, which are an essential part of children's holistic learning.

- Provide resources like ribbons and chiffon strips to use while dancing and to encourage free movement.
- Children can listen to music independently and as part of a social group to motivate imaginative and creative thinking.
- Invite musicians to come in to the setting and play their music, while giving the children a chance to talk and experience how artists create their music and be inspired.
- Practitioners can be good role models when they play instruments, for instance guitar or piano, and this provides an opportunity for the children to experience 'live' music in a relevant way alongside their own music making.
- Children can be taken on visits to a musical event as part of the broader community aspect of their education. This would be a cross-subject and holistic experience.

Books may also inspire children to act out stories through role play, puppets or dance. Picture book illustrations are a powerful and positive media that stimulate imagination and expression as seen in collections of children's drawings (Coates and Coates, 2011: 98). Story themes are often reflected and represented in children's play scenarios, their paintings and drawings and in small world play.

## Link to characteristics of effective learning

The characteristics of effective teaching and learning are:

- playing and exploring – children investigate and experience things, and 'have a go;
- active learning – children concentrate and keep on trying if they encounter difficulties, and enjoy achievements; and
- creating and thinking critically – children have and develop their own ideas, make links between ideas, and develop strategies for doing things.

Expressive arts and design enables all these characteristics to be present and practitioners can formulate how children will be able to engage and learn in these ways. The EAD in the Foundation Stage is one of the four specific areas of learning and development and this reflects the possible connections to other aspects of all the other areas. This can be made relevant in how practitioners plan for children's play and opportunities to be motivated and enable the children to construct their own learning to become critical and creative learners with confidence. By understanding the role of imagination and creativity in young children's development the learning environment can be designed to support an early years pedagogy that provides considered and relevant intervention by the adults to support the child in their process of learning.

**Figure 10.1** 'Sculpture show!' by Simeon, aged 5

**Case study**

Simeon attended a sculpture exhibition when he was just 5 years old as a guest of his father who ran the gallery where the sculptures were situated. Simeon has gifted the drawing to the sculptor and he has consented to include the drawing of the 'Sculpture show' (see Figure 10.1).

Observing children's drawings and representations can assist adults working with children in understanding children's meanings and development of their expressive identities and creativity (Matthews, 2003). In this drawing Simeon has shown his observational abilities and sense of art and design through his spatial relationships represented in the drawing. This shows some elements of perspective as the sculptures are depicted as in the reality of their positions around the exhibition gallery, where the sculptures sat on plinths in the middle space of the room and the foreground and on selected shelves around the three walls. Simeon was also able to place the sculptures at varied levels on the shelves and depict their sizes in addition to the range of forms and shapes. The sculptures are made from bronze and some from plaster and concrete and Simeon has also used shading and colour to represent the different pieces in the gallery emphasizing the detail of each sculpture. The sculptures are of different themes and are representative of animals and hybrid forms and shapes. The drawing shows some animation and the movement of certain sculptures.

Simeon has direct *access* to pencils and pens to choose and use and he appears to understand that he can observe and draw what he can see and experience from the opportunity to freely draw in this way. Simeon was allowed *time* to create and visualize his own view of the exhibition and achieve quite remarkable accuracy and detail. Observational drawing can also be an opportunity for concentration and refinement of the hand and eye coordination required in the technique and design of forms, whether they are representations of the imagination or real objects. So the concentration allowed by Simeon not being interrupted by a change in routine or adult demands to do something else meant he was able to become immersed in his drawing for a lengthy period of time, which resulted in high levels of engagement (Laevers, 1994). This, combined with his capabilities in the actual drawing produced a sense of satisfaction and achievement for Simeon. This kind of time and freedom to immerse himself in a creative process is reflective of the pedagogy of the Reggio Emilia approach in early childhood (Malaguzzi, 1994) where children engage in creative activities and projects for prolonged periods of time through a range of languages (modalities). Simeon has chosen to observe and draw and this was a meaningful experience that enabled his own creative drive and ability to be expressed, and importantly, shared with the artist who created the sculptures in the gallery with whom he could identify and express his own creative self. This is an opportunity for early years educators to understand that drawing is also a *process* and an emotional *response* to the observation or experience; in this case study the response to 'Sculpture show'.

## Transformations

Research studies have revealed that young children's drawing is part of their playful, meaningful and multimodal engagement with the world (Ring, 2010: 115). The concept of being playful has been promoted by many educationalists (Broadhead, 2004; Bruce, 1991, 2001; Moyles, 2010; Pahl, 1999; Wood and Attfield 2005) as essential to children's learning and involves the capacity to imagine and dream, to consider different ways to be, for example in role play. Children can be given opportunities to solve problems and have ideas that can be taken forwards in their play or shown by symbolic representations such as mark making, drawing and painting. To transform ways of constructing, designing and imagining the 'what if' is part of this creative thinking through EAD experiences. The transformation of materials in play and experimentation can be made visible by the resources and materials being made available for children to access and use independently and collectively. Creating the conditions for children to express themselves involves practitioners in understanding the ways children use the environment to 'transform' and revisit ideas and possibilities that are meaningful to them. In this way children are developing their ways of being and knowing, which is a creative process.

In imaginative play children can transform people, for example the child who changed the construction model they had made from a robot to a dinosaur! This was all achieved through model making using materials that the child selected from a variety of natural and junk resources. The creation of three-dimensional objects is an important progression in children's art and design capability. Children have to hold in mind a picture, thinking through it as part of the process of designing and constructing forms and models created entirely by them so making real something that they have imagined (Duffy, 2006). Time, open-ended materials that can be 'transformed' by being used in different ways for 'possibility thinking', and creative physical spaces are necessary to support children's design and creative abilities.

### Reflections

How is an enabling environment created to encourage the development of EAD?

How can this aid the holistic view of the child and support learning?

## Conclusions

This chapter has considered some of the experiences and opportunities for babies and young children in the revised EYFS. The EAD are discussed as a range of playful and experimental activities that afford the children freedom to develop and build their imaginative and critical thinking capacities, in particular through free-flow play and adult support and intervention in response to the children's interests and abilities.

A case study was presented to consider the creative process of drawing by a child as a way of seeing and thinking and making meaning in response to an event. The potential challenges resulting from change can be reflected upon in dialogue with other colleagues who are working with Foundation Stage children; this can be incorporated in planning and assessment meetings and by including close observation of the children's patterns of development and interests. Through the ongoing reflection on practice and ideas, the early years team can continue to explore their own ideas about children's learning and EAD as reflection is a process that is evolving. Therefore it is the early years educator's responsibility and commitment to reflect on how the changes may affect practice for the positive and for innovation in the future. This responsibility is also about how to sustain the elements that provide good experiences for exploration and creative thinking by the children in order to develop the characteristics of effective learning and teaching for all. This should be based on the relationships with and knowledge about the children in order to respond in a sensitive and respectful way to them, facilitating the children's voice and potentialities. The challenges may also be about acknowledging that children are not a homogenous mass and that the standardization of all educational experience will not enable children to become confident, creative and critical thinkers who will innovate for society in the future. How might you work towards sustaining the positive opportunities in your early years settings for all children to experience a creative learning environment that enables the imagination of the possible?

## References

Broadhead, P. (2004) *Early Years Play and Learning*. London: RoutledgeFalmer.

Bruce, T. (1991) *Time to Play in Early Childhood Education*. London: Hodder and Stoughton.

Bruce, T. (2001) *Learning through Play: Babies, Toddlers and the Foundation Years*. London: Hodder and Stoughton.

Coates, E. and Coates, A. (2011) The subjects and meanings of young children's drawings. In D. Faulkner and E. Coates, (eds) *Exploring Children's Creative Narratives*. Oxford: Routledge.

Davies, M. (2003) *Movement and Dance in Early Childhood*, 2nd edn. London: Paul Chapman Publishing.

DCSF (Department for Children, Schools and Families) (2009) *Learning, Playing and Interacting: Good Practice in the EYFS*. 00775-2009BKT-EN.

DfE (Department for Education) (2012) *Statutory Framework for the Early Years Foundation Stage: Setting the Standards for Learning Development and Care for Children from Birth to Five*. www.education.gov.uk/publications/standard/AllPublications/Page1/DFE-00023-2012 (accessed 27 March 2013).

Duffy, B. (2006) *Creativity and Imagination in the Early Years*. Maidenhead: Open University Press.

Hope, G. (2004) *Teaching Design and Technology 3–11*. London: Continuum International Publishing Group.

Hope, G. (2008) *Thinking and Learning Through Drawing*. London: Sage.

Laevers, F. (1994) *The Leuven Involvement Scale for Young Children*. Belgium Centre for Experiential Education.

Malaguzzi, L. (1994) History, ideas and basic philosophy. In C. Edwards, L. Gandini, and G. Forman (eds) *The Hundred Languages of Children: The Reggio Approach to Early Childhood Education*. Norwood, NJ: Ablex Publishing.

Marsh, J. (2005) *Popular Culture, New Media and Digital Literacy in Early Childhood*. London: RoutledgeFalmer.

Martin, E. (2005) Emotional development and learning. *Early Education*, 45: 11–13.

Matthews, J. (2003) *Drawing and Painting: Children and Visual Representation*. London: Hodder and Stoughton.

Moyles, J. (2010) *Thinking about Play: Developing A Reflective Approach*. Maidenhead: Open University Press/McGraw-Hill Education.

Pahl, K. (1999) *Transformations: Making Meaning in Nursery Education*. Stoke-on-Trent: Trentham Books.

Ring, K. (2010) Supporting a playful approach to drawing. In P. Broadhead, J. Howard and E. Wood (eds) *Play and Learning in the Early Years*. London: Sage.

Rogers, S. and Evans, J. (2008) *Inside Role-Play in Early Childhood Education: Researching Children's Perspectives*. London: Routledge.

Wood, E. and Attfield, J. (2005) *Play, Learning and the Early Childhood Curriculum*, 2nd edn. London: Paul Chapman.

## Further reading

Clarke, A. and Moss, P. (2001) *Listening to Young Children: The Mosaic Approach*. London: National Children's Bureau.

Flewitt, R. (2008) Multimodal literacies. In J. Marsh and E. Hallet (eds) *Desirable Literacies*. London: Sage.

Gascoyne, S. (2012) *Treasure Baskets and Beyond: Realizing the Potential of Sensory-rich Play*. Maidenhead: Open University Press/McGraw-Hill Education.

Lancaster, P. (2003) *Listening to Children*. Milton Keynes: Open University Press.

National Advisory Committee on Creativity and Cultural Education (NACCCE) (1999) *All Our Futures: Creativity, Culture and Education*. London: DfEE.

Young, S. (2008) Collaboration between three- and four year olds in self-initiated play with instruments. *International Journal of Educational Research*, 47(1): 3–10.

# Part 4

## Advanced early years pedagogy

Part 4 covers issues and challenges which might be experienced by those involved in early years and further consideration of new initiatives. Chapter 11 is written by Corinne Syrnyk, who has extensive experience in working with young children and teaching courses in higher education in the UK and Canada. Corinne considers a key aspect of development which causes concern, that is behaviour issues. She explores the nature of possible inappropriate behaviour, why it might occur and strategies to support the child. An understanding of the challenge can help to enable those around the child to support in the most appropriate ways. Nurture groups are also discussed. Corinne uses a case study example to highlight strategies which can be used when helping a child.

Chapter 12, written by Jane Murray, emphasizes the importance of incorporating problem-solving and thinking in the early years. Jane considers different forms of thinking, for example critical thinking and reasoning. Perceptions of thinking are raised, including psychologists' views. Case studies highlight the value of this approach. Links are made to encouraging children to use problem-solving and thinking as a preparation for a lifelong way of being to help them meet future challenges.

Jackie Musgrave uses her wealth of experience as a former nurse who has moved into higher education. In Chapter 13, 'Good practice for the welfare of the child', Jackie considers children's health and wellbeing in the early years and supports the identification of welfare issues. Suggestions are made for practitioners in how to promote young children's health and welfare, with reflections of good practice.

The final chapter, written by Pat Beckley and titled 'Challenges and convergence', draws on her experience in early years settings as well as in leading courses and participating in a number of institutions as an external examiner for early childhood courses in higher education. It also draws on her research examining approaches to early years learning and development in the UK and abroad, with possible implications for networks of collaborative practice which influence relevant policies.

While these issues provide challenges to practitioners to implement changes, they encompass interesting developments and innovative, stimulating practice to motivate children.

# 11

# Birth–5 issues: addressing challenging behaviour in the early years
## Corinne Syrnyk

## Introduction

This chapter considers behaviour issues in the early years. Why do they occur? How can children be supported? A case study is used to provide examples of how interventions can successfully be made to support a child's development. Nurture groups are discussed. The importance of the perception of children as a unique child is emphasized.

## The rise of behaviour issues in the early years

What distinguishes 'good' from 'bad' behaviour? The behaviour of others is always subject to our interpretation yet the boundaries and criteria that lead to such judgements are not always straightforward. For that reason it is useful to conceptualize children's behaviour as falling along a spectrum that encompasses a wide range of variables of differing complexities. Along this spectrum we acknowledge that most children behave in what we might deem an 'acceptable' manner. While it is normal to see deviations in children's behavioural patterns, children must learn how to moderate their behaviour and they typically do so in the early years of their life. For example, during the 'terrible 2s' children's behaviour can become amplified with tantrums. It is also around this time that young children start to engage in more rough and tumble play, which typically involves more aggressive behaviour and interaction on the part of the child. Aggressive behaviour is a common facet of early childhood and is thought to peak at around 4 years of age, declining after this point. So while a certain degree of variation in behaviour is to be expected from most children, what about those children whose behaviour extends farther along the spectrum and exceeds our expectations?

Due to the range and complexity of extreme behaviour in childhood, experts struggle to agree on a definition; however, a safe definition here might refer to this as a form of recurrent behaviour that interferes with a child's learning or engagement in social situations. There are a host of labels for children exhibiting more extreme types of behaviour, including: problematic behaviour, persistently disruptive behaviour, aggressive behaviour or, even broader, anti-social behaviour. For our purposes we will use the term 'challenging behaviour'. Characteristics of challenging behaviour in the early years includes indifference and/or noncompliance to adult direction, physical and/or verbal aggression towards others, and disruptive or maladaptive actions such as inappropriate verbal responses or episodes of withdrawal. While clinicians wield a set of specific diagnoses for children exhibiting the most extreme examples of challenging behaviour (e.g. operant defiant disorder, conduct disorder, etc.), in British early learning settings children who are found to exhibit difficulty managing their behaviour may be referred to as having social, emotional and behavioural difficulties (SEBD). This is a more holistic label that recognizes the often under-developed social and emotional knowledge and skills of children exhibiting complex challenging behaviours. As one of the most common types of SEN (special educational needs) statements, a child with SEBD may be described as '[being] withdrawn or isolated, disruptive and disturbing, hyperactive and lacking concentration; those with immature social skills; and those presenting challenging behaviours arising from other complex special needs' (DfES, 2001: 87). However, the wide nature of these criteria and a lack of agreement about what constitutes appropriate or inappropriate behaviour can contribute to uncertainty about who qualifies as having SEBD.

One thing early years professionals do agree on is that the incidence of challenging behaviour within settings is growing (e.g. Sodha and Margo, 2010). This is not just a UK phenomenon as evidence from other Westernized countries also reports more and more children are being excluded from preschool settings because of behaviour problems (e.g. Gilliam and Shahar, 2006). While it is tempting to believe that a young child's extreme behaviour may be a function of their age or stage of development, such explanations contradict the growing body of evidence that reports more children to be entering school *with* problem behaviours. This rise complements the fact that young school starters with SEN are eight times more likely to be excluded and this primarily extends to pupils with SEBD (DfE, 2011a). In fact, the government's latest SEN green paper recognizes that exclusions can be indicative of underlying causal factors, manifesting as SEBD, and recommends that excluded or at-risk children be subject to a multi-agency assessment to identify these factors (DfE, 2011b).

In sum, it is perhaps not surprising to learn that children exhibiting challenging behaviour during the early years tend to retain these behaviours throughout their childhood. While a recent report from the House of Commons Education Committee (Commons Education Committee, 2011) suggests that the true nature of behaviour in schools is difficult to ascertain because of insufficient data, we cannot ignore evidence from longitudinal studies that shows us that challenging behaviour in the early years is predictive of a range of negative long-term outcomes for children and wider society. In order to address the growing number of young children with challenging behaviour we must first set about gaining a better understanding of its origins.

## Understanding the behaviour epidemic

The reasons behind early challenging behaviour are complex and often include a combination of genetic, psychological and social factors. Timing also plays a role here as poor behaviour can be triggered by instability in transition periods. For example, individual children can struggle to adapt as they make the change from preschool to school (Dunlop, 2003).

It is well established that genes play a significant role in a variety of areas that affect behaviour during the early years, including learning difficulties, the ability to maintain attention, the tendency to help and share (prosocial behaviour), and hyperactivity (for a review see Raine, 2002). Interestingly, children who experience breathing problems during sleep are more likely to have behavioural problems in later childhood (Bonuck et al., 2012). However, biological factors do not act alone – environmental factors are equally important here.

As such, other key risk factors for challenging behaviour in the early years are of a more social nature, centring around the family. A UK investigation by the Department for Education (DfE, 2012a) found parenting style to be a major risk factor for challenging behaviour in the early years. Harsh and inconsistent parenting that includes corporal punishment and inadequate supervision has long been associated with poorer outcomes for children, leading to an increased risk of challenging behaviour. However there are also other factors at work as a variety of studies have established correlations between child temperament, parenting style and challenging behaviour (e.g. Deater-Deckard and Dunn, 1999). Children with difficult temperaments (who are irritable and difficult to soothe) tend to attract more coercive parenting, setting the stage for a 'vicious cycle' of negativity in the parent–child relationship. Indeed, parenting stress can have a negative impact on parenting practice and ultimately a child's behaviour (Deater-Deckard, 2006). Negative behaviours learned within families are not isolated to the home but spread to other settings, putting added pressure on public and social systems. Other risk factors for challenging behaviour include adverse maternal behaviour during the prenatal period (i.e. drug addiction, malnutrition), family poverty, and family dysfunction (Keenan et al., 1998). Indeed, a UK study by the Sutton Trust (2010) found that children from poorer families are more likely to have challenging behaviour than children from more affluent backgrounds and that challenging behaviour is becoming a problem of more disadvantaged families. Overall, a tense early relationship between parent and child that results from a combination of child and parent characteristics is known to contribute to an increased risk of negative outcomes, including challenging behaviour (Belsky et al., 1996). In fact, evidence from longitudinal studies shows that persistent aggressive behaviour during early childhood is a very strong predictor of violent behaviour in adolescence (e.g. Nagin and Tremblay, 1999). It seems that a combination of nature and nurture serves as a potent mix in most cases of challenging behaviour.

## Addressing behaviour early

It is accepted practice that all manner of early years settings in the UK establish guidance and aims that are in accordance with national legislation and frameworks. The topic of behaviour is not an exception and as a result behaviour policies are becoming a common working component in many early years settings. The Department for Education's recent guidance for managing behaviour in schools

(DfE, 2012b) suggests developing policies that aim to promote good behaviour, self-discipline and respect, and that prevent bullying and regulate the conduct of pupils. While policies can be helpful in recognizing different behavioural needs and the responsibilities of the settings in managing these needs, they also need to emphasize problem-solving.

**Reflections**

How can we encourage children to develop a sense of self in the community?

Furthermore, how can we instil positive change where there is challenging behaviour?

## Intervention

There is an arsenal of time-tested methods that may be of some use to educators and parents dealing with less severe examples of challenging behaviour. These include, for example, verbal praise, sticker charts and certificates (see Table 11.1 for an overview). These types of strategies tend to follow the school of behaviourism as they stipulate that rigorous training and repetition, when accompanied by reward or punishment, can shape behaviour into something more socially acceptable. As short-term forms of intervention these may be effective for children exhibiting mild forms of challenging behaviour and/or give the impression of 'fixing' particular behaviours. However, these methods do not penetrate to the issues underlying more extreme examples of challenging behaviour (i.e. SEBD) in the early years.

Longer-term, more intensive intervention strategies that address behaviour are multifaceted but share similar foundations that centre on developing children's social skills. With this in mind, it is worth noting that over the years a number of programmes have been created to be delivered as an embedded aspect of the curriculum. For example, in the USA the Incredible Years Programme includes early years educators instilling positive management and discipline strategies within the classroom, and places emphasis on developing children's social competence. Meanwhile in the UK programmes such as the nurture approach have been growing and gaining attention for their effectiveness and early applicability.

## The nurture approach

Nurture doctrine stipulates that children who lacked the opportunity to build trusting relationships with adults during their formative early years do not have the skills or knowledge to thrive in a traditional learning environment (Bennathan and Boxall, 2005). As a result these children tend to exhibit challenging behaviour which is typically regarded as a form of SEBD. Unsurprisingly, the nurture approach is firmly entrenched in both attachment theory and hierarchy of needs theory. Here, the early positive attachment between the child and caregiver(s) is seen to be essential for

**Table 11.1** Short-term and longer-term approaches to managing challenging behaviour

| Short-term approaches | Description |
|---|---|
| *Reward schedules* | Includes charts, logs and diaries which measure desirable behaviour using tangible tokens (e.g. stickers) which are accumulated towards a larger reward |
| *Rules and boundaries* | A simple, straightforward set of rules and boundaries should be made clear from the start and repeated often. These should be constructed in a manner that is positive and clearly delineates consequences |
| *Positive sanctions* | Includes those larger rewards that children have had to work towards. A popular example is 'choosing time', a designated time of the week where a child may choose their preferred activity provided they have met specific behavioural criteria over a set amount of time. (May be retracted as a consequence of a serious breach of rules/boundaries) |
| *Comments* | Positive verbal reinforcement is a powerful tool for shaping good behaviour and performance, but it must be delivered in a consistent and genuine manner to be effective. Punitive comments tend to be ineffective and may damage self-esteem and are to be avoided in general. Comments that relate disappointment might be used occasionally to reinforce learning through consequence |
| *Negative sanctions* | Consequences are integral when children are learning about behaviour and its impact. A popular example are 'time-outs' wherein a child must give a certain amount of time lost (to bad behaviour/choices) in a safe but often silent and regimented context (sitting still and/or with arms crossed) |

| Longer-term approaches | |
|---|---|
| *Patience and commitment* | Required characteristics of adults who aim to instil positive change in children with challenging behaviour |
| *Role models* | Adults (particularly teachers, teaching assistants) are not only 'instructors' but should demonstrate through their own actions, the key roles of responsible adults. This can include engaging in more physical contact (e.g. hugs) and empathy to encourage the development of trust |
| *Talking-over* | Adults provide a running commentary about the behaviour of the children and its impact. This is more successful when done in tandem across a pair of adults (e.g. teacher and teaching assistant) of the opposite sex, as it has the additional function of providing role model material (see above) |
| *Transparency* | As with the above, key adults need to provide explanations for their choices (why is particular behaviour being rewarded or favoured?) so that the child can understand where their behaviour went right or wrong and how their actions affect others. The intention here is to get the child to learn to apply reason to their own decisions before they act |

healthy child development (Ainsworth and Bowlby, 1991). This is complemented by the idea that basic needs such as food and warmth must be met before individuals can realize their need to feel safe and secure, and likewise progress to fulfil more psychological needs such as love and trust (Maslow, 1987). By affording children with SEBD the opportunity to 'catch up' on early childhood, the nurture approach acts as a psychotherapeutic model of educational intervention that attempts to fill in the gaps in children's early social and emotional development. This is done by making a 'home' experience available to children within the context of the classroom. This comprises a balance of routines, structure and affection combined with a focus on play and social activities appropriate for varied levels of developmental delay. To achieve this, the approach has typically been delivered by means of nurture groups (NGs): a specialized class that operates within a mainstream educational setting and consists of a select group of pupils who meet the SEBD profile and whose behaviour tends to put them at risk of exclusion. Conventional NGs contain approximately 10 pupils, one support staff and one specialist teacher. The embedded design of NGs aims to return children to full-time mainstream provision, following successful intervention. This complements the UK's inclusion agenda which advocates that at-risk children stay in or return to mainstream education wherever possible (DfES, 2001).

As the nurture approach, specifically NGs, continues to gain momentum within UK schools and classrooms, research-based evidence has sought to demonstrate the positive impact of the approach on children's educational progression. So far, longitudinal studies examining a subset of children participating in NGs have found that most children could be reintegrated into full-time mainstream classes less than a year after starting with the NG (Iszatt and Wasilewska, 1997). In addition, while large scale research has found the social, emotional and behavioural functioning of NG pupils to improve (Cooper and Whitebread, 2007), it also appears that involvement in NGs has a positive impact on children's academic attainment (Binnie and Allen, 2008; Reynolds et al., 2009).

## Case study

### Nurturing challenging behaviour

Liam is 5 years old and lives with his mother and three siblings. His parents are no longer together and Liam's father has spent time in prison for assault and battery. Although Liam's father is now out of prison, contact with him has been difficult. There have been reports of domestic violence in the home, which Liam has been witness to on more than one occasion. As a result Liam's father is no longer allowed to be in the family home and any contact with Liam must be supervised. Liam finds his familial situation difficult but often talks about his father in a positive manner, suggesting attachment difficulties. Liam also suffered a bereavement three years ago when an uncle, with whom he had a close relationship, passed away suddenly. It is thought that the early loss of this father-figure also had a negative impact on Liam as he did not comprehend the abrupt nature of his uncle's departure, causing Liam to become even more anxious and ill-trusting of adults.

Despite his young age Liam has been excluded from his mainstream placement because of consistently disruptive and aggressive behaviour. School reports show a colourful history for such a young pupil describing incidents of throwing furniture/equipment, uncontrollable screaming, violence towards peers and adults, and absconding. This extreme behaviour extends to all aspects of Liam's home and school life. Liam's challenging behaviour has been evident throughout his early childhood and started to be documented at his nursery placement during which he was issued an SEN statement for SEBD.

Following his exclusion Liam is placed in a special state-run school for children with SEBD that employs the nurture approach. Upon entry into his new class Liam quickly engages in disruptive behaviour. It is the job of his new class teacher, Mr Bee, to assess Liam and he starts by noting that Liam struggles to be in a room with others and to share space; Liam seeks out conflict rather than solutions. Liam also appears to be poor at regulating his emotional state and is delayed here compared to same-age peers. For example, it is noted that, with support, Liam listens well, can stay on task and displays a desire to complete tasks. However, it is also clear that Liam finds it very difficult to settle on any kind of play or free activity that does not have a supervised boundary. That is, Liam quickly engages in aggressive play, smashing toys together, destroying what his play partner has made and giving over to uninhibited and boisterous behaviours. Liam is often more interested in what other children are doing and uses such comparisons to make negative judgements about his own play ('they are having more fun than I am'). In addition, Liam has quickly formed a dependency on Mr Bee and is reluctant to share him with his classroom peers and 'burns' with jealousy when Mr Bee is playing with and attending to other pupils.

To a practising 'nurture' teacher who is familiar with challenging children, this is a classic case of 'behaviour as communication' – through careful observation of Liam's actions and responses, Mr Bee can identify the gaps in Liam's emotional development and start to implement strategies to help fill these gaps with meaningful experiences from which Liam may grow emotionally. That is, by giving Liam the opportunity to catch up on his emotional development Mr Bee hopes that Liam will attain the social skills necessary to manage everyday situations so that he may further his learning.

To work towards this Mr Bee adopts a gradual approach. First, to address how Liam interacts with others Mr Bee incorporates 'belly games' into planned PSHE play sessions. These typically consist of marbles, pick-up sticks or building activities that involve the children lying on the floor next to each other during play. These play-based sessions involve games that include elements of competition, the possibility of conflict and the risk of losing and are conducted in a safe and enjoyable manner. They provide Liam with the opportunity to begin to negotiate and form tentative relationships. They also teach Liam how to resolve conflicts through turn-taking and how to lose without the loss of self-esteem as he contributes towards a group goal. Over time Mr Bee gradually withdraws his participation in these play sessions to the point where he only provides support, in the form of verbal encouragement and warnings, from a distance. This type of graduated scaffolding helps Liam learn to overcome his anxieties and to feel secure when not in the presence of a key adult. This is the first step towards building up Liam's emotional security.

Next, to address Liam's emotional development, Mr Bee specifically targets Liam's difficulty making trusting relationships with others. Mr Bee suspects that Liam's challenging behaviour manifests from early attachment problems. Indeed, Mr Bee observes that Liam is overly sensitive to the states of adults, watching key adults and their interactions with others closely. In doing so, Liam is always trying to monopolize adult attention. To cope with his anxiety here Liam employs strategies that include intentionally and repeatedly doing work incorrectly, pretending not to know an answer to a question, or dominating, bullying or withholding equipment from other children (all of which require adult assistance). To deal with this behaviour Mr Bee consciously ignores Liam's attention-seeking behaviour without thwarting or singling him out. At the same time Mr Bee is careful to also provide Liam with dedicated one-on-one time (to help him build up experience of positive emotional attachments) and to praise or discredit (using the 'talking-over' method) any behaviour that does or does not contribute to the aims of the class. This is a demanding process that requires commitment and patience from Mr Bee as Liam's behaviour often raises the emotional temperature of the whole class and also because it is simply very difficult to ignore repetitive, annoying behaviours.

Overall, the aim of this process of intervention is to show Liam the importance of recognizing and talking about his emotional state so that he can learn to manage how he chooses to act in different situations. With time and commitment Mr Bee aims to teach Liam that all behaviours are communication.

*Contributed by Steven Bentham, an 'outstanding' primary nurture teacher*

Along with more established intervention programmes such as the nurture approach, the UK boasts many other associations that offer training and support for challenging behaviour to families, children and educators. These include, for example, the National Society for the Prevention of Cruelty to Children (NSPCC), the Social, Emotional and Behavioural Difficulties Association (SEBDA), Children 1st and Chance UK. While the breadth of available supports gives us confidence that the additional needs associated with challenging behaviour are being recognized, research suggests that the application of these varied approaches is less then superior. This is because provision here tends to result in staff who are not adequately prepared in their own roles due to a lack of coordination within and between services, along with the inconsistent application of intervention programmes themselves (Coe et al., 2003). Furthermore, pupils' challenging behaviour is associated with increased staff stress and 'burn-out' (e.g. Hastings and Bham, 2003). Despite the supports available for challenging behaviour and the growing awareness of its impact on pupils and their educators, it would seem a more joined-up approach is needed to tackle challenging behaviour. That is, more work needs to be done to disseminate knowledge on this topic to educators and practitioners so they may feel better prepared to cope with and respond to cases of challenging behaviour.

## Prevention

It is clear from the direction of intervention programmes that preventing rising levels of challenging behaviour in young children lies in better education and, ultimately, a greater appreciation for the sensitivity of early learning and relationships. This includes early years provision in terms of education and care. Research shows that high-quality early educational experiences that emphasize children's social development can reduce challenging behaviours in the short term and protect children from developing challenging behaviour in the longer term (e.g. Reynolds et al., 2007). As children from challenging familial backgrounds who attend nursery have been found to be less aggressive than peers who did not experience early child care (Borge et al., 2004), diluting their exposure to high-risk environments might help. This reinforces the purpose of programmes like Sure Start, a government initiative to promote early development (the UK equivalent to the USA's Head Start programme). These programmes aim to improve outcomes of the most disadvantaged young children and their families. One of the main ways that Sure Start attempts to meet its aims is by raising parental aspirations, self-esteem and skills. This complements the current UK coalition Government aim to reform early years practice to have a greater emphasis on engagement with parents. A recent direct investigation into the impact of parenting styles for challenging behaviour (DfE, 2012a) calls for more support for parents in need. Indeed, parents are a central point in the guidance for pre-school education and care, the 2012 EYFS framework (DfE, 2012d), which specifically calls for more emphasis to be placed on socialisation during the early years. This is underlined by the *Supporting Families in the Foundation Years* framework (DfE, 2012c) which sets out the UK's overarching commitment to providing quality services during the early years. This includes, for example, making family-support services more accessible to parents and improving the uptake of parenting, family learning and relationship programmes. All in all these frameworks are promising from a preventative perspective as they recognize the pivotal role of good parenting for all aspects of healthy child development, including social skills and behaviour, and appear to be willing to adopt a more proactive stance.

## Conclusion

So what can be done? Professionals, practitioners, parents and policy-makers can start by adopting a proactive and informed ethos towards challenging behaviour. This should be followed up by a community-wide commitment to challenging behaviour that is met not only in policy but through action. This is no small task. Such a stance requires communities to commit themselves to adopting a hands-on approach to prevention and intervention by making sure that all, particularly early years staff, have adequate knowledge, practical guidance and training. It also requires individuals within communities to re-envision challenging behaviour as a form of communication on behalf of the child. Although they may be born with a certain disposition that may lend itself to negative reactions from others (and ultimately challenging behaviour), it is probably safe to say that children are not 'born bad'. When children behave in undesirable, aggressive ways, they are sending a message the only way they know how; challenging behaviour is a child's way of communicating their internal state with the world. While a typically developing child from a nurturing family background will have benefited from ample, positive learning and developmental experiences, enabling them with the skills and capacity to engage with others in a meaningful way, not all children are so lucky. With this in mind, it is important that key adults working directly with children with challenging behaviour keep positive. Kids exhibiting challenging behaviour have enough to cope with. So while negative or punitive stances have their time and place, these are best kept to a minimum as they can lead to more unwanted behaviour and do not favour the long-term emotional development of the child.

This leads us to the question of whether it is time that society re-examines its priorities towards children's early learning. Perhaps we can take a lesson from the nurture approach and recognize that in order for children to learn we must first address their emotional, social and behavioural needs. A preoccupation with paper-work and results can, at times, appear to undermine the central tenant of a healthy childhood: wellbeing. When faced with challenging behaviour it is worth remembering that at the heart of every argument about 'behaviour' is a child – and keeping them in focus as a young, learning and feeling individual is paramount.

## References

Ainsworth, M.D.S. and Bowlby, J. (1991) An ethological approach to personality development. *American Psychologist,* 46: 331–41.

Belsky, J., Woodworth, S. and Crnic, K. (1996) Trouble in the second year: three questions about family interaction. *Child Development,* 67: 556–78.

Bennathan, M., and Boxall, M. (2005) *Effective Intervention in Primary School: Nurture Groups,* 2nd edn. London: David Fulton.

Binnie, L. and Allen, K. (2008) Whole school support for vulnerable children: the evaluation of a part-time nurture group. *Emotional and Behavioural Difficulties,* 13(3): 201–16.

Borge, A.I.H., Rutter, M., Côté, S. and Tremblay, R.E. (2004) Early childcare and physical aggression: differentiating social selection and social causation. *Journal of Child Psychology and Psychiatry,* 45(2): 367–76.

Bonuck, K., Freeman, K., Chervin, R. and Xu, L. (2012) Sleep-disordered breathing in a population-based cohort: behavioural outcomes at 4 and 7 years. *Pediatrics*, doi: 10.1542/peds.2011-1402.

Coe, C., Spencer, N., Barlow, J., Vostanis, P. and Laine, L. (2003) Services for pre-school children with behaviour problems in a midlands city. *Child Care and Health Development*, 29(6): 417–24.

Commons Education Committee (2011) *Behaviour and Discipline in Schools*. House of Commons London: The Stationery Office.

Cooper, P. and Whitebread, D. (2007) The effectiveness of nurture groups on student progress: evidence from a national research study. *Emotional and Behavioural Difficulties* 12(3): 171–90.

Deater-Deckard, K. and Dunn, J. (1999) Multiple risks and adjustment of young children growing up in different family settings. In M.E. Hetherington (ed.) *Coping with Divorce, Single Parenting and Remarriage*. Hillsdale, NJ: Lawrence Erlbaum.

Deater-Deckard, K. (2006) Parenting stress and child adjustment: some old hypotheses and questions. *Clinical Psychology: Science and Practice*, 5(3): 314–32.

DfE (Department for Education) (2011a) *Permanent and Fixed Period Exclusions from Schools in England 2009/10*. London: DfE.

DfE (2011b) *Support and Aspiration: A New Approach to Special Educational Need and Disability*. London: DfE.

DfE (2012a) *How is Parenting Style Related to Child Anti-Social Behaviour? Preliminary Findings from the Helping Children Achieve Study*. London: DfE.

DfE (2012b) *Behaviour and Discipline in Schools: A Guide for Headteachers and School Staff*. London: DfE.

DfE (2012c) *Supporting Families in the Foundation Years*. London: DfE.

DfE (2012d) *Statutory Framework for the Early Years Foundation Stage: Setting the Standards for Learning, Development and Care for Children from Birth to Five*. www.education.gov.uk/publications/standard/All Publications/Page1/DFEE-00023-2012 (accessed 27 March 2013).

DfES (Department for Education and Skills) (2001) *Special Educational Needs: Code of Practice*. London: DfE.

Dunlop, A-W. (2003) Bridging early educational transitions in learning through children's agency. *European Early Themed Monograph Series, Childhood Education Research Journal*, 1: 67–86.

Gilliam, W.S. and Shahar, G. (2006) Prekindergarten expulsion and suspension: rates and predictors in one state. *Infants and Young Children*, 19: 228–45.

Hastings, R.P. and Bham, M.S. (2003) The relationship between student behaviour patterns and teacher burnout. *School Psychology International*, 24(1): 115–27.

Iszatt, J., and Wasilewska, T. (1997) NGs: an early intervention model enabling vulnerable children with emotional and behavioural difficulties to integrate successfully into school. *Educational and Child Psychology*, 14(3): 121–39.

Keenan, K., Shaw, D., Delliquadri, E., Giovannelli, J. and Walsh, B. (1998) Evidence for the continuity of early problem behaviors: application of a developmental model. *Journal of Abnormal Child Psychology*, 26(6): 441–54.

Maslow, A.H. (1987). *Motivation and Personality*, 3rd edn. New York: Addison-Wesley.

Nagin, D. and Tremblay, R. (1999) Trajectories of physical aggression, opposition, and hyperactivity on the path to physically violent and non-violent juvenile delinquency. *Child Development*, 70: 1181–96.

Raine, A. (2002) Biosocial studies of antisocial and aggressive behaviour in children and adults: a review. *Journal of Abnormal Child Psychology*, 30(4): 311–26.

Reynolds, S., MacKay, T. and Kearney, M. (2009) Nurture groups: a large-scale, controlled study of effects on development and academic attainment. *British Journal of Special Education*, 36(4): 204–12.

Reynolds, A.J., Temple, J., Suh-Ruu, O. et al. (2007) Effects of a school-based early childhood intervention: a 19-year follow-up of low-income families. *Archives of Pediatric Adolescent Medicine 2007*, 161: 730–9.

Sodha, S. and Margo, J. (2010) *Ex Curricula: A Generation of Disengaged Children is Waiting in the Wings*. London: Demos.

Sutton Trust (2010) *A Cross-cohort Comparison of Childhood Behaviour Problems – Summary of Preliminary Finding for the Sutton Trust*. London: The Sutton Trust.

# 12

## Problem-solving and thinking in the early years

Jane Murray

## Introduction

The shaping of young children's early experiences prior to starting school provides 'the initial stage of organised instruction' of the 'pre-primary tradition' (Bennett, 2005: 11) in a context where education is regarded as preparation for work (DfE, 2010). Focus on 'school readiness' in the EYFS (DfE, 2012) reflects this approach, yet it also emphasizes 'creating and thinking critically' for children aged birth to 5 years (p. 7), aligning with the 'social pedagogic tradition' in which young children enjoy significant autonomy (Bennett, 2005). The 'school readiness' agenda is a government reaction to employers' concerns (DfE, 2010): the Confederation of British Industry (2011) expresses disquiet regarding school leavers' abilities in literacy, mathematics and problem-solving. However, while there is significant focus on literacy and mathematics in the 2012 EYFS framework, there is relatively little emphasis on problem-solving. This chapter addresses the nature of young children's problem-solving and the thinking processes that they may adopt to find solutions. The chapter concludes with examples of young children's problem-solving behaviour and thinking in their settings and at home.

## What is problem-solving?

Problem-solving definitions vary but there are common features. Problem-solving is an important cognitive skill (Keen, 2011; Meadows, 2006) yet Piaget (1972) theorizes that even neonates solve problems to construct knowledge. Hope (2002) claims that 'when we solve a problem we learn something new' (p. 265), while Meadows (2006) and DeLoache et al. (1998) include goals, obstacles and strategies as problem-solving stages. Planning, memory, organization, joint decisions and partnership seem to contribute to problem-solving in social contexts (Rogoff, 1990).

Educators debate whether *problem-solving* or *problem-seeking* is most important (Lipman, 2003: 64). Schön (1983) argues that problems are set in 'situations which are puzzling, troubling and uncertain' (p. 40), potentially requiring synthesis and evaluation (Bloom, 1956), whereas problem-solving may not necessarily require these higher-order cognitive skills. Helm and Katz (2001) suggest that children setting their own problems classify, sort, categorize, quantify, represent data, investigate, experiment, observe and compare, yet supporting young children to devise problems that extend thinking can present challenges for adults (Edwards, 1998). Brown and Campion (2002) note that school curricula often exclude young children from higher-order thinking, directing them towards acquiring 'basic skills'; they argue that 'thinking and reasoning should be part of the curriculum from the earliest years' (p. 120).

## What are thinking skills?

Kant (1787) suggests that we derive knowledge from two sources: *intuitions* which are mediated by information our senses provide, and *concepts* which require us to actively conduct thinking in order to construct knowledge (Engstrom, 2006; Mensch, 2011). Dewey (1933/1991) defines thinking as: 'that operation in which present facts suggest other facts (or truths) in such as way as to induce belief in the latter upon the ground or warrant of the former' (pp. 8–9). Emerging from a context of behaviourism, Bloom's 'taxonomy' (1956) and Flavell's metacognition – 'knowledge concerning one's own cognitive processes' (1976: 232) – sparked interest in *thinking about thinking*: 'thinking skills' became tools for attainment (Glevey, 2006). Gardner (1993) suggests people have propensities for thinking via different 'intelligences', providing the 'ability to solve problems or fashion products that are of consequence' (p. 15). De Bono's 'lateral thinking' (1973) engages thinkers to explore inductively; his 'parallel thinking' (1985/2000) is a collaborative problem-solving tool which he illustrates with 'Six Thinking Hats', each symbolizing a different thinking mode.

Attuning to the discourse surrounding thinking skills in the late twentieth century, teachers began to teach thinking about thinking through models featuring skills, collaboration, metacognition, application and development of dispositions for thinking (Adey and Shayer, 1994; McGuinness, 1999). However, the argument for teaching thinking skills is contested (Wegerif, 2004); some see capacity for building knowledge through conceptual processing as innate (Piaget, 1972) so that adult intervention is not always deemed necessary for children's development of thinking for problem-solving. Equally, Gardner (1993) notes that young children do not need 'explicit tutelage' to conceptualize, but do so through 'spontaneous interactions with the world' (p. 36). Furthermore, Dewey (1933/1991) posits that not all thinking results in problem-solving: while the ability to acquire, retain and transfer new information may be valuable, only the ability to *act* on information can solve problems.

**Reflections**

In what ways can we support children's thinking and their confidence in their considerations of risk-taking?

## Different views of thinking

This section considers how philosophers and psychologists view thinking and explores different modes of thinking.

### Philosophers' views of thinking

Thomas (2007) lists different forms of thinking identified by ancient Greek philosophers: *aesthesis* (perception or observation), *doxa* (common knowledge), *episteme* (knowledge derived from reasoning), *heuriskein* (discovery), *logos* (pure reasoning), *phronesis* (practical wisdom) and *techne* (knowledge of a craft, not requiring understanding) (pp. 149–50). Equally, within the 'philosophy for children' movement, thinking modes include information processing, enquiry, reasoning, creative thinking and evaluation (Fisher, 2001); moral reasoning, argument and epistemology (Costello, 2000); analogy, ethics, logic and metaphysics (Matthews, 1990).

### Psychologists' views of thinking

Psychologists also identify different types of thinking, including representation, logic, concepts, analogies, images and connections (Thagard, 2005; Barkley, 2001) suggests that these may be controlled by the brain's 'executive functions'. Psychologists have tended to measure thinking (Terman, 1916; Torrance, 1974) and recent developments in neuroscientific techniques have led to exponential progress in psychologists' understanding of the brain's operation (Goswami, 2010): neuroimaging tools have demonstrated that a 1-year-old infant's brain closely resembles that of an adult (Chugani, 1997).

### Critical thinking

Critical thinking is 'a defining concept of the Western university' (Barnett, 1997: 2), yet defies a single definition (Kuhn, 1999). Glaser (1941) describes critical thinking as 'a persistent effort to examine any belief or supposed form of knowledge in the light of the evidence that supports it and the further conclusions to which it tends' (p. 6). This focuses on the *processes* of critical thinking, but some definitions focus on *outcomes*. For example, Facione (1990) defines critical thinking as 'purposeful, self-regulatory judgment which results in interpretation, analysis, evaluation, and inference, as well as explanation . . . upon which that judgment is based' (p. 2), while Moon (2008) defines it as 'the ability to consider a range of information . . . to process this information in a creative and logical manner, challenging it, analysing it and arriving at considered conclusions which can be defended and justified' (p. 21). Smith (2002) characterizes critical thinkers as flexible, sceptical and able to identify assumptions, discern fact from opinion, infer logically and base judgements on evidence.

Critical thinking and metacognition are correlated (Paul and Elder, 2002): critical thinking is underpinned by knowledge of how one thinks oneself *and* how others think (Kuhn, 1999). The ability to 'recognise mental states in [oneself] and others' signals 'theory of mind' (TOM) (Astington et al., 1989: 1). The stage at which children acquire TOM has been debated (Davies and Stone, 1995; Wellman, 1989), though 'theory theorists' believe that the brain's mechanisms for TOM are innate and can be triggered by environmental factors within the first year (Meltzoff, 1995; Kovács et al., 2010). Neonates suggest they recognize 'something like me' by imitating facial gestures (Meltzoff, 1999: 261).

## Dialogic thinking

Babies and young children appear 'hard-wired' to interact socially to make sense of the world (Burnard et al., 2006; Meltzoff, 1999); Vygotsky's (1978) argument that 'what a child can do with assistance today she will be able to do by herself tomorrow' (p. 57) is well established. Social environments which include 'guided participation', with verbal and non-verbal interaction, are important for cognitive development (Wood et al., 1976; Rogoff, 1990). Learners' and teachers' shared understanding of the *nature* of their interaction also seems an important basis for dialogue underpinning children's thinking (Mercer and Littleton, 2007). This resonates with Bakhtin's theory that language can only be a meaningful tool in context (1981) as well as Crossley's 'egological intersubjectivity' (1996: 23): the ability to empathize.

Alexander (2008) recognizes equal dialogue as a valuable tool for supporting thinking. He sees 'dialogic teaching' as a reciprocal enterprise in which teachers engage with children's articulation of ideas. Alexander's thinking resonates with Dahlberg and Lenz Taguchi's 'meeting place' (1994: 2), Schaffer's 'joint involvement episodes' (1992: 101), 'sustained, shared thinking' (Siraj-Blatchford et al., 2002: 8) and 'relational pedagogy' (Papatheodorou and Moyles, 2009).

## Reasoning and logical thinking

Bonjour (1998) notes that 'for a person's belief to constitute knowledge it is necessary . . . that the person have an adequate *reason* for accepting it' (p. 1). However, the nature of 'reason' is contested (Thomas, 2007): Aristotle cleaves to experiential reasoning as a basis for reason while Socrates and Plato adopt a model of abstract thinking (Pappas, 2004). This dualism was reiterated later by Hume (1748) advocating empiricism – an experiential 'synthetic' approach – and Kant (1787) who explored 'pure reason': an abstract 'analytic' approach.

Empiricists view the senses as the only verifiable source of knowledge (Hume, 1748; Thomas, 2007). This idea of verification was developed further in the 1920s within 'logical positivism' (Ayer, 1959). Twentieth-century behaviourists reiterated empiricist approaches for researching children's development; these developed into the 'what works' approach which assumes universal truth (Bridges, 2003): 'rules for action . . . the only thing practitioners need to do is to follow these rules' (Biesta, 2007: 11). However, when working with children, we may construct multiple versions of 'truth' (Guba and Lincoln, 1989). Conversely, Kant (1787) argues that mental activity, rather than sensation, provides basis for judgement. He divides mental activity into two conceptual categories: *a priori* (analytic) propositions which are not experiential and *a posteriori* (synthetic) propositions which are predicated on first-hand experience combined with mental activity.

Deduction is high-order pure abstract reasoning which 'yields a conclusion that must be true given that its premises are true' (Johnson-Laird and Byrne, 1991: 2). Deductive logic is is exemplified in different ways, for example, 'first order logic' (Frege, 1879/1972) and Aristotlean syllogism. When children are required to solve mathematical problems such as 'doubling, halving and sharing' (DfE, 2012: 9), they may engage in deductive reasoning. Hume (1739/2000) saw deductive reasoning as superior to inductive reasoning which relies on inference, yet, while empiricists regard inductive reasoning as fallible (Ayer, 1940), it is still considered valid logical reasoning (Coderre et al., 2003).

## Analogous thinking

Analogies are perceived as 'tools for thought and explanation' (Johnson Laird, 1989: 313) based on complex structural principles embedded in the mind (Brown, 1990). Vosniadou and Ortony (1989) claim analogy is 'crucial for recognition, clarification and learning and it plays an important role in scientific discovery and creativity' (p. 1). Young children's abilities to extend knowledge to new contexts for problem-solving have only been established quite recently (Goswami, 1991). Once the cause of a problem is understood, toddlers are able to transfer knowledge to new contexts (Goswami and Brown, 1989; Hope, 2002; Singer-Freeman and Bauer, 2008; Singer-Freeman and Goswami, 2001). This suggests that *'knowing how'* may be as important as *'knowing what'* (Ryle, 1949) in empowering young children to solve problems. Adults support young children to know 'how' by modelling because humans possess innate ability to learn by observing others (Meltzoff and Williamson, 2010): infants as young as 13 months can apply modelled solutions to new problems (Chen et al., 1997).

## Creative thinking

'Making links between ideas' is statutorily required of English children aged 0–5 years as part of 'Creating and thinking critically' (DfE, 2012: 7). Since 'thinking critically' has been addressed, I turn now to the nature of creating in the early years and the thinking that may relate to it. Definitions of creativity often allude to innovation, for example, 'processes that lead to solutions, ideas, conceptualisations, artistic forms, theories or products that are unique and novel' (Johnson-Laird, 1988: 203). Definitions of creativity embracing absolute innovation are often referred to as 'big C creativity' (Duffy, 2006: 17); however, Craft (2000) proposes that we can value young children's personal 'new findings' as 'little c' creativity (p. 3). Yet defining creativity remains problematic because definition provides a template, which diminishes innovation (Duffy, 2006). Creativity is a conflicted area; it is seen as divergent and convergent (Craft, 2000; McCrae, 1987), destructive and constructive (Ferguson, 2011; Knauss, 1999), social and solitary (Gruber, 1989; Lloyd and Howe, 2003) as well as an outcome and a process (Hargreaves, 2012).

Creative thinking 'is novel and produces ideas that are of value' (Sternberg, 2003: 326); it is regarded as a transferable and 'important skill' to acquire in the early years (Wheeler et al., 2002). Characteristics of creative thinking include fluency, flexibility, originality and elaboration (Torrance, 1974) while young children's creative thinking requires social, cognitive, emotional and motivational 'foundations' (Hargreaves, 2012). Equally, young children seem likely to think creatively when they have opportunities to explore, experiment, hypothesize, analyse, take risks, set themselves challenges, become involved, play and interact in contexts that are meaningful and enjoyable with their peers and with adults who scaffold, model and question (Duffy, 2006; Fumoto et al., 2012). Pondering 'possibility' is regarded as key to creative thinking (Craft, 2000); Burnard et al. (2006) suggest that this happens when children progress from asking 'What is this and what does it do?' to 'What can I do with this?' (p. 245). Craft (2000) posits that exploring possibilities encourages imagination to develop and creativity and imagination are often linked (Duffy, 2006; Fumoto et al., 2012; NACCCE, 1999).

## Images and mental modelling

Mental imagery features significantly in literature on human thinking (Thagard, 2005). Wittgenstein (1922) refers to beliefs we construct by observing as a 'picture' (1922: 4.012): 'a model of the reality as we think it is' (4.01). Craik (1943) proposed *mental model* theory in which humans make sense of the world by 'spontaneously and systematically constructing and manipulating special image-like and map-like ... mental representations' (Hanna, 2006: 136). The capacity to engage in mental modelling may involve deductive argument (Craik, 1943) or inference (Hanna, 2006). Mental models are defined as small-scale components which we build and synthesize into reasoning (Johnson-Laird, 1983); they may complement schemas, familiar to early years practitioners as important expressions of young children's thinking (Athey, 2007), while schemas may, in turn, support the internal organization of mental models (Craik, 1943).

## Epistemological thinking

Epistemological thinking is 'concerned with the nature and justification of human knowledge' (Hofer and Pintrich, 1997: 88): thinking about how we know that we know. Epistemological thinking is seen as highly sophisticated critical thinking (Kuhn, 1999). Yet Isaacs (1930) observes that 'epistemic interest and enquiry ... is in every respect the same in the child as in the adult' (p. 322) and more recently, Meltzoff (1999) notes that even neonates may have epistemological capabilities, indicated by their responses to others' facial gestures (Meltzoff and Moore, 1977).

## Young children's thinking for problem-solving

A challenge for anyone interested in young children's thinking is that it is 'invisible' (Salmon, 2006: 457; Wittgenstein, 1967). Therefore, practitioners and parents wishing to establish young children's development observe *behaviours*. The Young

Children as Researchers (YCaR) project (Murray, 2011a; 2011b) focused on observing natural research behaviours of children aged 4–5 years, eliciting evidence to reinforce the view that young children have 'capabilities' (Sen, 1993: 31) to construct knowledge which may result in problem-solving (Gardner, 1993; Piaget, 1972). Examples of YCaR problem-solving behaviours are shared below, with the modes of thinking they indicated.

---

**Case studies**

### Johnny

In his Reception setting, Johnny decided to create a 'wristwatch' using paper, glue and scissors. He measured a strip [of paper] around his wrist and cut a bit off the end. He adjusted and readjusted it four times until satisfied with the fit. He admired it, then moved to another activity. The 'strap' came unstuck. Johnny returned to the 'making table' to fix it successfully. In this vignette, Johnny set a problem and found a solution by engaging in logical, critical and analogous thinking.

### Pedro

In his Reception setting, Pedro chose to attempt to construct an igloo using sugar cubes: a practitioner-planned activity. His attempts were unsuccessful: Pedro predicted correctly that a child nudging the table would result in his construction breaking. Consequently, Pedro decided to build a tower instead, designing and successfully constructing it with a sturdy base and surrounding it with a protective wall. This construction had a successful outcome because Pedro solved his problem by engaging in logical and analogous thinking.

### Gemma

At home, Gemma, her mother and grandmother were in the sitting room. Gemma's mother tried on new shoes that were too big. She said: 'I don't think the smaller size would fit because I need the size for the width.' Gemma suggested: 'Why don't you just push a tissue up the back? Why don't you put an extra heel?' Here, Gemma empathized and provided solutions for her mother's problem, indicating theory of mind (Meltzoff, 1995), a factor in critical thinking, and she developed her ideas through dialogic thinking.

### Martin

At home, Martin was filming with a new camcorder when his father said to him: 'I don't know how this works mate – how does this . . .? Are you recording or not?' Martin responded: 'When the red dot is on it means it's recording.' Here, Martin engages in logical *a posteriori* thinking to solve his father's problem.

Findings from the YCaR Project suggest that participating children aged 4–5 years engaged in thinking that led to problem-solving when they experienced characteristics of the 'social pedagogic tradition' (Bennett, 2005). These included free access to resources, opportunities to draw on their own prior experiences, time and opportunity to seek and find solutions, autonomy to choose to engage in social or solitary contexts, all within 'free flow play' environments (Bruce, 2005: 149).

## Conclusion

This chapter has addressed the nature of thinking that young children in the EYFS may adopt to solve problems they either encounter or set themselves. As the examples from the YCaR project indicate, observing young children's problem-solving behaviours can provide clues to the modes of thinking children aged 4 and 5 years may engage in that otherwise remain 'invisible' (Salmon, 2006: 457; Wittgenstein, 1967). Furthermore, evidence from the YCaR project suggests that children aged 4–5 years are likely to engage in thinking that leads to problem-solving in environments that are characteristic of the 'social pedagogic tradition' (Bennett, 2005). This may be important to bear in mind in our efforts to provide for children's current needs as well as securing their future employability (CBI, 2011; DfE, 2010).

## References

Adey, P. and Shayer, M. (1994) *Really Raising Standards: Cognitive Intervention and Academic Achievement.* London: Routledge.

Alexander, R.J. (2008) *Towards Dialogic Teaching: Rethinking Classroom Talk,* 4th edn. York: Dialogos.

Astington, J.W., Harris, P.L. and Olson, D.R. (eds) (1989) *Developing Theories of Mind.* Cambridge: Cambridge University Press.

Athey, C. (2007) *Extending Thought in Young Children.* London: PCP.

Ayer, A.J. (1940) *The Foundations of Empirical Knowledge.* London: MacMillan.

Ayer, A.J. (Ed.) (1959) *Logical Positivism.* New York: The Free Press.

Bakhtin, M.M. (1981) *The Dialogic Imagination.* Austin, TX: University of Texas.

Barkley, R.A. (2001) Executive functions and self-regulation: an evolutionary neuro-psychological perspective. *Neuropsychology Review,* 11: 1–29.

Barnett, R. (1997) *Higher Education: A Critical Business.* Milton Keynes: SRHE and Open University.

Bennett, J. (2005) Curriculum issues in national policy making. *European Early Childhood Educational Research Journal,* 13(2): 5–23.

Biesta, G. (2007) Why 'what works' won't work: evidence-based practice and the democratic deficit in educational research. *Educational Theory,* 57(1): 1–22.

Bloom, B. (1956) *Taxonomy of Educational Objectives.* Boston, MA: Allyn and Bacon.

Bonjour, L. (1998) *In Defense of Pure Reason.* Cambridge: Cambridge University Press.

Bridges, D. (2003) *Fiction Written Under Oath.* Dordrecht: Kluwer Academic Publishers.

Brown, A. (1990) Domain-specific principles affect learning and transfer in children. *Cognitive Science,* 14: 107–33.

Brown, A.L. and Campion, J.C. (2002) Communities of learning and thinking, or a context by any other name. In P. Woods (ed.) *Contemporary Issues in Teaching and learning.* London: Routledge.

Bruce, T. (2005) *Developing Learning in Early Childhood*. London: PCP.

Burnard, P., Craft, A., Cremin, T. et al. (2006) Documenting 'possibility thinking': a journey of collaborative enquiry. *International Journal of Early Years Education*, 14(3): 243–62.

Chen, Z., Sanchez, R.P., and Campbell, T. (1997) From beyond to within their grasp: Analogical problem solving in 10- and 13-month-olds. *Developmental Psychology*, 33: 790–810.

Chugani, H.T. (1997) Neuroimaging of developmental non-linearity and developmental pathologies. In R.W. Thatcher, G.R. Lyon, J. Ramsey and N. Krasnegor (eds) *Developmental Neuroimaging: Mapping the Development of Brain and Behaviour*. San Diego: Academic Press.

Coderre, S., Mandin, H., Harasym, P.H. and Fick, G.H. (2003) Diagnostic reasoning strategies and diagnostic success. *Medical Education*, 37(8): 695–703.

Confederation of British Industry (CBI) (2011) *Building for Growth: Business Priorities for Education and Skills*. London: Confederation of British Industry.

Costello, P. (2000) *Thinking Skills and Early Childhood Education*. London: David Fulton.

Craft, A. (2000) *Creativity across the Primary Curriculum*. London: Routledge.

Craik, K. (1943) *The Nature of Explanation*. Cambridge: Cambridge University Press.

Crossley, N. (1996) *Intersubjectivity: The Fabric of Social Becoming*. London: Sage.

Dahlberg, G. and Lenz Taguchi, H. (1994) *Förskola och skola och om visionen om en mötesplats* [Preschool and school and the vision of a meeting-place]. Stockholm: HLS Förlag.

Davies, M. and Stone, T. (eds) (1995) *Folk Psychology*. Oxford: Blackwell.

De Bono, E. (1973) *Lateral Thinking: Creativity Step-by-step*. London: Harper and Row Publishers.

De Bono, E. (1985/2000) *Six Thinking Hats*. London: Penguin.

DeLoache, J.S., Miller, K.F. and Pierroutsakos, S.L. (1998) Reasoning and problem solving. In D. Kuhn and R. Siegler (eds) *Handbook of Child Psychology, 5e, Vol. 2: Cognition, Perception and Language*. New York: Wiley.

Dewey, J. (1933/1991) *How We Think*. New York: Prometheus.

DfE (Department for Education) (2010) *The Importance of Teaching*. https://www.education.gov.uk/publications/standard/publicationDetail/Page1/CM%207980 (accessed 3 November 2011).

DfE (2012) *Statutory Framework for the Early Years Foundation Stage: Setting the Standards for Learning, Development and Care for Children from Birth to Five*. www.education.gov.uk/publications/standard/AllPublications/Page1/DFE-00023-2012 (accessed 27 March 2013).

Duffy, B. (2006) *Supporting Creativity and Imagination in the Early Years*. Maidenhead: Open University Press.

Edwards, C. (1998) Partner, nurturer and guide: the role of the teacher. In C. Edwards, L. Gandini and G. Gorman (eds) (1998) *The Hundred Languages of Children*. Westport, CT: Ablex Publishing.

Engstrom, S. (2006) Understanding and Sensibility. *Inquiry*, 49(1): 2–25.

Facione, P. (1990) *The Delphi Report*. Millbrae, CA: The California Academic Press.

Ferguson, R. (2011) Meaningful learning and creativity in virtual worlds. *Thinking Skills and Creativity*, 6(3): 169–78.

Fisher, R. (2001) Philosophy in primary schools: fostering thinking skills and literacy. *Reading, Literacy and Language*. July: 67–73.

Flavell, J.H. (1976) Metacognitive aspects of problem solving. In L.B. Resnick (ed.) *The Nature of Intelligence*. Hillsdale, NJ: Erlbaum.

Frege, G. (1879/1972) *Conceptual Notation and Related Articles*, Trans. T.W. Bynum. Oxford: Oxford University Press.

Fumoto, H., Robson, S., Greenfield, S. and Hargreaves, D. (2012) *Young Children's Creative Thinking*. London: Sage.

Gardner, H. (1993) *Multiple Intelligences*. New York: Basic Books.

Glaser, E.M. (1941) *An Experiment in the Development of Critical Thinking*. New York: Teachers College Press.

Glevey, K.E. (2006) Promoting thinking skills in education. *London Review of Education*. 4(3): 291–302.

Goswami, U. (1991). Analogical reasoning: what develops? A review of research and theory. *Child Development*, 62: 1–22.

Goswami, U. (ed.) (2010) *The Wiley-Blackwell Handbook of Childhood Cognitive Development*, 2nd edn. Chichester: John Wiley and Sons.

Goswami, U. and Brown, A.L. (1989) Melting chocolate and melting snowmen: Analogical reasoning and causal relations. *Cognition*, 35: 69–95.

Gruber, H. (1989) Networks of enterprise in scientific creativity. In B. Gholson, W.R. Shadish, R.A. Neimeyer and A.C. Houts (eds) *Psychology of Science: Contributions to meta-science*. Cambridge: Cambridge University Press.

Guba, E.G. and Lincoln, Y. (1989) *Fourth Generation Evaluation*. Newbury Park, CA: Sage.

Hanna, R. (2006) *Rationality and Logic*. Cambridge, MA: MIT Press.

Hargreaves, D. (2012) Creative thinking, social relationship as an early childhood practice. In H. Fumoto, S. Robson, S. Greenfield and D. Hargreaves *Young Children's Creative Thinking*. London: Sage.

Helm, J.H. and Katz, L. (2001) *Young Investigators*. New York: Teachers' College Press.

Hofer, B.K. and Pintrich, P.R. (1997) The development of epistemological theories: Beliefs about knowledge and knowing and their relation to learning. *Review of Educational Research*, 67(1): 88–140.

Hope, G. (2002) solving problems: young children exploring the rules of the game. *The Curriculum Journal*, 13(3): 265–78.

Hume, D. (1739/2000) *A Treatise of Human Nature*. Oxford: Oxford University Press.

Hume, D. (1748) An enquiry concerning human understanding. In T. Beauchamp (ed.) (2000) *David Hume: An Enquiry Concerning Human Understanding*. Oxford: Oxford University Press.

Hume, D. (2000) An enquiry concerning human understanding. In T. Beauchamp (ed.) *David Hume: An Enquiry Concerning Human Understanding*. Oxford: Oxford University Press.

Isaacs, S. (1930) *Intellectual Growth in Young Children*. London: George Routledge.

Johnson-Laird, P.N. (1983) *Mental Models*. London: Cambridge University Press.

Johnson-Laird, P.N. (1988) Freedom and constraint in creativity. In R.J. Sternberg (ed.) *The Nature of Creativity: Contemporary Psychological Perspectives*. Cambridge: Cambridge University Press.

Johnson-Laird, P. (1989) Analogy and the exercise of creativity. In S. Vosniadou and A. Ortony (eds) *Similarity and Analogical Reasoning*. Cambridge: Cambridge University Press.

Johnson-Laird, P.N. and Byrne, R.M.J. (1991) *Deduction*. Hillsdale, NJ: Lawrence Erlbaum Associates.

Kant, I. (1787) *The Critique of Pure Reason*. Prepared in e-text by C. Aldarondo (2003) Project Gutenberg. http://www.gutenberg.org/dirs/etext03/cprrn10.txt (accessed 5 May 2012).

Keen, R. (2011) The development of problem solving in young children: a critical cognitive skill. *Annual Review of Psychology*, 62: 1–21.

Kovács, Á.M., Téglás, E. and Endress, A.E. (2010) The social sense: susceptibility to others' beliefs in human infants and adults. *Science*, 330(6012): 1830–4.

Knauss, W. (1999) The creativity of destructive fantasies. *Group Analysis*, 32(3): 397–411.

Kuhn, D. (1999) A developmental model of critical thinking. *Educational Researcher*, 28(2): 16–26.

Lipman, M. (2003) *Thinking in Education*. Cambridge: Cambridge University Press.

Lloyd, B. and Howe, N. (2003) Solitary play and convergent and divergent thinking skills in preschool children. *Early Childhood Research Quarterly*, 18(1): 22–41.

Matthews, G. (1990) *Philosophy and the Young Child*. Cambridge, MA: Harvard University Press.

McCrae, R.R. (1987) Creativity, divergent thinking, and openness to experience. *Journal of Personality and Social Psychology*, 52 (6): 1258–65.

McGuinness, C. (1999) *From Thinking Skills to Thinking Classrooms. Research Report No. 115*. Norwich: Her Majesty's Stationery Office.

Meadows, S. (2006) *The Child as Thinker*. London: Routledge.

Meltzoff, A.N. (1995) Understanding the intentions of others: re-enactment of intended acts by 18-month-old children. *Developmental Psychology*, 31(5): 838–50.

Meltzoff, A.N. (1999) Origins of theory of mind, cognition and communication. *Journal of Communication Disorders*, 32(4): 251–69.

Meltzoff, A.N. and Moore, M.K. (1977) Imitation of facial and manual gestures by human neonates. *Science*, 198(4312): 75–8.

Meltzoff, A.N. and Williamson, R.A. (2010) The importance of imitation for theories of social-cognitive development. In G. Bremner and T. Wachs (eds) *Handbook of Infant Development*, 2nd edn. Oxford: Wiley-Blackwell.

Mensch, J. (2011) Intuition and nature in Kant and Goethe. *European Journal of Philosophy*, 19(3): 431–53.

Mercer, N. and Littleton, K. (2007) *Dialogue and the Development of Children's Thinking: A Sociocultural Approach*. London: Routledge.

Moon, J.A. (2008) *Critical Thinking: An Exploration of Theory and Practice*. Abingdon: Routledge.

Murray, J. (2011a) Young children's explorations: young children's research? *Early Child Development and Care*. DOI:10.1080/03004430.2011.604728. (Print forthcoming).

Murray, J. (2011b) Knock, knock! Who's there? Gaining access to young children as researchers: a critical review. *Educate~*, 11(1): 91–109.

NACCCE (National Advisory Committee on Creative and Cultural Education) (1999) *All our Futures: Creativity, Culture and Education*. London: DfEE. http://sirkenrobinson.com/skr/pdf/allourfutures.pdf (accessed 26 June 2012).

Papatheodorou, T. and Moyles, J. (eds) (2009) *Learning Together in the Early Years: Exploring Relational Pedagogy*. Abingdon: Routledge.

Pappas, E. (2004) Teaching Thinking and Problem Solving in the University Curriculum: A rationale. Paper presented at the 2004 American Society for Engineering Education (ASEE) Southeastern Section Meeting. Auburn University, United States, April.

Paul, R.W. and Elder, L. (2002) *Critical Thinking: Tools for Taking Charge of Your Professional and Personal Life*. Upper Saddle River, NJ: Pearson Education/FT Press.

Piaget, J. (1972) *The Principles of Genetic Epistemology*. London: Routledge and Kegan Paul.

Rogoff, B. (1990) *Apprenticeship in Thinking*. New York: Oxford University Press.

Ryle, G. (1949) *The Concept of Mind*. London: Hutchinson.

Salmon, A.K. (2006) Promoting a culture of thinking in the young child. *Early Childhood Education Journal*, 35(5): 457–61.

Schaffer, H. (1992) Joint involvement episodes as context for development. In H. McGurk (ed.) *Childhood Social Development: Contemporary Perspectives*. Hove: Lawrence Erlbaum.

Schön, D. (1983) *The Reflective Practitioner*. New York: Basic Books.

Sen, A. (1993) Capability and well-being. In M. Nussbaum and A. Sen (eds) *The Quality of Life*. Oxford: Oxford University Press.

Singer-Freeman, K.E. and Bauer, P.J. (2008) The ABCs of analogical abilities: evidence for formal analogical reasoning abilities in 24-month-olds. *British Journal of Developmental Psychology,* 26: 317–35.

Singer-Freeman, K.E. and Goswami, U. (2001) Does half a pizza equal half a box of chocolates?: Proportional matching in an analogy task. *Cognitive Development,* 16(3): 811–29.

Siraj-Blatchford, I., Sylva, K., Muttock, S., Gilden, R. and Bell, D. (2002) *Researching Effective Pedagogy in the Early Years (REPEY) RR356.* London: Department for Education and Skills.

Smith, R. (2002) *Challenging your Preconceptions: Thinking Critically about Psychology.* Belmont, CA: Wadsworth/Thomson Learning.

Sternberg, R.J. (2003) Creative thinking in the classroom. *Scandinavian Journal of Educational Research,* 47(3): 325–38.

Terman, L. (1916) *The Measurement of Intelligence.* Boston, MA: Houghton Mifflin.

Thagard, P. (2005) *Mind.* Cambridge, MA: MIT.

Thomas, G. (2007) *Education and Theory.* Maidenhead: McGraw-Hill Education/Open University Press.

Torrance, E.P. (1974) *Torrance Tests of Creative Thinking.* Bensenville, IL: Scholastic Testing Service, Inc.

Vosniadou, S. and Ortony, A. (eds) (1989) *Similarity and Analogical Reasoning.* Cambridge: Cambridge University Press.

Vygotsky, L. (1978) *Mind in Society.* Cambridge, MA: Harvard University Press.

Wegerif, R. (2004) Towards an account of teaching general thinking skills that is compatible with the assumptions of sociocultural theory. *Theory and Research in Education,* 2(2): 143–59.

Wellman, H.M. (1989) First Steps in the child's theorising about the mind. In D.R. Olson, J.W. Astington and P.L. Harris (eds) *Developing Theories of Mind.* Cambridge: Cambridge University Press.

Wheeler, S., Waite, S.J. and Bromfield, C. (2002) Promoting creative thinking through the use of ICT. *Journal of Computer Assisted Learning,* 18(3): 367–78.

Wittgenstein, L. (1922) *Tracticus Logico-Philosophicus,* Trans. C.K. Ogden. London: Routledge and Kegan Paul Ltd.

Wittgenstein, L. (1967) *Philosophical Investigations.* Oxford: Blackwell.

Wood, D., Bruner, J. and Ross, G. (1976) The role of tutoring in problem solving. *Journal of Child Psychology and Psychiatry,* 17: 89–100.

# 13

## Good practice for the welfare of the child
Jackie Musgrave

### Introduction

The 2012 EYFS framework (DfE, 2012) in the revised statutory guidance relating to safeguarding and welfare requirements states 'children learn best when they are healthy, safe and secure' (p. 13). Welfare can be defined as addressing both *health* and *wellbeing*. These are two different concepts and there is not one definition of what each concept means; however, definitions of the terms are considered below.

The aims of this chapter are:

- to define what is meant by 'welfare', 'health' and 'wellbeing';
- to identify the welfare issues for children and families in the early years;
- to explore the role of the practitioner in promoting, educating and planning for the welfare of children and families;
- to reflect on good practice in relation to the welfare of children.

### Policy relating to health and wellbeing

There has been an increased understanding of the inextricable links between good health and good social and emotional wellbeing in the early years and the effect of positive developmental outcomes and improved health in adulthood. There has also been an increased emphasis on identifying children who are at risk of poor wellbeing and health. Early identification means that interventions can be made that can reduce the long-term effect on individuals. Early years professionals play a key role in working with children and families in order to identify such children and families in order to achieve this goal. Since the Every Child Matters agenda (DfES, 2003) there has been a cross-government approach to initiatives designed to address education, health and wellbeing. As a result of the Every Child Matters agenda there has been a move to a multi-agency approach emerging in order to promote the wellbeing of children in the early years. The revised EYFS has personal, social and emotional development as a prime area of learning and development for children. This means that there is a statutory requirement for day care settings to create environments that are conducive to maintaining and promoting health and wellbeing. The National Institute for Clinical Excellence (NICE) public health guidance on social and emotional wellbeing in the early years (2012) has endorsed the importance of promoting children's wellbeing. The key professionals who are charged with this responsibility include health professionals and early years practitioners.

The timeline in Table 13.1 aims to summarize the main policies that have helped to shape contemporary approaches to health and wellbeing in the early years.

## Defining wellbeing

The EYFS has made it a statutory requirement for practitioners to promote the welfare of children; that is, to promote health and wellbeing. The Oxford English dictionary defines wellbeing as 'the state of being comfortable, healthy or happy'. However, there is not a universal understanding and definition of what wellbeing means. This is problematic, because in order to know what to do in practice it is essential that there is an understanding of what is meant by the concept of wellbeing. The NICE public health guidance on social and emotional wellbeing in the early years (2012) states that wellbeing is not a straightforward concept to define and there is not a universal definition. The NICE guidance (2012: 33) does offer a consensus of what constitutes social and emotional wellbeing as follows:

> Emotional wellbeing – this includes being happy and confident and not anxious or depressed
> Psychological wellbeing – this includes the ability to be autonomous, problem-solve, manage emotions, experience empathy, be resilient and attentive
> Social wellbeing – has good relationships with others and does not have behavioural problems; that is, they are not disruptive, violent or a bully.

Underdown (2007) defines wellbeing as the ability to experience healthy self-esteem, feeling worthwhile and able to make a positive contribution. The Children's Society report (Layard and Dunn 2009) researched children's views about what factors contribute to a good childhood. The authors of this report add another dimension to the definition and suggest that positive wellbeing includes enabling children to develop a sense of fulfilment.

These definitions suggest that 'wellbeing' is linked to emotional and social development as well as having a sense of achievement; however, Layard and Dunn state the importance of children developing resilience in order to overcome drawbacks, which implies that teaching children to cope with disappointment is an important factor in developing good wellbeing.

The NICE guidance acknowledges that they have drawn on the EYFS definitions and this example of working with a pre-existing policy is possibly an attempt to promote a common understanding of what is meant by wellbeing. It may appear that definitions are simply a case of semantics, but this is not so. Adopting a universally accepted definition means that there can be greater understanding of the factors that can impact on children's wellbeing and helps to identify what needs to be done in order to promote good wellbeing. This is particularly important for practitioners who

**Table 13.1** Policy timeline

| Year | Policy | Aims |
|---|---|---|
| United Nations 1989 | The United Nations Convention on the Rights of the Child | Article 24 outlines the right to the best possible health and health services |
| Department for Children, Schools and Families 1989 | The Children Act | The welfare of the child is paramount |
| Department for Education and Skills 2003 | Every Child Matters | Being healthy |
| Department of Health 2004 | National Services Framework for Children | |
| Department for Education and Skills and Department of Health 2005 | Managing Medicines in Schools and Early Years Settings | Guidance to help staff support children with medical needs who require access to medicines when in out of home care or school |
| Department of Health 2009 | Healthy Child Programme (formerly Child Health Promotion Programme) | Universal and targeted services for pregnant women and the first five years of life |
| Department for Education 2012 | Early Years Foundation Stage | Outlines welfare requirements to create an environment that keeps children healthy, safe and secure. A prime area of development is personal, social and emotional wellbeing |
| Department for Education and Department of Health 2011 | Supporting Families in the Foundation Years | To encourage partnerships between health and early years services |
| National Institute for Health and Clinical Excellence 2012 | Social and emotional wellbeing: Early Years | To define how the social and emotional wellbeing of vulnerable children aged under 5 can be supported through home visiting, childcare and early education |

observe, assess and plan care and education for children in order to promote their development. A universal definition also means that professionals with a responsibility for promoting good wellbeing will have a shared understanding. In turn, a shared understanding means that planning services and interventions can be more effective.

As well as an absence of a universally accepted or universally appropriate definition, there is a complex range of factors that can impact on children's social and emotional development. Wellbeing also needs to be considered in the context of global, cultural, religious and economic influences. At present, there appears to be an agreement that vulnerable children are more likely to have 'poor' (NIHCE, 2012: 18) social and emotional development. This point will be returned to below. The next section outlines the benefits of good social and emotional wellbeing for children and society.

## Benefits of good social and emotional wellbeing

The introduction of the EYFS states that 'a secure, safe and happy childhood is important in its own right' (p. 2) but is also important as part of what is needed by children as part of the foundation to children making the most of their potential to achieve in the future. The NICE guidance is a powerful endorsement of the importance of the adults in children's lives working together to promote social and emotional development in the early years in order to promote good wellbeing in children. The NICE guidance draws on a limited range of evidence-based research to make this claim. Part of the reason why there is limited research that can support the claim that good wellbeing is so important links back to the point made above about the absence of a universal definition of what wellbeing means. However, NICE recommends that society adopts a 'life course' perspective of children by recognizing disadvantage that can be present in children's lives from before birth and in the early years. Early disadvantage can have lifelong and negative effects on health and wellbeing. Children who are not happy because of factors in their lives that disadvantage them can be vulnerable to poor developmental outcomes and achievement. Happy children are more likely to learn and in turn reach their potential and make a positive contribution to society. Conversely, unhappy children are more likely to have behaviour problems and there is increasing evidence that children who are deemed to be vulnerable to poor social and emotional development are more likely to be involved in criminality and anti-social behaviour as adults.

Therefore, the benefits of good wellbeing can be to individuals as well as to society. The Good Childhood Children's Society (Layard and Dunn, 2009) report suggests that children who learn to live in harmony with others in society are more likely to lead happy lives and in turn this will impact positively on society. NICE offer an economic benefit to society by taking into account the costs of addressing the legacy of criminality and anti-social behaviour that is the outcome of children having poor wellbeing developed in the early years.

## Defining vulnerable children

Vulnerable means being susceptible to physical or emotional injury. When the term vulnerable is used in relation to children it usually means that there are factors in their lives that put them at risk of not developing and learning optimally. The risk factors that make children vulnerable to poor social and emotional development are most notably:

- children with parents who have drug, alcohol and mental health problems;
- difficult family relationships especially if domestic violence and criminality are features of family relationships.

Vulnerable children *may* also include those who:

- are living in a single parent family;
- have physical disabilities;
- were born to young parents (under 18);
- have parents who were/are looked after in the care system.

Specific health-related issues are not included in the factors most likely to cause poor wellbeing. However, there is an increasing number of children who are obese, especially in the minority world. Hall and Elliman (2006) report that as well as the health implications caused by increased obesity (see below) there is an increased risk of depression in later life caused by the effect of being obese.

It is important to note that children's vulnerability can vary depending on the family circumstances, meaning that the level of vulnerability can change. Once a child is deemed to be vulnerable, it does not mean that they will remain so for ever. The changing status of children's vulnerability means that practitioners have to know the children for whom they are caring and educating. It is also important to be aware of the signs that children who are vulnerable can exhibit and these signs can include:

- withdrawn behaviour
- unresponsiveness to stimulation
- behavioural problems
- delayed speech
- poor language and communication skills.

## Implications for early years practitioners

The revised EYFS has personal, social and emotional development as a prime area of learning and development for children. This means that there is a statutory requirement for settings to create a nurturing and loving environment that enables the development of good wellbeing.

The revised EYFS makes it a statutory requirement for 2-year-old children to have a progress check. This requirement is possibly compensatory because it is estimated that about 50 per cent of children do not access the Healthy Child Programme. Children who do not access universal services, such as developmental checks, and are found to have developmental delay are at greater risk of not reaching their potential developmental outcomes. Early intervention is known to be an effective approach to maximizing long-term developmental outcomes.

The welfare requirement for children to have a Key Person means that children have a practitioner who knows their key children and is equipped to take the responsibility of caring for their welfare requirements. In order to fulfil this role it is vital that practitioners have in-depth knowledge of child development and are confident in using the EYFS assessment process to identify vulnerable children.

The NICE guidelines for social and emotional wellbeing outline the role of practitioners in promoting the use of early years' services. The guidance states that practitioners should be systematic and persistent in their efforts to encourage vulnerable parents to take up the range of universal services as well as targeted services.

**Reflections**

The benefit of positive social and emotional development for children in the early years is that this is more likely to lead to good wellbeing. In turn, this has implications for a successful economic and harmonious society. Consider how you can promote good wellbeing in your practice.

Think about the following:

- What do you need to know about the children and families?
- What factors in their lives could make them vulnerable to poor wellbeing?
- What do you know about policy and child development that helps you understand the factors that can make children and families disadvantaged and more likely to develop poor wellbeing?
- How do you and your colleagues create an enabling environment for children to develop good wellbeing?

Think of the policies in your settings that are designed to promote good wellbeing in children; consider how they help and what may be improved. Which other services are available for children who are at risk of developing poor wellbeing in your setting?

This section has examined definitions of wellbeing and highlighted the importance of the roles of early years practitioners working with parents and other professionals to promote social and emotional development in order to maximize the chances of children developing good wellbeing. It is acknowledged that a powerful impact on children's wellbeing is health. The next section examines children's health and makes links to the EYFS welfare requirements.

## Promoting and maintaining the health of children in day care settings

The EYFS states 'children learn best when they are healthy' (3.1: 13), and it also states that 'the provider must promote the good health of children attending the setting' (3.42: 21). In order to think about how practitioners can achieve these aims, this section aims to put 'health' into context by considering the following factors:

- what is meant by 'health';
- child health policy in the UK;
- inequalities in health;
- contemporary child health issues;
- implications for practice.

## Defining health

In recent years there has been a range of government policy that has brought together services aimed at improving health for children, as summarized in Table 13.1. This is because the link between physical health and wellbeing are increasingly being recognized; and as discussed above, good emotional and social wellbeing has a positive impact on children's developmental outcomes and learning. As well as children becoming acutely unwell, many children have chronic medical conditions and there are an increasing number of children in day care settings who were born, or develop, medical needs that are complex (see Table 13.2, p. 162).

In the same way that wellbeing is difficult to define, so is the concept of health. The Oxford Dictionary defines health as 'the state of being free from illness or injury'. Clearly this is a simplistic definition and does not reflect the complexities of what contributes to health in the contemporary world. The World Health Organization (2013) define health as:

> The extent to which an individual or group is able on the one hand to realise aspirations and satisfy needs; and, on the other hand, *to change or cope with the environment*. Health is, therefore, seen as a resource for everyday life, not the objective of living; it is a positive concept emphasizing social and personal resources, as well as physical capacities.

This definition takes an holistic view of the impact of health on each area of development. It also takes a pragmatic view of health and acknowledges that people may need *to change or cope with the environment* in order to overcome the effect of a disease or condition. The role of practitioners in helping to change the environment or helping children to cope with the environment is fundamental to meeting some of the welfare requirements of the EYFS; how practitioners can achieve this will be discussed below. A lack of a universal definition can in part be explained by the diversity of explanations that individuals say that health means to them. It is usually only when we feel unwell that we become aware of what it is like to be without health. Feeling unhealthy and unwell makes us value our health. It is interesting to ask children what they think health means; they frequently respond with comments about healthy eating.

## Health provision for children in the UK

Over the last hundred years the UK government has legislated in order to improve the health of mothers and young children. The United Nations *Convention on the Rights of the Child* (1989) changed perceptions of children's rights. For the first time it was recognized that children have an entitlement to health. Article 24 states that children have a right to the best possible health and health services available. Again, it is important to look at the child in the context of their environment when considering health services and what is available to improve children's health. For example, children in the majority world are unlikely to be able to access organized services that are universally available in the UK. A primary aim of child health policy in the UK is to prevent disease, or to identify conditions that can affect health and wellbeing and offer early treatment and/or interventions aimed at minimizing the signs and symptoms of diseases and conditions.

Health services are structured in two ways. First, the *Healthy Child Programme* (DoH, 2009) provides services aimed at a) preventing disease and b) the identification of children with conditions that can result in ill health and in turn impact on children being prone to poor emotional and social developmental outcomes. These are referred to as *universal* services and are available free to all children in the UK. Examples of universal services include immunizations and screening activities. The other aim of the *Healthy Child Programme* is to provide early intervention based on a range of screening activities. *Screening,* in relation to health, can be defined as a tool that is used on a defined section of the population in order to identify individuals who are likely to benefit from further tests or treatment in order to minimize the impact of a disease or the complications of a disease. The second way that the *Healthy Child Programme* aims to improve children's health, wellbeing and developmental outcomes is by identifying children who are vulnerable (see definition above). If children and families are identified as being vulnerable, the relevant services available can then be *targeted* in order to reduce inequalities in children's health.

The EYFS and *Healthy Child Programme* work together to promote the health of children as described above. For example, the EYFS progress check at age 2 is an initiative that is an example of a screening tool that is universally offered in order to review the child's development in the three prime areas of the EYFS. Detailed guidance for practitioners about the 2-year-old progress check is available in the National Children's Bureau publication '*A Know How Guide: The EYFS Progress Check at Age Two*' (NCB, 2012). To briefly summarize the rationale, the aim of screening all 2-year-olds by carrying out a 2-year-old check is to assess what children can do as well as to identify any developmental delay or health needs that have not been identified. So the 2-year-old check is not just a screening tool, but an opportunity to review the progress of all children and assess any unmet needs from the developmental and health point of view. The 2-year-old check is an example of the current understanding of how health, wellbeing and developmental outcomes are interrelated. Another part of the rationale for screening and assessing developmental outcomes is that any needs that are identified can have interventions planned in order to meet the needs.

## Inequalities in health

The EYFS seeks to achieve equality of opportunity for all children; however, despite the robust attempts to prevent, identify and correct as many diseases and conditions that can negatively affect children's health, there are inevitably children who do not enjoy optimal health. This situation results in inequalities in health for children which leads to poorer health. The reasons for inequalities are complex. The overriding reason for children having poor health is as a result of living in poverty.

Inequalities in health are not the only reason for children not having the right to health; there are cultural, religious and socio-economic factors that impact on children having access to health services. For example, travelling communities are known to have poorer health than settled communities. Wilkin et al. (2009) report that travellers are 17 times more likely to experience stillbirth than the national average. In addition to this, travellers are more likely to have asthma and overall there is a lower life expectancy than in the settled population. One reason for the poorer health outcomes in travellers is that there is reluctance to discuss health issues with strangers and they can experience difficulties accessing services. These facts are shocking and mean that children are being denied the right to health. However, it also suggests that accessing health services that are offered is health enhancing and life saving.

## Contemporary child health conditions

Despite the best efforts to provide universal and targeted health services that are free for all children in the UK, there remain health conditions affecting children that cannot be avoided or are proving difficult to prevent. This section examines contemporary child health conditions in the UK.

The EYFS states that 'practitioners must consider the individual needs of children' (1.7: 6) and this requires considerable knowledge of medical conditions in order to be able to manage the health needs of children. Practitioners are likely to come across a wide range of conditions that impact on children's health and wellbeing. Table 13.2 categorizes some descriptions of conditions.

## Acute medical conditions

Acute medical conditions are usually caused by an infection caused by the spread of micro-organisms which are viruses, bacteria and fungi. Micro-organisms enter the body in the following ways:

- Inhalation: breathed into the airway
- Ingestion: swallowed via the digestive system
- Inoculation: through a cut in the skin.

**Table 13.2** Medical conditions impacting on children's health and wellbeing

| Description of types of conditions | Definition | Examples of conditions | Management |
|---|---|---|---|
| Acute | Sudden onset | Viral infections (the common cold), bacterial infections (measles), fungal infections | Minimize the symptoms of the conditions, for example fever can be reduced with paracetamol medicine |
| Chronic | Lasting longer than three months Incurable | Asthma, anaphylaxis (severe allergy to food or substances such as latex or animal hair), diabetes mellitus, eczema, sickle cell anaemia | Signs and symptoms can be minimized by medications (including creams and inhalers) and management of the environment |
| Chronic complex medical conditions | Ongoing and requiring frequent interventions and treatment | Congenital (present at birth), for example spina bifida, complications as a result of being born prematurely, cystic fibrosis | Medication to minimize the symptoms of the condition, or interventions such as physiotherapy to maintain or promote physical functions. Toilet needs may have to be managed by staff. Tube-feeding may be required |

Infections can be prevented, or their impact minimized, by health education and health promotion activities, for example immunizations (see below). However, there are acute conditions that are not caused by infection, for example appendicitis.

Trying to find out what is wrong with acutely sick children can be difficult for all adults, including medical staff, and can cause anxiety to all concerned. The majority of illnesses affecting children are caused by an infection as described above. Illness can affect children in ways that are different to adults and also in ways unique to each child. Children are very likely to be unpredictable in the way they respond to illness and the speed with which they can become unwell. The symptoms of an acute medical condition can affect children in a matter of a few hours and tragically there are reported cases of children who appeared mildly unwell, only to die a few hours later because of meningitis. Meningitis can be difficult to diagnose and can be fatal; however, successful health education campaigns and the introduction of the Hib and meningococcal immunizations (see the section below on immunization) has reduced the numbers of children who contract the condition. However, the vast majority of acute illnesses caused by infections are thankfully not fatal.

## Infectious diseases that are not preventable by immunization

The most common infectious diseases that are not preventable by immunization programmes include:

- diarrhoea and vomiting (gastrointestinal infections);
- the common cold (upper respiratory infections);
- middle ear infections (otitis media) usually as a result of an upper respiratory infection.

The conditions listed above are acute because children can show symptoms over a short period of time. Children can be very well and healthy, but within hours can have a high temperature and other symptoms associated with the infection that is affecting them. Children's understanding of illness is related to their age and stage of development (Eiser, 1985) and their limited vocabulary and understanding of their bodies can make it difficult to ascertain how and where the symptoms of the illness are affecting them. Fortunately, children generally respond well to treatment of the symptoms that usually accompany infectious diseases. For instance, reducing a high temperature with appropriate medicine can help children to feel much better and can avoid children having a febrile convulsion as a result of their body temperature going too high.

Acute infectious diseases can have an underestimated impact on the health and consequent wellbeing of young children and their families and practitioners in day care settings. An upper respiratory infection can make a child feel very unwell for a few days and can cause a regression in children's developmental achievement during an illness and the following days when they are recovering. Most children recover from acute infectious illnesses without any long-term developmental consequences. However, an acute upper respiratory tract infection, such as the common cold, can result in middle ear infections (otitis media). Middle ear infections can become chronic and difficult to cure and repeated middle ear infections are a significant negative factor for children's overall development. Vernon-Feagans and Manlove (2005) noted that 12–18-month-old infants who had repeated middle ear infections used language less and had lower levels of attention. They also reported that children in day care with chronic ear infections showed lower levels of social development. However, if the quality of care was good, this reduced the negative outcomes that could be caused by the combination of a chronic health condition and poor quality care.

## Implications for practitioners

There is no room for complacency about the importance of preventing and minimizing the spread of infection in early years settings. The EYFS states that settings 'must have a procedure, discussed with parents and/or carers, for responding to children who are ill or infectious, take necessary steps to prevent the spread of infection, and take appropriate action if children are ill' (DfE, 2012: 22). The considerations that need to be addressed in order for practitioners to be able to meet these requirements relating to preventing the spread of infection can be summarized as the following:

*   *policies and practices* within the setting aimed at preventing infections;
*   *health education* and training of staff aimed at preventing the spread of infection – effective handwashing techniques, health education to teach children about good habits in preventing infection and managing their own hygiene;
*   *health promotion* – can include informed information about universal services such as immunization programmes.

### Preventing infectious diseases in day care settings

One of the EYFS early learning goals for physical development is that 'children know the importance of good health and they can manage their own basic hygiene and personal needs successfully' (p. 8). The most powerful way of avoiding cross-infection is for individuals to develop effective handwashing techniques that remove micro-organisms and avoid transfer of micro-organisms and cross-contamination. Practitioners must be aware of their role in modelling good hand hygiene by following recommended techniques and educating children about the reasons they are washing their hands. Practitioners must teach children effective handwashing techniques and support children to develop hygienic toilet habits as well as teaching children to manage all their bodily fluids, such as secretions from the nose.

The provision of food requires careful consideration in day care settings. The storage and preparation of food is a complex area and there are many points in the provision of food where lack of hygiene can lead to a gastrointestinal infection that can result in diarrhoea and vomiting. Therefore, the EYFS requires all staff involved in the preparation and storage of food to receive food handling training in order to understand the required careful attention to maintaining hygiene standards. The EYFS also requires practitioners to notify Ofsted within 14 days of any food poisoning that affects two or more children in a setting.

Children who have an infectious disease should not be cared for in their day care setting because of the risk of spreading the infection to other children and staff. Therefore, it is important that a policy that includes the infectious conditions that will require children to be excluded, as well as an explanation of why it is important to exclude children and for how long, is written and shared with parents.

---

**Case Study**

Millie is 2 years 10 months old and was accompanied to nursery early in the morning by her Dad. He mentioned to Millie's Key Person, Marie, that she was not her normal self and that she had not had her breakfast, but if there were any concerns, staff could call her mum because he was about to go to work and would be in a day-long meeting. Millie has a quiet morning and is pale and lacking in energy. After three hours, Millie starts to become grizzly, is very hot and refuses to eat or drink. When her Key Person asks Millie if she has a headache, Millie nods. Her Key Person asks her where her headache is; Millie points to her tummy! The manager decides that Millie's mum needs to be contacted and asked to come and collect her. However, Millie's mum's mobile number is not correct and they realize that her dad is not available.

Consider this situation from the perspectives of Millie, her parents and your setting. What are the considerations for policy (both locally and EYFS) and practice?

---

This section has considered the implications for practitioners to prevent the spread of infection by adopting policies that educate individuals about good practice in minimizing the spread of infection. Some of the issues that can arise when trying to minimize infection and keep children well and work with parents have been discussed. The next section considers how the health of children is promoted by immunization against a range of infectious diseases.

## Preventing infectious diseases by immunization of children

Immunizations are a universal service aimed at reducing the risk of disability and death to children as a result of contracting diseases such as diphtheria, tetanus, polio, mumps and measles. Until the 1950s, these infections were some of the most common threats to children's health.

The aim of immunization schedules is to achieve what is known as 'herd immunity', which means that the majority of the population is protected from the disease. This is important for children who genuinely cannot receive immunizations. There are few reasons why children should not receive immunizations, but children who are receiving treatment for cancer should not be immunized. There are also reasons why immunization should be delayed, for example children who require high dose steroids or are receiving immuno-suppression (in order to prevent rejection of transplanted organs). However, if herd immunity has been achieved, that is most of the population has been immunized, children who have genuine medical reasons for not being immunized will be protected.

Immunization is an area where practitioners can play a key role in educating staff and parents about the part that immunizations play in promoting the health of children. It is important that practitioners are aware of the background to stories that are widely reported in the media and cause concerns for parents. An example of how negative reporting has affected immunization uptake is illustrated by the measles, mumps and rubella (MMR) immunization controversy. In 1998, Andrew Wakefield claimed to have found a link between children developing autism after having been given the MMR immunization. This claim has been discredited and Wakefield was struck off the General Medical Council in 2010 for serious professional misconduct as a result of the claims he made in his research. The controversy that surrounded the MMR immunization has left a legacy of suspicion about the safety of immunizations. This has resulted in a drop in the number of parents who are taking up the offer of MMR for their children; herd immunity has now been lost for measles and the disease is now endemic in the UK. Measles is a serious disease that can be fatal and can leave children disabled, therefore there is an urgent need to prevent the spread of measles as well as other infectious diseases by increasing immunization uptake by parents in order to reduce the risk of unnecessary death or disability.

### Reflections

Consider your role in promoting the immunization schedule that is available for children in the UK. How can you link the need to prevent the spread of infection as required by the EYFS with promoting immunizations?

How can you encourage parents to have their children immunized?

Current guidance about immunization schedules is available from the Health Protection Agency (see Useful websites at the end of the chapter).

## Chronic medical conditions

Although there is much that can be done to prevent disease and to promote health for children, it is inevitable that some children will develop conditions that are chronic (see Table 13.2). The effects of a chronic condition can have a significant impact on the lives of children and can interfere with normal childhood activities (Brown et al. 1995). The most common contemporary medical conditions that affect children in the UK include:

- allergy/anaphylaxis
- asthma
- diabetes mellitus (type 1)
- eczema
- epilepsy
- sickle cell anaemia
- obesity.

Further information about each of these conditions can be found in the guidance *Managing Medicines in Schools and Early Years Settings* (DfES/DoH, 2005) which is a joint publication by the Department for Education and Skills and the Department of Health. The guidance includes information for staff involved with storing, administering and recording of medication for children with anaphylaxis, asthma, diabetes mellitus and epilepsy. There is not information relating for eczema or sickle cell anaemia; however, further information can be found on the websites set up by the charities to help support adults caring for young children with these conditions, (see p. 172).

## Obesity

Obesity is an example of how eating habits, in the case of increasing calorie intake and reduced energy output because of less physical activity, have had a dramatic effect in the number of children who are overweight. Since the early 2000s there has been an increase in childhood obesity to the extent that Hall and Elliman (2006) refer to this alarming trend as an 'epidemic of obesity' (p. 179). Research about children who are overweight reveals that there can be greater levels of emotional and psychological distress and this can lead to poor wellbeing. In addition to poor wellbeing, childhood obesity is causing children to develop conditions such as type 2 diabetes mellitus. This is a form of diabetes that until recently was only seen in people over the age of 40. Overweight adults often have increased blood pressure and an increased risk of cancer and strokes. It remains to be seen how the current epidemic of obesity affects children in later life, and it is clear that early years professionals have a vital role in addressing obesity in young children.

## Implications for practitioners

The obesity epidemic is serious and practitioners are ideally placed to try to shape children's eating and activity habits. Although Hall and Elliman (2006) point out that there is 'no single health promotion measures to reverse the emerging problem of obesity' (p. xix), there remains a need to address it as a public health issue. Therefore, the problem of children's obesity can partly be addressed through the requirements of the EYFS as follows:

- *policies and practices* within the setting aimed at providing healthy meals, snacks and drinks;
- *health education* and training of staff, parents and children aimed at teaching about the benefits of physical exercise and healthy eating;
- *health promotion* activities that are sensitive and appropriate for the children and families in settings that are aimed at increasing physical exercise and healthy eating.

## Managing chronic medical conditions

The effects of a chronic condition on a child's life can be minimized by under-standing the condition and how it affects children. If we look again at the WHO's definition of health, the first sentence includes 'the extent to which an individual or group . . . is able to . . . change or cope with the environment'. These words sum-marize the approach required in order to minimize the impact of the symptoms of chronic conditions on children. For example, outdoor play on a cold day may provoke or 'trigger' wheezing for children who have asthma. However, the environment can be changed for children whose asthma is triggered by running on a cold day by giving preventer inhalers (following the setting's medicines policy) before they go out. It is also important to work with parents to ensure that as much as possible is done to reduce the impact of the symptoms on children. In the example of a child with asthma it would be important that parents supply a scarf for practitioners to ensure that it is worn over the child's face so that air is filtered and warmed before breathing in, thus reducing the risk of triggering the child's asthma symptoms. If children with chronic medical conditions are not supported in changing their environment or not helped to cope with their environment, then chronic medical conditions can impact on inclusion of children in their education setting. Mukherjee et al. (2000) researched children with chronic conditions in primary and secondary schools. Their findings highlighted the children's need to have support from teachers in order to take part in school activities and manage peer relationships because of difficulties caused by their condition. Research relating to the effect of chronic medical conditions on children in the early years is limited, but early findings of my research suggest that including children with chronic conditions in all aspects of the EYFS may raise some challenges for practitioners (Musgrave, 2012).

In addition to chronic medical conditions there is an increasing number of children with complex medical conditions. They may require feeding by gastric tubes as well as other treatments to keep them well and healthy.

## Implications for practitioners

As previously stated, the EYFS requires practitioners to 'promote the good health of children attending the setting' (DfE, 2012: 21). This requirement means that practitioners need to have a deep understanding of what may affect the health of each child and this is particularly true when children have chronic medical conditions. Knowledge and training are essential to staff in settings being able to identify and meet the needs of children. However, training about specific chronic health conditions is sometimes difficult to access and can depend on the professional network of practitioners. Children with complex medical needs are more likely to have a network of multi-agency professionals to work with practitioners to support their care needs in day care settings.

The EYFS welfare requirement of a 2-year-old check is a welcome opportunity to review children's medical care and to identify any health needs and if necessary, to refer the child to other professionals. The 'Know How Guide' (NCB, 2012) for progress checks for a child with an identified disability, medical or special educational need. Children with chronic medical conditions such as asthma need special consideration because the complexity of such conditions is frequently under-estimated.

## Children who are unwell in day care settings

It is inevitable that there will be times when children become ill while in their day care setting. The section above looks at issues relating to managing children who become acutely unwell and emphasizes the need to minimize the spread of infection and protect other children from becoming unwell. Children who have a chronic medical or complex medical condition are more likely to have bouts of illness connected with the symptoms of their condition. Such bouts of illness are less likely to be infectious; however, there are considerations about sick children in day care settings and it is important that practitioners have a policy and develop good practice to manage such occurrences. For instance, there are practical considerations about caring for children who are unwell: is there a quiet area for children to rest and are there sufficient staff numbers to cope with the extra needs of children? There are not necessarily easy solutions to these considerations but at all times the welfare of the child should be the most important consideration.

### Paediatric first aid training

First aid is a vital part of maintaining health and the EYFS recommends that at least one person who has a current paediatric first aid certificate is on the premises in order to manage first aid emergencies. While it would be desirable for all practitioners to hold a first aid certificate, this may be unrealistic. As well as being available for cuts and bumps and more serious accidents, children who have a chronic condition can become unwell as a result of the symptoms of their condition being 'triggered'. For example, a child with diabetes may have a hypoglycaemic attack and need to have emergency first aid treatment, therefore practitioners will need to work with parents to ensure that all staff know the correct first aid response.

### Safe administration and storage of medicines

The EYFS requires practitioners to obtain written permission before administering medication to children. The *Managing Medicines in Schools and Early Years Settings*

(DfES/DoH, 2005) guidance outlines good practice in relation to developing policies around the storage, administration and recording of medication.

## Food and drink

The EYFS requires children's food and drink to be healthy, balanced and nutritious and has been discussed in relation to reducing obesity in a previous section. However, children with chronic medical conditions often have dietary requirements in order to keep them healthy. Providing special diets for children can present practitioners with challenges. This is especially so when providing food to children who have anaphylaxis or allergy to foods. Anaphylaxis, in rare cases, can be fatal, and children who are allergic to foods such as eggs or milk can react to very small amounts of the allergy-causing food. This can make the management of food for children a stressful occasion for staff trying to ensure that children do not inadvertently come into contact with other children's food that could trigger a reaction in an allergic child. It is understandable that practitioners exercise high levels of surveillance in order to try and reduce accidental cross-contamination from occurring. Some practitioners exercise caution by feeding children separately in order to minimize the risk; however, this can have the unintended consequence of excluding children from the sociable aspects of eating together. Again, this is a difficult dilemma to resolve.

## Conclusion

This chapter has highlighted the considerations for practitioners meeting the welfare of children in the Foundation Stage. The depth of knowledge required for this to be achieved requires considerations that are complex. Identifying children who are vulnerable to poor wellbeing and understanding the impact of health on wellbeing has been endorsed by the NICE guidelines. Early intervention by implementing policies that offer universal and targeted services are known to be effective and early years practitioners are well placed to be key players in meeting the aims of government policies to improve and maintain the health of children.

Key messages for practitioners include:

- prevention of infection: promoting health by educating parents and practitioners about immunization programmes;
- understanding chronic medical conditions, recognizing the triggers of conditions in order to reduce the impact of symptoms on children;
- adapting and managing the environment in order to promote inclusion of children with health conditions;
- being aware of the factors that can create inequalities in child health.

## References

Brown, D., Krieg, K. and Belluck, F. (1995) A model for group intervention with the chronically ill: cystic fibrosis and the family. *Social Work in Pediatrics*, 21(1): 81–94.

DfE (Department for Education) (2012) *Statutory Framework for the Early Years Foundation Stage: Setting the Standards for Learning, Development and Care for Children from Birth to Five.* http://www.education.gov.uk/publications/standard/AuPublications/Page1/DFE-00023-2012 (accessed 27 March 2013).

DfES (Department for Education and Skills) (2003) *Every Child Matters.* Norwich: TSO.

DfES/DoH (Department for Education and Skills/Department of Health) (2005) *Managing Medicines in Schools and Early Years Settings.* London: DfES. http://www.teachfind.com/national-strategies/guidance-managing-medicines-schools-and-early-years-settings (accessed 17 December 2012).

DoH (2009) *Healthy Child Programme: Pregnancy and The First Five Years of Life.* http://www.dh.gov.uk/en/Publicationsandstatistics/Publications/PublicationsPolicyAndGuidance/DH_107563 (accessed 4 January 2012).

Eiser, C. (1985) *The Psychology of Childhood Illness.* New York: Springer-Verlag.

Hall, D. and Elliman, D. (2006) *Health for All Children,* 4th edn. New York: Open University Press.

Layard, R. and Dunn, J. (2009) *A Good Childhood: Searching for Values in a Competitive Age.* London: Penguin.

Mukherjee, S., Lightfoot, J. and Sloper, P. (2000) The inclusion of pupils with a chronic health condition in mainstream school: what does it mean for teachers? *Educational Research,* 42(1): 59–72.

Musgrave, J. (2012) How are inclusive environments created in day care settings for children aged 0–3 years with common chronic conditions (anaphylaxis; asthma; diabetes, eczema; epilepsy)? Briefing Paper for paper presented at TACTYC Conference, November 2012. http://www.tactyc.org.uk/workshop/Jackie%20Musgrave_Inclusion%200-3_Chronic%20Conditions.pdf (accessed 19 December 2012).

NCB (National Children's Bureau) (2012) *A Know How Guide: The EYFS Progress Check at Age Two.* www.ncb.org/uk/ey/peertopeersupport (accessed July 2012).

NICE (National Institute for Health and Clinical Excellence) (2012) *The NICE Public Health Guidance.* http://publication.nice.org.uk (accessed 3 May 2013).

NIHCE (2012) *Social and Emotional Wellbeing.* Manchester: NICE.

Underdown, A. (2007) *Young Children's Health and Welll-being.* Maidenhead: Open University Press.

United Nations (1989) *Convention on the Rights of the Child.* Available at www.unicef.org (accessed 3 May 2013).

Vernon-Feagans, L. and Manlove, E.E. (2005) Otitis media, the quality child care and the social communicative behaviour of toddlers: a replication and extension. *Early Childhood Research Quarterly,* 20: 306–28.

Wilkin, A., Derrington, C. and Foster, B. (2009) *Improving the Outcomes for Gypsy, Roma and Traveller Pupils: A Literature Review.* www.dcsf.gov.uk/research (accessed December 2009).

World Health Organization (2013) *Environmental Health.* Available at http://www.whoint/topics/enviornmental_health/en/ (accessed July 2012).

## Further reading

Albon, D. and Mukherji, P. (2008) *Food and Health in Early Childhood.* London: Sage Publications.

DCSF/DoH (Department for Children, Schools and Families/Department of Health) (2009) *Healthy Lives, Brighter Futures: The Strategy for Children and Young People's Health.* http://

www.dh.gov.uk/en/Publicationsandstatistics/Publications/PublicationsPolicyAnd Guidance/DH_094400 (accessed 4 January 2012).

DfE/DoH (Department for Education/Department of Health) (2011) *National Child Measurement Programme: Guidance for Schools 2011/12.* https://education.gov.uk/ publications/standard/publicationDetail/Page1/NCMP-406358 (accessed 4 January 2012).

Health Protection Agency (2012) *Health Protection Report.* http://www.hpa.org.uk/hpr/ archives/2012/news4-812.htm#prtsss1210 (accessed 2 December 2012).

Health Protection Agency (2012) *Health Protection Weekly Report: Immunization.* http:// www.hpa.org.uk/hpr/infections/immunisation.htm#coverQ312 (accessed 15 December 2012).

## Useful websites

Anaphylaxis Campaign http://www.anaphylaxis.org.uk/schools/help-for-schools

Asthma UK http://www.asthma.org.uk/how-we-help/teachers-and-healthcare-professionals/ schools-and-early-years/

Diabetes UK http://www.diabetes.org.uk/Professionals/Shared_Practice/Care_Topics/ Diabetes-Care-in-Schools/

Epilepsy Society http://www.epilepsysociety.org.uk/WhatWeDo/Schoolsawareness

Health Protection Agency http://www.hpa.org.uk

National Eczema Society https://www.education.gov.uk/publications/standard/publication Detail/Page1/ECZEMA-RESOURCES

Sickle cell anaemia http://www.gosh.nhs.uk/medical-conditions/search-for-medical-conditions/sickle-cell-anaemia/sickle-cell-anaemia-information/

# 14
## Challenges and convergence
Pat Beckley

## Introduction

This chapter considers challenges posed to early years provision in general terms. This is followed by a discussion of possible challenges concerning the introduction of the 2012 EYFS framework, where practitioners implement the changes building on their existing knowledge, understandings, beliefs and values. Aspects of the framework, such as partnerships with parents, safeguarding, and continuing professional development are considered in the light of new perspectives on these issues. Finally, consideration is given to possible convergence of policies, where the changes have been a possible response to wider policies and understandings from other providers.

## Challenges to early years provision

> In the twenty-first century it is probably evident to every parent, professional worker, kindergarten and primary teacher that early childhood is high on the political agenda almost everywhere.
>
> (Gammage, 2006: 235)

Changing patterns of work and a growing desire to help children perceived to be disadvantaged have created further childcare requirements. Changes on a global scale have led to new challenges. Communication links can forge an international sharing of ideas regarding early years provision. Politicians urge us to consider our place in a global economic society and how best the learning we provide for young children can serve them to enable them to be confident adults in an ever-changing and challenging world. A tightening financial climate means costs have to be scrutinized. Yet the United Nations International Children's Emergency Fund (UNICEF) in 2002 urges 'no nation today can afford to ignore opportunities for maximising investments in education in a competitive economic environment based on knowledge, flexibility and lifelong learning' (Dahlberg and Moss, 2007: 5). Similarly Musgrave claims the future might 'require the personal attributes associated today with zero production growth rather than with inevitable and endless development' (1965: 334). Therefore consideration is needed of ways in which children could be prepared for future challenges.

In the 2012 EYFS framework the characteristics of effective learning equip children with the means to be resilient, positive and resourceful. The framework also supports parents if there is a need to move to find work in challenging times. Ease of sharing information with colleagues at an international level, for example through internet links, fosters collaboration and discussion. In Europe these can include networks for those concerned with the care and education of young children, such as the European Early Childhood Education Research Association (EECERA). Moss writes 'Being at the heart of Europe means having a mature and sustained engagement with other countries, using this opportunity to exchange experience, discuss issues of shared interest and reflect on policy and practice' (Dahlberg and Moss 2007: 39). These global communities influence thoughts of what is required for early years provision, sharing and implementing new ideas. The importance of partnerships with parents is deemed to be high on the agenda for early years provision where there can be a combined concern for the welfare of the children. However it could be an equal partnership, or in a market place where there are many providers parents might be felt to have a strong voice in what happens, while in others the setting takes the lead. Staff can liaise with parents/carers to give an awareness and understanding of what is happening in the provision and why it is beneficial to the children.

## Partnerships with parents/carers

Partnerships with parents and carers are of huge importance in the early years environment. Successful relationships give clear messages to the children that adults are working together to support their welfare and progress. There are many ways these can effectively be forged and the manner in which they are approached will depend on the way of working and the number of adults present.

In a home environment it is useful to keep a learning journey diary to share achievements and give a record of happenings during the day. Larger settings may have more formal arrangements, including open days, fairs or parents meetings. Communication between parents/carers and the EYFS provision is essential for securing children's progress and wellbeing. Successful communication can be developed before the child enters the proffered setting.

If it is a childminder's provision the child could visit the establishment to gain knowledge of the adults involved, other children accessing the setting and the routines in place. A learning journey diary could be begun and a memento of the visit kept for the child to see when they return.

In a larger setting if a parent indicates an interest in securing a place for their child in the provision and completes a form for entry, an arrangement can be made for the child to visit the facility or a time could be made for a home visit, in which case necessary safety issues for the visiting adults would need to be considered. Families can often feel more at ease in their own surroundings which could contribute to helping to discuss their child. If the child and parent/carer visited a facility a small gift or made item could be brought from the setting to enable the child to have a positive recollection of the provision and be excited about the prospect of returning.

Such visits are important in helping to prepare for the child's smooth transfer to the new environment and to implement any requirements or special needs resources that might be needed. Visits to the setting help parents/carers to gain an understanding of its aims, ethos and routines while supporting knowledge of the child, such as possible health issues, concerns voiced by the family and the achievements of the child. Networking between parents can be encouraged to be a valued part of the children's development in the learning community, promoting a positive atmosphere from the outset. By the time a child enters the provision parents/carers and the child should be able to get to know the staff, routines, environment and resources in the setting, know who has been designated as the Key Person and be able to communicate with adults in the setting, participating in the sharing of knowledge about their child.

The importance of the relationships, ensuring continuity and shared understanding between home and early years provision, should be demonstrated as an ongoing part of the experiences of the child. Practitioners should do their utmost to welcome parents/carers and children, welcoming children who should be eager to participate. The Key Person can support new visitors to settings by showing them the facilities, helping them to get to know some of the other children and the resources available. If a child does not attend frequently procedures should be in place to ascertain why. Colleagues can promote liaison by planning, cooperating and working well together, providing good role models for the children in their care.

Fathers can be welcomed by ensuring they are aware they are valued. Discussions can lead to an understanding of their fears for or interests relating to their children. Family support groups, such as parents meetings, language, numeracy or literacy workshops can be used as a means of including fathers in their child's learning and development. Expertise could be harnessed through items made or events supported, always ensuring necessary health and safety checks are covered.

In a positive, carefully considered, enabling environment parents and staff can work together through liaison regarding health concerns, ensuring children remain safe and secure while promoting achievements and sharing the enjoyment of learning and development. It is important to build on strengths described by parents prior to the child's arrival at the setting, provide a firm foundation for future progress through strong relationships with staff and parents, and promote a sound background for the development of every child as an individual.

Most practitioners, if not all, have devised ways of encouraging this cooperation and useful communication between themselves and parents/carers. Further consideration can be made concerning parental wishes for the learning accessed by their children. Some parents may wish to support the setting as 'Friends of . . .' while others may help to provide their time to make resources or use their expertise. In a Scandinavian country visited recently parents had a strong voice in the running of the provision, concerning aspects such as timings, how the sharing of achievements was accomplished, which areas of learning should be given prominence and how this should be delivered. In the 2012 EYFS framework practitioners can use their professional expertise to share how the provision addresses the areas of learning to enable parents/carers to know how the learning is being organized, for example through the beneficial characteristics of learning through play.

## Wellbeing and safeguarding

Babies and young children are dependent on the people who are responsible for their care and for the safety of the environment they inhabit and play in. Safeguarding issues have been emphasized in the 2012 EYFS framework (DfE, 2012). Most settings had already begun to address this aspect of provision before the framework, for example making sure that a record of visitors to the setting was maintained and Criminal Records Bureau (CRB) checks were made. Many settings enhanced their security procedures for adults entering buildings where children in their early years and older were busy. Effective collaboration between all those concerned with the welfare of individual children is essential in providing a good level of care in early years practice.

It is a priority for homes and settings with young children to maintain a safe and secure environment for them where they can flourish and feel confident that their welfare is being considered. Health and safety aspects can be scrutinized to ensure that any failings or weaknesses in the environment through such events as constant use or the effects of the weather are made safe. These might include for example water from taps which is running at too high a temperature, spillages on the floor which may cause slipping, broken toys or items of furniture. It will be necessary to keep dangerous materials away from young children and ensure they cannot be reached by them, such as some cleaning equipment.

Children's welfare can also be considered through the lifestyle they lead, for example too sedentary a routine can lead to obesity. Children's use of resources needs to be considered too, such as the use of internet sources. Care should be taken to protect children from inappropriate sites through the use of safety devises such as Firewall, where children are excluded from inappropriate information.

> **Reflections**
>
> How do I share information when I have concerns about a child?
>
> Who do I pass the information to?

In an age where new technologies are being developed practitioners have to ensure that the settings and the children who visit them remain safe and secure. Practice in different countries varies, where some settings have little control over who visits the establishment. For example, in one setting I visited abroad a group of young children greeted me on my arrival and one of them opened the gate to let me enter. Practitioners need to be vigilant to maintain an up-to-date knowledge and awareness of safety aspects for the welfare of their children and the adults who work there.

## Continuing professional development

The 2012 EYFS framework and corresponding profile assessments provide a broad basis which practitioners can use to formulate their plans for the provision and children in their care, responding to the need of the children and the community the setting serves. This allows practitioners to use their professional judgement in devising appropriate strategies to enhance their provision and relies on the commitment and dedication of the adults who are involved in early years learning and care. It is an exciting time to be involved in early years provision. Practitioners can respond to new initiatives, innovations and ideas, following the prescribed guidelines, within their own beliefs and values. National conferences, such as the annual TACTYC national and international conference or research conferences, for example EECERA, highlight new ideas and the sharing of differing pedagogies and varying practice. Local networks enable practitioners to compare and discuss different practice, reflecting on provision and enabling the enhancement of the settings they organize and manage.

## Challenges and convergence

New challenges have been faced by practitioners when implementing the 2012 EYFS framework. Changes have included the inclusion of physical development as a prime area and the split between communication and language as a prime area and literacy as a specific one. It is interesting that these aspects appear to have been influenced by discussions with colleagues on an international scale; for example in Norway physical development is deemed most important and language abilities a crucial aspect of a child's learning. However, Moyles (ed.) (2002: 60) state 'Early Years pedagogy is extremely complex and difficult to define precisely. It is more than 'practice' alone, for it is what practitioners think about as well as do, and the principles, theories, knowledge and qualities that inform and shape their practice.' The cultural contexts of practitioners shape the manner in which policies are implemented. The implementation of the new policies reflects 'personal thinking and beliefs concerning the way learning is fostered' (David, 2003: 7).

Humphries and Simpson (2005: 16) suggest 'Europeanisation' refers to 'both the development of a regulatory framework at the European level and its impact on domestic structures and policies'. Convergence consists of 'the degree to which there is an 'institutional fit' between the European model and the domestic one' (p. 16). Knill (2006: 4) believes this is achieved through a process of 'spreading policies across countries' through such means as policy measures and through policy convergence by voluntary methods where aspects of practice are felt to be beneficial. Modern uncertainties, cross-national policy convergence caused by transnational communication such as OECD (The Organisation for Economic Cooperation and Development) and pressure from international league tables encourage policy convergence. Changes partly driven through convergence bring challenges to those implementing the changes. The new EYFS framework enables practitioners to implement the changes for the benefit of the early years children, the provision they access and the communities they serve.

## References

Dahlberg, G. and Moss, P. (2007) *Ethics and Politics in Early Childhood Education*. London: RoutledgeFalmer.

David, T. (2003) *What do we Know About Teaching Young Children? Early Years Research: Pedagogy, Curriculum and Adult Roles, Training and Professionalism.* Macclesfield: BERA Academic Review.

DfE (Department for Education) (2012) *Statutory Framework for the Early years Foundation Stage: Setting the Standards for Learning, Development and Care for Children from Birth to Five.* www.education.gov.uk/publications/standard/AllPublications/Page1/DFE-002023-2012 (accessed 27 March 2013).

Gammage, P. (2006) *Early Childhood Education and Care: Politics, Policies and Possibilities.* TACTYC, Colchester: Routledge.

Humphries, P. and Simpson, S. (2005) *Globalisation, Convergence and European Telecommunications Regulation.* Edward Elgar. eScholar ID: 4b56.

Knill, C. (2006) *Cross National Policy Convergence: Causes, Concepts and Empirical Findings.* Abingdon: Routledge.

Moyles, J. (ed.) (2002) *Beginning Teaching, Beginning Learning in the Primary Schools.* Buckingham: Open University Press.

Musgrave, P.W. (1965) *The Sociology of Education.* London: Methuen.

Pugh, G. and Duffy, B. (eds) (2010) *Contemporary Issues in the Early Years: Working Collaboratively for Children* London: Paul Chapman Publishing.

# Conclusion

The perceived characteristics of effective learning continue to be discussed and deliberated upon. The three identified in the EYFS framework – playing and exploring, active learning, creating and thinking critically – covering children's engagement, motivation and thinking – provide a useful basis on which to plan and prepare a suitable enabling environment for young children's learning and development. They provide a sound foundation for practice while giving the professional responsible for the early years setting the scope and professional judgement to respond to the needs of the children in their care and the community the setting serves. The characteristics are 'child friendly' and let children enjoy their childhood and progress in learning through active participation in it. They also encourage children's resilience to attempt challenges they set themselves, opportunities to rely on their own ideas, and an ability and self-confidence to seek challenges through a 'can-do' attitude, qualities which will be of great value in later life.

The challenges faced by practitioners implementing the changes will be ongoing as new initiatives are incorporated into existing practice and adults working with young children reflect on the value of changes made and refine them. New networks in localities and communities will continue to discuss pedagogy and practice, bringing fresh ideas to new challenges. Collaboration and the sharing of ideas from colleagues working with young children in wider contexts, such as the national association TACTYC, the Association for the Professional Development of Early Childhood Educators, and those working on the learning and development of young children in other countries, strive to improve practice.

The 2012 EYFS framework gives practitioners a basis on which to work and the prime and specific areas of learning and development. However, these are broadly based and allow practitioners to use their own expertise to cater for the children they are responsible for. Children are being allowed to be children and learn qualities which will help them through life, while practitioners are given opportunities to develop their provision, striving to make it the best it possibly can be. This happens in a continual state of change with new children, new initiatives, further insights into appropriate practice, changing communities, new technologies and greater ease with which ideas can be shared worldwide. It is in this context that the 2012 EYFS will provide a basis for practice where practitioners can meet the changes and challenges, reflecting on them in preparation for the unknown challenges of the future.

# Appendix 1

# Continuous provision

| Key learning: Communication and language | Key learning: Literacy |
| --- | --- |
| Key learning: Physical development | Key Learning: Mathematics |
| | Key learning: Understanding the world |
| Key learning: Personal, social and emotional development | Key learning: Expressive arts and design |

| Resources and organization (environment) | Possible children's activities | My role: scaffolding learning/ differentiation |
| --- | --- | --- |
| | | |
| | | |

# Appendix 2

**Appendix 2** Example of short-term Early Years Foundation Stage free-flow plan

Theme:              Nursery rhymes and stories

Focus for day:      Literacy

Topic:              Little Red Riding Hood

Learning environment – use of whole setting, indoors and outdoors

| Date/time | Learning objectives | Development Matters/ELGs | Focused activities | Independent activities | Resources/organization | Observational assessments and ways forward |
|---|---|---|---|---|---|---|
| 9–9.20 a.m. | PSE<br>Relate and make attachments to members of their group | All levels | Small construction activities. Whiteboard, emergent writing, Lotto games | Activities available if desired to be used by children but they are able to devise activities using indoor and outdoor resources as they wish | Pastoral groups. Welcome parents/carers and children. Named adults help each group | |
| 9.20–9.55 a.m. | L<br>Attempt writing for a purpose | 40–60+ (ELGs, HA) | Make own books about favourite story or own story – discuss sequence, characters, etc. | | **Teacher focus group**<br><br>Pupils who are more able to make own books. Show younger children, tell story and describe how they made the books. | |
| | CD | 30–50 (AA) | Finger puppets made based on story chosen – discuss story and materials, textures used for puppet | Letters to wolf, Little RR Hood | **OA** to help children make puppets and discuss materials. | |
| | Create different textures | 30–50 (AA) | Choose filling for sandwiches for grandma record choice | Large bricks – make grandma's house | **OA** record choice of sandwich filling Red, older group – copy for profile records | |
| | L | 30–50 (LA) | Bake strawberry jam tarts – make recipe books | Dolls house – room plans, positional language | **OA** to help yellow group bake tarts. | |
| | | 22–36 (LA) | Red monoprint paintings | Listen to tapes of stories/rhymes | **OA** to help children with monoprint paintings | |
| | Use writing as a means of recording | 22–36 (LA) | Finger pathways | Red playdoh – 'sausage' letters, matching and identifying | | |
| | L | All groups | Puppet play based on Little Red Riding Hd | | | |

| Time | Learning objective | | Review | Activities | OA / Support |
|------|------|------|------|------|------|
| | Know information can be relayed in the form of print<br>Draw/paint<br>Ascribe meaning to marks | 22–36 (LA) | | Red water – movement – vocabulary – pouring, filling, full, empty, etc.<br>Sand toys – pathways for cars<br>Painting pictures of favourite rhyme/story<br>Nursery rhyme/story jigsaws – colour coded for level of difficulty<br>Role play – grandma's house<br>Computer programme – Bailey's Book House | **OA** help pupils identified as SEN<br>Whole class tidy resources for group time<br>Children share in groups with named adults |
| | Begin to be aware of the way stories are structured | 22–36 (LA) | | | |
| 9.55–10 a.m. | | | Review work achieved – share and discuss | | |
| 10–10.15 a.m. | PSE Relate and make attachments to members of group | | | | |

# Index